Johanna Johnston has written several biographies, including one of Harriet Beecher Stowe. She lives in New York.

'Johanna Johnston's new biography is well worth publishing for its portrayal of her extraordinary and resilient figure with sympathy and understanding.'   Herbert van Thal, *Daily Telegraph*

'Few women of her time and class can have known such violent reversals of fortune, with bankruptcy, penury, three-to-a-bed and actual hunger on the one hand and even grandeur on the other. Johanna Johnston's *Fanny Trollope* very entertainingly shows how and why it all happened.'   Isabel Quigly, *Guardian*

'Mrs Johnston's story is full of colour, and is as briskly and attractively told as one of Mrs Trollope's own.'   David Skilton, *Books and Bookmen*

The Life, Manners and Travels of Fanny Trollope

A Biography

Johanna Johnston

Quartet Books

London Melbourne New York

Published by Quartet Books Limited 1980
A member of the Namara Group
27 Goodge Street, London W1P 1FD

First published in Great Britain by
Constable and Co. Ltd, London, 1979

Copyright © 1978, 1979 by Johanna Johnston

ISBN 0 7043 3325 2

Reproduced, printed and bound in Great Britain by
Hazell Watson & Viney Ltd, Aylesbury, Bucks

To Ann R

Contents

Contents

Acknowledgments

I would like to express gratitude to the New York Public Library not only for its unrivalled resources but for use of the Frederick Lewis Allen Room. The New York Historical Society was also helpful. Gerald Raftery of the Martha Canfield Memorial Library in Arlington, Vermont, gave assistance far above the call of duty, in obtaining various rare books. My thanks also to Sandra Pease of the Guy W. Bailey Library of the University of Vermont, in Burlington, for her patience, and to Dr N. John Hall for useful suggestions. Special acknowledgment is owed to all Trollope biographers who have blazed a trail to various sources, chief among them the late Michael Sadleir with his *Trollope, A Commentary*, and Lucy Poate Stebbins and Richard Poate Stebbins with their book *The Trollopes; The Chronicle of a Writing Family*. The bibliography of Frances Trollope's complete works was compiled by Michael Sadleir.

The Life, Manners and Travels of Fanny Trollope

PART ONE

English Ways
1780–1827

Heckfield Vicarage –

'Manners Makyth Man' – 'Au Mieux-ing'

She left a monument to her name in Cincinnati, Ohio—an extravagant building known to the residents of the city as Trollope's Folly, until they finally demolished it in 1898, fifty years later. The outrage she provoked in every state of America by the book she wrote about America after her return to England made her just as well known. For several decades people bought the book in order to enjoy the fury it engendered in them. One American edition (pirated from the English publication, as, of course, all editions were) had a semi-humorous editorial preface, doubting that the book actually could be the production of an English lady. 'The English ladies are not what I believe them to be, if they, or any one of them, would so far forget what was due to themselves and the character of their country, as to lend their name and sanction to a gross violation of the common decorums of life.' That editor was writing with tongue in cheek, basically, but there were thousands who echoed the sentiment quite seriously. Mrs Trollope (what a name! in itself an offence! could it be true?)—whoever she was—was certainly no lady.

She never troubled to certify her status as a lady to the Americans. She never did much apologizing or explaining all her life long. Neither did she reminisce about her life in autobiography or memoirs. What was past was past to Fanny Trollope.

She was born on 10th March 1780 (five years later than Jane Austen, whom she never knew—more's the pity—since they both observed 'manners' with an ironic eye). She was the daughter of the Reverend William Milton and his wife, who were living, at the time, in the village of Stapleton, near Bristol. They christened her, their second daughter, with a name so popular during those years that it seems half the girl children of England in the last of the eighteenth and beginning of the nineteenth century were named Frances and called Fanny.

Soon after her birth, the Reverend Milton was awarded the living at Heckfield, in north Hampshire and sixty miles from London. A year or so later, a son, Harry, was born, and shortly thereafter the mother of Mary, Frances, and Henry died. The Reverend Milton waited a suitable period of time and then married a Miss Partington, who was an acceptable if unremarkable stepmother.

William Milton, the vicar of Heckfield, was a more interesting parent—a gentleman in the great English tradition of mild eccentricity. He was the son of a Bristol saddler but had risen in life by attending the famous school at Winchester, which had been established four centuries earlier by William of Wykeham. From there he had gone on to its pendant institution of higher learning, New College, Oxford. William of Wykeham had chosen the same motto, 'Manners makyth man', for both these institutions, and at both Latin was the preferred language. William Milton had finished this schooling a creditable Wykehamist. His manners were delightful, his Latin excellent, and he conducted the services at Heckfield and in the nearby village of Mattingly to everyone's satisfaction. But the main vent of his mind was toward invention.

Using French rather than Latin, he said he liked to look at life with a view as to how it would be changed *au mieux*. One of his minor inspirations was a specially designed dinner plate. For years family meals tormented him because the sound of his knife squeaking against china as he cut his meat rasped his nerves. Finally he invented a way to better this situation. He had plates moulded and fired with a coin-sized depression in the centre and had the centre filled with silver.[1]

'Aha!' he said as he sawed back and forth on a slice of mutton, silver sliding softly against silver. 'Definitely *au mieux*.'

His chief interest, however, was in wheeled vehicles. Something (perhaps some personal upset) had alerted him to the tendency of stage-coaches, gigs, and other conveyances to overturn. During the many hours he had free of pastoral duties he was often busy in the coach house that adjoined the Heckfield vicarage, inventing newer and safer wheeled carriages. He drew, he experimented, he created models. Translating these models to life-size reality involved some expense for blacksmithing and allied crafts and further expense as he applied for patents. But his children, Mary, Fanny, and Henry, found a good deal of entertainment in watching him as he hummed about his work in the coach house or took some new contraption on to the yew-bordered lawn outside to give it a trial run. After which, they could tag at his heels as he relaxed by working on another of his hobbies, his rose garden.

Just how Mary and Fanny were educated was never recorded. Young Henry, of course, was sent off at the proper time to Winchester to become a Wykehamist like his father. There was no such traditional route to learning for girls. But Mary and Fanny did learn reading, writing, and arithmetic, and also picked up a certain knowledge of French and Italian. Like the heroines of Jane Austen's novels—and like the heroines of Fanny's own novels, some years later—they emerged as young women with an excellent vocabulary, a pretty talent for singing and playing the pianoforte, an eye for art, and a smattering of foreign languages. Actually, Fanny had more than a smattering of Italian. She translated many stanzas of Dante into English and wrote original verses of her own in Italian. It is conceivable that she was tutored from time to time by her father's friend Dr Nott, a prebendary at Winchester and a well-known Italian scholar, who often visited Heckfield. Years later, one of Fanny's sons remembered Dr Nott, still a family friend, as a spare figure with 'pale and delicately cut features', soberly dressed in black gaiters, his chin half-muffled in an elaborate white neck stock. Undoubtedly this spare, elegant scholar read Fanny's translations and original verses and encouraged her to keep on with her Italian studies. He must have talked to her of Italy, describing its hills studded with yew trees, its romantic little kingdoms, the unique blue of its sky. Years later, Fanny said that the dream of visiting Italy someday was born in her girlhood years.

Apart from such mild fantasies, she was not an especially dreamy girl. Small, slender, and healthy, with wide-set eyes in a heart-shaped face, she liked brisk walks every day when the weather was not too 'dirty'. Above all, she enjoyed any kind of social activity.

Small as Heckfield was, there was enough of that going on to keep
her from becoming bored. Since William Milton was the vicar, he
and his family were automatically accepted among the local gentry,
which meant that they both gave and received invitations to tea,
dinner parties, picnics, or excursions now and then to nearby
Reading for an evening at the theatre.

Dinner parties could be rather splendid, especially at the hospitable mansion of Mr Shaw Lefevre, the Member of Parliament for
the borough of Reading.

'We had some delightful eels at the top, soup in the middle, and
a haunch of Lord Stowell's venison at the bottom, a boiled chicken
on my side, and what was on the other I do not recollect,' one guest
reported in a letter to her daughter. 'We had after, a brace of
partridge at top, a very fine rabbit at the bottom, a dish of pease
in the middle, tipsey-cake on one side, and grape tart on the other.
Except some pease, I dined on the fish and venison, and tasted
nothing else.'[2]

This particular guest was Mrs George Mitford, and the daughter
to whom she wrote was young Mary Russell Mitford, who would
one day win a good deal of fame as an author and playwright.
Mrs Mitford's letters to young Mary not only detailed some of the
lavish dinners that were served around Heckfield but also gave a
glimpse of a typical day's activities when guests were visiting a house
like the Lefevres': 'The gentlemen dedicated the morning to field
sports, the ladies accompanied me round the grounds and afterwards we took a ride round Lord Rivers' park before we dressed
for dinner.' Finally, they show us young Fanny herself, for the
Lefevre house party was joined at one dinner by 'Mr. Milton, his
wife, and two daughters, the younger of whom, Miss Fanny Milton,
is a very lively pleasant young woman. I do not mean to infer that
Miss Milton may not be equally agreeable, but the other took a far
greater share in the conversation, and playing casino a great part of
the evening with Mr. S. Lefevre, Mr. Monck, and your old Mumpsa,
it gave me an opportunity of seeing her in a more favourable light
than her sister.'[3]

So there, for a moment, we can also see Fanny Milton, sitting at the wonderfully laden table, with its choices at top, middle, and bottom, and later, 'lively and pleasant' as she played cards with Mrs Mitford and two gentlemen. Her older sister, Mary, was less visible, having little of her younger sister's energy or curiosity. She was content to join her stepmother in the day's domestic routines, checking on the activities of the cook and the maids, and then to sit quietly at her books or her needlework. Young Harry, who had more of Fanny's vitality, was away most of the year at Winchester, learning his Latin and his manners. So Fanny expended her energy in whatever ways were available, walking a lot, reading the latest novels from the local lending library, working at her Italian, and enjoying herself tremendously whenever she was invited out or when guests came to the vicarage. Now and then there was the excitement of a journey, sometimes to Exeter, to visit her mother's cousin, Fanny Bent, a spinster of slender means who had such a fresh and independent view of life that young Fanny loved her dearly.

Sociably and placidly, the days slipped along, and Fanny was nineteen, twenty, twenty-one—and that at a time when a young woman was considered on the shelf if she had not found a husband by the time she was twenty.

What was wrong? Why had neither she nor Mary, properly gentle daughters of a proper vicar, found no suitor by such advanced ages? Were there few young men in the country houses of her father's parish, or were there perhaps too many young women in the neighbourhood, vying for their attention? Or, more likely, were most of the suitable young men being lured from the country to the excitement of the war?

English alarm over the tumultuous events in France had been a constant through most of Fanny's girlhood. She was nine when the mobs of Paris stormed the Bastille, and from then on, there had always been something going on across the Channel to rouse British concern. A French king and queen were beheaded (Good God! was this what revolution led to?), new governments were being improvised, French armies were marching here and there on the Continent, winning frightening victories over English allies. Plainly, England had to move in on the side of her friends. By the time Fanny was seventeen, Napoleon Bonaparte was well embarked on his meteoric rise from military success to political power. In 1798 he was invading Egypt, and England's Admiral Nelson had most of the English fleet spreading canvas all over the Mediterranean and South Atlantic in an attempt to trap him.

As a result, the chief goal for many young Englishmen was to go to sea and take part in the storming of an enemy warship, and perhaps become wealthy with a share of the prize money. For young men with few advantages, a naval career loomed as the one possible way to rise in the world. Even for young men of wealth and position there was a glamour to joining the navy that was lacking in the army, and undoubtedly the navy had taken some of the young men from the Heckfield district just when Mary and Fanny needed them.

Still and all, it was that seemingly endless conflict with France and Napoleon that finally offered Fanny and Mary a chance to move out into a wider world than Heckfield. Henry finished his years at Winchester and came home for what he feared would be an unhappy interview with his father.

'Please, sir, I would rather not go on to New College. I know how much you think of it, but I don't feel I'm cut out to be a scholar *or* to hang on all those years to win a living as a cleric.'

'Mmmmm,' said the vicar of Heckfield, taking in the information. 'And what do you feel you are cut out to be?' he asked mildly.

Henry spoke of an interest in art and literature. His father nodded and then said that worthy as those interests were, they hardly provided a young man with an income, and he feared that Henry would have to take that mundane item into consideration.

Henry had thought about that. He had heard that the War Office in London needed young men. The pay was good, the hours easy. If he could obtain a post in the War Office, he could support himself and in his free time take advantage of London's cultural resources, gradually preparing himself for some sort of career in the arts.

His father pondered the suggestion. He was an equable man, pleased to indulge his children whenever it seemed reasonable. Henry's plan seemed reasonable enough. The vicar said he would speak to Mr Lefevre and any other parishioners who might be helpful. He did so, and before long a position in the War Office was offered to Henry.

A new question presented itself. Where and how was Henry to live in London?

Perhaps it was Fanny who was inspired. Mary and she should go with him. They could rent a house in some nice section of the city. Mary and she could preside over the housekeeping and make a home for Henry. Meantime, the two sisters could, like Henry, enjoy the city's cultural advantages and widen their circle of friends. There had never been any difficulties between the girls and their stepmother. On the other hand, they felt no special bond to their home.

In the spring of 1803, Mary, Fanny, and Henry moved from Heckfield into a tall, narrow, terraced house in Keppel Street off Russell Square, Bloomsbury.

For Fanny, the move was definitely *au mieux*.

2

London – Thomas Anthony Trollope – Letters

Quizzing was all the thing in the fashionable world of London just then. No one knew where the word had come from, but everyone knew what it meant. Quizzing was talking to someone in a teasing manner, trying to have the last witty word, talking about someone or something in a mocking way, or just simply answering an ordinary remark in a wry, off-putting manner.

Beau Brummell, the almost constant companion of the young Prince of Wales, was a master of the art. Some of his quizzes were quoted from one drawing room to another. There was the time when he was confined with a lame leg to his luxurious chambers and was visited by a friend. 'I am sorry your leg is in such bad shape,' said the friend. 'I'm sorry for it too,' replied Brummell, 'particularly as it's my favourite leg.' The ladies and gentlemen of the court were convulsed by the story, as though a man like Beau Brummell carried his perfectionism to such an extreme that he had a preferred leg.

Fanny, Mary, and Henry hardly moved in the circles where Beau Brummell was a familiar, but they knew a good deal about him. He had been a young nobody (although his father was a wealthy merchant) when George, Prince of Wales, discovered him. His christened name of George Bryan Brummell had been forgotten after the perfection of his wardrobe had won him the nickname of Beau. Fanny, Mary, and Henry enjoyed hearing every tidbit of gossip about him—how nothing was ever really good enough for him. The Prince of Wales was used to having his own way, whether he wanted to build a new palace in London, a pleasure dome in Brighton, or to attract the beautiful young widow, Maria Fitzherbert. If all else failed, George, Prince of Wales, ran a fever, became delirious, and got what he wanted. But Beau Brummell, it seemed, did set limits.

Everyone had heard the story of how Beau had shrugged in disapproval when the Prince had asked his opinion of a new coat and how the tears had welled in the Prince's eyes.

The world that centred around George, Prince of Wales, was very special—it was a world made up of men and women wholly devoted to amusing themselves with clothes, parties, conversation, and sex. Infidelity between husbands and wives was almost mandatory. Without it, what would they have to talk about? It was always entertaining to try to guess the father of the latest infant born to one noblewoman or another. And in most cases the betrayed husband accepted the role of nominal father, immune to quizzing. In this world, during the first years of the Prince's infatuation with Maria Fitzherbert, gossip had centred around whether or not he had secretly married her. It was unthinkable that he could have—under the religious act, he would forfeit all rights to the throne by marrying a Roman Catholic, which Maria Fitzherbert was. On the other hand, it was impossible that he had *not* married her, because the devout Maria was still faithfully going to morning mass, which she surely would not dare to do if her relationship with the Prince had not been regularized by the church. Had they been married? Hadn't they? Before the speculation became boring, the Prince confounded everyone by breaking with Maria and publicly marrying his cousin, Caroline of Brunswick. A whole new level of conjecture was achieved. Obviously, the Prince could not have married Maria Fitzherbert, or he would now be committing bigamy, and surely even George, Prince of Wales, would stop at that. Caroline gave birth to a daughter, after which the Prince, who seemed dedicated to providing fresh gossip, disassociated himself from his wife and resumed his affair with Maria. Perhaps it was fortunate for the endlessly forgiving Mrs Fitzherbert that she was unable to conceive. Quite different from the experience of King George III's third son, William, Duke of Clarence, who had had eight children with the energetic actress Dorothy Jordan by 1803—and there were more to come.

Carlton House, the Prince's new establishment just down the Mall from Buckingham Palace, was only two miles or so from the Keppel Street house where Henry, Fanny, and Mary had established themselves. They could walk past it, or drive past it in a Hackney coach if some call or errand took them in that direction, but it enclosed a world remote from them.

And yet, some eddies of its frivolity drifted out into the general London atmosphere. The solid, professional middle class might prefer the morality of old King George III and his wife, settled in domesticity at Windsor or Kew, worrying about their fourteen children (all legitimate), and fearful always that the wing of madness that had brushed the king several years before might do so again. But the air of gaiety that surrounded the Prince's circle, the interest in theatre, dancing, every sort of holiday, were part of the London atmosphere. And quizzing was everyone's game.

Fanny Milton took to it naturally. She had always been quick with a certain light mockery. Once the household in Keppel Street was in running order, she had more opportunities for exercising that talent than Heckfield had ever offered. With letters from friends in Heckfield, Reading, and Winchester, the young Miltons had no trouble finding new acquaintances in the city. Henry met a variety of presentable young men at the War Office whom he could invite to the house in Keppel Street, and soon Mary and Fanny were presiding over small dinners, evening card parties, or impromptu suppers. They went to Covent Garden to see the latest plays—Miss Duncan in *The Provoked Husband* and *The Forty Thieves*, or John Kemble, old 'glorious John', or Charles Kemble, or any of the other acting Kembles in whatever their latest production might be. Afterwards, the young Miltons and their friends quizzed each other merrily on the merits of the performances and the plays.

Mrs Mitford (the same Mrs Mitford who had been favourably impressed by Fanny at a Heckfield dinner party) came to London with her husband and daughter and called upon the young Miltons. Fanny met the plump, gentle, and talented Mary Russell Mitford who, though seven years younger, became a lifelong friend. Sir Thomas and Lady Dyer, acquaintances from the vicar's Winchester days, came to call, and Lady Dyer also became a friend, soon bringing friends of her own to swell the group.

In the Keppel Street drawing room they talked at times about the progress of the war and Napoleon's seemingly unlimited ambitions.

Good heavens, now he had made himself emperor of the French and Josephine his empress. He had elevated all his family to various princedoms in the European countries that he was picking off, one by one. In November 1805 there was news that Admiral Nelson and his fleet had scored a magnificent victory over the French and their allied fleets at Trafalgar. But these good tidings were dimmed by national mourning when it was learned that Nelson had been fatally wounded in the battle. Still, it was reassuring to know that England continued to rule at sea, since it was evident that Napoleon and his armies dominated on land, defeating the Prussians at Austerlitz, entering Berlin, making tentative moves towards Russia. Only in Spain was the Duke of Wellington beginning to cause Napoleon's forces a little difficulty. But the war had been going on so long by now and was so far away. Conversation at 22 Keppel Street turned much more frequently to the latest novel by Maria Edgeworth, the latest poems by Walter Scott, or the new play at Covent Garden.

Sometime in the summer of 1808, Henry brought home yet another friend, an earnest young barrister who had chambers in Lincoln's Inn and the additional credentials of being an old Wykehamist and a fellow of New College.

'Fanny, my dear, may I introduce Mr Trollope?'

'Mr Trollope, my sister Miss Frances Milton.'

Thomas Anthony Trollope, large and heavy-set, bowed over the hand of the slight young woman who curtsied and smiled up at him. There is no record that Fanny ever quizzed the new acquaintance about his last name, which had the same colloquial meaning then as now. Instead, she was soon seated near him and listening attentively as he discoursed on poetry. He could not accept the excesses of such modern poets as Wordsworth and Coleridge, he said. Did not Miss Milton agree that they really went too far in their raptures about nature? Fanny nodded in serious agreement. Few of the new writers could compare with the great old classicists. Mr Trollope, encouraged by her interest, expounded further. They had a long tête-à-tête, and when the evening was over, Mr Trollope expressed the hope that they would meet again in the near future.

Henry obliged with another invitation to Mr Trollope and then another. During each visit, Mr Trollope concentrated most of his attention on Fanny.[1]

Accustomed though she was to male company, Fanny was now becoming a little fluttered. She was twenty-eight years old, and despite the young men who had been in and out of the house during the last five years, Mr Trollope was the first to show her this particularly marked sort of attention. She was surprised and pleased one day when the post brought her a book from him, along with two Latin odes and his translations of the same. Naturally she read the book and the poems with great care and responded appreciatively.

On another visit to Keppel Street, Mr Trollope found it raining heavily when it was time to go. Henry pressed an umbrella upon him and told him to consider it his own. This necessitated another exchange of notes the next day as Mr Trollope hurried to arrange for the return of the umbrella. For some reason, Fanny, who saved so little, preserved these notes.[2]

Lincoln's Inn
23rd Sept. 1808

My Dear Madam,

As your brother will probably have left Keppel Street before my servant is able to get there with the umbrella he was so good as to lend me last night, I take the liberty of addressing this note to you expressing my best thanks for the loan of it. At the same time I really hope you will indulge me in the request that it may henceforth be safely deposited in your house, since experience has shown that they are very apt to ramble from mine. Altho' the stern unrelenting heart of your brother may be inexorable, permit me, on the behalf of my trembling client now at your doors, to indulge better hopes from the clemency of the female disposition. In full expectation of this my humble request being complied with I shall consider myself as ever bound to pray etc. etc.

I am, my dear Madam, with my best respects to your sister whom I hope to enlist as an advocate in my cause,

Your most true and very humble servant
Thos. Anth. Trollope

Fanny wrote her answer on the blank back sheet of Mr Trollope's note.

My Dear Sir,

I am afraid you have applied to a very bad place, for *all my eloquence* has proved in vain. Henry still feels it *impossible* to accept your umbrella, and therefore like an honest council I really advise you to give up the cause. To you I will confess that I think he sees this problem in a right point of view. Whenever the said umbrella met his sight I think it would give him a disagreeable sort of sensation. But as I was engaged on the other side, you may be sure I did not hint this to *him*. He desires me to say that he wishes you would prove you forgive his so pertinaciously insisting on having his own way, by giving him the pleasure of your company to dinner on Friday.

Ponderous notes, both of them, and if Mr Trollope was being quizzical about the umbrella, the joke is rather baffling. But his attraction to Fanny was soon apparent to everyone. He came to dinner as requested, and Fanny lent him Maria Edgeworth's *The Modern Griselda*. After returning home with it, he stayed up most of the night reading so that he might acknowledge the book, with comments, very promptly.

They looked an ill-matched pair. He was large and slow, and she was small and quick. She used words lightly, glancingly, and not always correctly. He was meticulous about the meaning of a word or phrase and tortured an idea half to death with his literalism. None of this bothered either of them just then. By 1st November 1808, Mr Trollope had made his decision and sent Fanny Milton an extremely long letter that he began with a laboured attempt at lightness.

My Dear Madam,

In the course of the last Spring I was no little delighted with the subject a certain debating society had chosen for their weekly discussion, which to the best of [my] recollection was in the words, or to the effect following: 'Is it most expedient for a man to make

avowal of his attachment to a lady viva voce (*anglice* in tête-à-tête),
or by epistolary correspondence?'

I well remember, and probably, my dear Madam, you may also,
that there was one, altho' not of this honourable society, who
expressed a most decided opinion upon the subject; and to that
opinion I now think myself bound to submit.

Could it have been Fanny herself, in a quizzing mood, who spoke
up for written proposals, thus giving women some tangible evidence
of intentions on the part of suitors? Presumably both he and she
understood the reference. Mr Trollope lumbered on:

This preface explains the motive of my now addressing you. It
will save me the necessity of a more explicit avowal, and sufficiently declare to you that my future happiness on earth is at
your disposal.

If indeed, as I trust is the case, you are not entirely unaware
that my chief delight has long since had its source in your society
and conversation; and if, permit my vanity to indulge the hope,
there has been the slightest degree of mutuality in this delight,
then perhaps—I confess I scarcely know what I was going to say,
but perhaps you would not require *three weeks* for passing a
sentence on which I must so anxiously depend.

There is no one perhaps that has a greater contempt for those
who are induced to contract alliances upon motives of a pecuniary
nature than I have; but at the same time I have had experience
enough to teach me that happiness is not to be expected where the
parties are no longer capable of enjoying those necessaries and
comforts of life to which they have been accustomed, and which
are commonly incident to the rank and situation they hold in
society.

With these sentiments, and believing them to be your own, as
indeed they must be those of every sensible and considerate person
of either sex, I deem it an indispensable duty, in addressing myself to you on this subject in which all my dearest interests are
involved to make an open declaration of what ground I have to
hope for the enjoyment of those comforts above alluded to.

My present income, tho' somewhat uncertain since part of it arises from my profession, is about £900 per annum; but as near £200 of this proceeds from my fellowship etc. at Oxford, this last emolument would drop, should I no longer be deemed a fit member of that society. I should also add that this income, trifling as it is, is subject to certain incumbrances, but as it is much beyond my present expenditure as a single man, they are gradually wearing away.

I must now draw this long letter to a conclusion; a letter perhaps chiefly to be remarked by its singularity, and particularly in its manner and style being so little adapted to its subject. If I have erred in this I must admit that it has been in a great measure with design, as my sole object has been to make a declaration which I could no longer conceal, and at the same time to state those circumstances, a knowledge of which, in case you should think the subject of my writing worthy your consideration, would be necessary for that purpose. In doing this in the most simple manner, and in rejecting the flippant nonsense which I believe to be commonly used on occasions of this nature, I doubt not I have acted as well in conformity of your sentiments as those of, my dear Madam,

Your sincere admirer and most devoted servant

Thos. Anth. Trollope

It was Fanny's first proposal, and she had to look for a few signs of 'the flippant nonsense' that was customary in such offers. 'My future happiness on earth is at your disposal. . . . My chief delight has long since had its source in your society and conversation.' Having drawn reassurance from those avowals, she had the rest of the letter to attend to, those long paragraphs about her suitor's financial views and situation. Fanny pondered. To what sorts of necessaries and comforts did Mr Trollope imagine her accustomed? He had seen her only in her brother's house, her allowance and Mary's supplementing Henry's income from the War Office. Perhaps it seemed to Mr Trollope that they lived lavishly. He knew nothing about the modest vicarage in Heckfield and the Reverend Milton's extravagances in the way of patents.

That very day she wrote her reply, as forthright as anyone could wish in confessing that so far as worldly goods were concerned, she was not a very desirable match.

It does not require three weeks consideration, Mr. Trollope, to enable me to tell you that the letter you left with me last night was most flattering and gratifying to me. I value your good opinion too highly not to feel that the generous proof you have given me of it, must for ever and in any event, be remembered by me with pride and gratitude. But I fear you are not sufficiently aware that your choice, so flattering to me, is for yourself a very imprudent one. You have every right in an alliance of this kind to expect a fortune greatly superior to any I shall ever possess, and I agree too perfectly with you in your ideas on this point not to think that you ought to be informed of the truth in this particular, *before* you decide on so important a subject. All I have independent of my father is £1300, and we each receive from him at present an annual allowance of £50. What he would give either of us, were we to marry, I really do not know.

In an affair of this kind, I do not think it any disadvantage to either party that some time should elapse between the first contemplation and final decision of it; it gives each an opportunity of becoming acquainted with the other's opinion on many important points which could not be canvassed before it was thought of, and which it would be useless to discuss after it was settled. I have to thank you for choosing that manner of addressing me, which I once so vaguely said I thought the best, but I have more than once since I began writing this, wished I had not said so. I have not, nor can I, express myself quite as I wish. There is something of cold formality in what I have written, which is very foreign to what I feel,—but I know not how to mend it.

                                                    Fanny Milton

Thomas Anthony Trollope made some amends for the 'cold formality' of that exchange by an instant response to her letter, delivered to her by penny post on the very same day.

'My Dearest Madam,' he called her now, and told her how happy her answer had made him. 'I will not trouble you with another long letter. . . . May I request you to permit me to have the pleasure of calling upon you at half past three o'clock? . . . One word by the bearer will be sufficient.'

Fanny gave the 'one word', Mr Trollope came, and undoubtedly there was less cold formality between them.

A few weeks later, Fanny took the stagecoach to Reading, where she was met by her father's servant, who drove her home through the cold moonlight in one of the Reverend Milton's 'patent' gigs. Fanny's mind was full of concern about her own future, and what her father's reaction would be to her proposed engagement.

3

Marriage – Children – Social Life

'It is a solemn business, my dear friend. Does not the near approach of it almost frighten you? I tremble lest you should love me less a twelvemonth hence than you do now. I sometimes fear you may be disappointed in me, that you will find me less informed, less capable of being a companion to you, than you expect, and then—but I am growing very dismal—this will never do. I must go and sun myself a little upon the heath.'[1]

It was the first of May 1809 when Fanny wrote so apprehensively to Thomas Anthony, and the date for their marriage had been set for the end of the month. The financial details had been settled satisfactorily. The Reverend Milton had journeyed to London to assess Thomas Anthony Trollope and discuss his prospects. The vicar had examined the young man and found nothing to disapprove. He already knew that both Thomas Anthony and his late father (who had been a vicar like himself) were Wykehamists, and this was an immediate bond. So far as the Reverend Milton could tell, young Trollope was properly learned in his profession of Chancery law. The vicar may have felt that the younger man's manner was rather ponderous, but then he could comfort himself with the hope that marriage to his light-hearted daughter might soften his edges a bit.

It was reassuring to the vicar to learn that Thomas Anthony Trollope had considerable expectations from the future. His mother had been Penelope Meetkerke, a descendant of an eminent Dutchman who had come to England as an ambassador from the Netherlands during Elizabeth's reign and remained there to establish his home. Thomas's mother had died when her son was still in school, but she had a childless older brother, squire of a prosperous estate called Julians, in Hertfordshire, and it had been long understood that this Adolphus Meetkerke considered his sister's only son as his heir. Since Adolphus and his wife were both in or approaching their sixties, Thomas Anthony, without being at all covetous, could look forward to inheriting a handsome estate some day. The vicar of Heckfield nodded approvingly. He said he would continue to give Fanny her annual allowance of fifty pounds after her marriage. Then in a burst of whimsy he added that he would also make over to her a one-eighth interest in the proceeds of one of his patent vehicles. (Since none of the vicar's inventions had ever brought in a shilling, this offer provided even Thomas Anthony with the makings of a proper quiz. He wrote to Fanny that he would expect her to pay the taxes on any income from that source.)

No, Fanny had no reason to feel apprehensive financially. Dr Nott, that longtime family friend, had also travelled to London, trumping up some small legal difficulty as an excuse to visit Fanny's suitor. Thomas Anthony was somewhat offended when he learned that Dr Nott's legal problem was a triviality worthy only of an attorney's attention. He was rather short in pointing out the mistake to his visitor, but Dr Nott overlooked it and also returned with a satisfactory report on Mr Trollope.

Then why was Fanny feeling dismal? Did she really fear that she was incapable of being an acceptable companion to the learned Thomas Anthony, or was she inverting her fears and wondering what sort of companion Thomas Anthony might be for her? Twice she wrote him diffident letters, trying to make a joke of her desire to hear from him more often and her worry as to how frequently he wanted to have her write to him. Plainly, Fanny craved some more impetuous, impulsive avowals of love than she was receiving. Both times Thomas Anthony responded quickly, trying to reassure her. He wrote that he had no patience with a man 'too vehement in his expressions . . . and always felt afraid of raising doubts as to the prejudice of my own sincerity by professing too much or declaring myself in too vehement a manner.'[2] Reading and rereading such stilted and repressed explanations, Fanny tried to tell herself that Thomas Anthony's very reticence showed his love, and though he might be more learned than she, she would accept the situation: That was simply as it should be in marriage.

And so everything went forward as planned. Trees and fields were wearing their first spring green, and hedgerows around Heckfield were flowering when Frances Milton and Thomas Anthony Trollope took their places before the altar in the little Heckfield church.

'Dearly beloved,' the vicar intoned as he began the ritual. The words slipped over them. They affirmed the promises and exchanged rings. There were kisses, smiles, tears, and a modest collation at the vicarage.

After that, foregoing a honeymoon, Fanny and her husband boarded a coach for London, where they were going to take up residence in a house that Thomas Anthony owned at 16 Keppel Street, just a few doors away from the house where Henry and Mary were still residing. The house at 16 Keppel Street was somewhat larger than No. 22, allowing the newly married pair to begin housekeeping in pleasantly spacious quarters.

Here, any doubts Fanny might have had about marriage disappeared. For the first time in her life, she had the entire responsibility for furnishing and decorating a home, and she liked it very much. The latest styles in chairs, tables, and loveseats might be in the spare, elegant manner of Adam or Chippendale, or the over-ornamented and constricted formality that Napoleon was making popular. But as Fanny picked her way from one cabinetmaker or draper to another, studying, frowning, imagining, she felt very sure of herself. Piece by piece, fabric by fabric, she was creating a home for herself and Thomas Anthony that would be not only proper but warm and welcoming as well. Their drawing room, long, dark, and narrow, as the drawing rooms in most London town houses seemed to be, would offer inviting areas for conversation around a tea table and places where people could sit at ease.

During these weeks of furnishing, Fanny liked to wait for Thomas Anthony's return from his chambers in Lincoln's Inn and then, after the greeting kiss, she would rush him to view the latest finished area, the latest inspired arrangement. Her sheer muslin skirts fluttering above small kid slippers, her brown curls caught up with a ribbon, Fanny looked very young and pretty. As she sparkled up at him, Thomas Anthony's serious countenance relaxed into a smile.

She had servants to engage: a cook, a maid, a footman. Most

young couples in the Trollopes' circumstances considered a footman a necessity, and Fanny was pleased to deck him out in Trollope livery. After all Thomas Anthony's grandfather had been Sir Thomas Trollope, a baronet, and a relative still bore the title. The livery was a valid family insignia, as appropriate as the marking on the Trollope silver.

Fanny was even happier when she could begin to entertain. Henry and Mary had been dropping in to observe progress from the time she and Thomas Anthony moved in. Now she could invite the friends who had visited the other house on Keppel Street. She could plan small dinners or evening parties for Thomas Anthony's friends and associates. She could entertain any of Thomas Anthony's family who might be visiting London—his sister, Diana, who was married to a clergyman and lived in Lincolnshire, or his sister, Penelope, married to Thomas Partington.

Thomas Anthony seemed not to object to an increasingly active social life and was a grave and welcoming host. Fanny did wish, however, that he was a little less given to insisting on his own views whenever some matter came into discussion, whether it was poetry, politics, or the proper play in whist. Strange. Had he been so dogmatic during their courtship? Well, perhaps, a little—dismissing Wordsworth and Coleridge out of hand.

Fanny was surprised also to find her husband curiously careful about small expenditures. He had made no complaint about the lavish purchases of furniture and fabric and other household items, but soon he was cautioning her that they could not afford to use expensive wax candles when they were alone. Cheap tallow candles were quite adequate for every day.[3]

'And about the wine,' he said, there was no need to put out the best bottles when there were just the two of them. An ordinary port would be sufficient. He spoke also about the fires. Wasteful for Joseph to light the fire in the downstairs dining room for breakfast. They could breakfast just as comfortably in the back drawing room, where a fire was lit anyway. And so he went on, totting up the ways in which they could economize.

Fanny nodded dutifully and saw that Thomas Anthony's wishes were respected. After all, one had to expect some adjustments in marriage. Thomas Anthony loved her. She was sure of that now and was therefore happy to tell him, a few months after their marriage, that she was pregnant.

His delight was warming, but she was not so pleased by his insistence that she now curtail all social activities. 'I'm fine,' Fanny protested. 'And I expect I shall keep on being so. I'm a very healthy young woman, you know.'

Thomas thought that had nothing to do with it. He believed that an expectant mother should spend most of her time resting or lying down. Fanny should not rush about entertaining people at tea, dinner, or cards. Above all, he and Fanny must now give up the idea of visiting Uncle Adolphus and his wife at Julians in Hertfordshire as they had planned.

Here Fanny was resistant to her husband's demands. She had set her heart on visiting Uncle Adolphus. She begged Thomas Anthony to reconsider and to remember that if they did not make the visit now, it would be well over a year before they could do so. At last Fanny prevailed. They made the journey to Julians.

Fanny was pleased by everything, the journey in the gig, the wide extent of Uncle Adolphus's lands, the large, old-fashioned but comfortable manor house. Uncle Adolphus was a red-faced country squire with the booming voice of authority. Aunt Meetkerke was a spare and rangy woman, dressed in a green riding habit of ancient cut. Fanny soon learned that this was her usual costume, since she spent most of her days riding around the parish keeping herself informed of everything that went on. Mrs Anne, Uncle's spinster sister, was the third member of the household, and she oversaw the housekeeping while Aunt rode around overseeing the parish. A shy, plump little woman, Mrs Anne trotted through the house with a basket over her arm that held the keys to all the cupboards, cellars, and keeps, and also a novel. Whenever she sat down to rest for a while, she read a few pages, and when she finally finished the book, placidly turned back to the beginning to read it through again.

Fanny found all these people quite charming and was only amused by Uncle Adolphus's political opinions, which were fiercely Tory and which he voiced loudly at the slightest provocation. Unfortunately, Thomas Anthony was not so objective. Proud of his own liberal views, he was outraged by his uncle's shouts of 'Hang 'em. Hang 'em all by their heels!' when the talk turned to the demands of peasant and factory workers. He found it impossible to restrain himself from responding angrily to his uncle's intemperate remarks. It seemed an eternity until the evening was over and the Trollopes could retire to their room. Fanny was not surprised that Thomas Anthony had a raging headache. She had noted his tendency towards headaches when over-excited. Watching him take some of the calomel with which he dosed such attacks, she realized that the visit to Julians was not going to be a success. She had to tell her husband that it was foolish of him to take his uncle's bluster so seriously and that everything he said simply encouraged Uncle Adolphus to more vehemence. But having said so and noting his stubborn and injured gaze, she sighed. She was learning that such counsel was apt to drive Thomas Anthony into even more rigid attitudes.

Returned to London, she pushed thoughts of the visit behind her and, in spite of Thomas Anthony's protests, continued the lively social life at 16 Keppel Street. Once again Mary Russell Mitford was in the city with her mother, this time bearing a sheaf of poems for which she was trying to find a publisher. Fanny had to have a small party for them and do what she could to help. Sir Thomas and Lady Dyer were in town, and they introduced Fanny to a handsome Italian general, Guglielmo Pepe, a refugee from one of the revolutionary ventures designed to win freedom for one or another small Italian kingdom. Soon General Pepe was a regular visitor at 16 Keppel Street. In any social gathering he was so given to pompous bromides that Fanny and some of her friends referred to him privately as *Le Gâteau Plombé*, but he was also so kind, loyal, and affectionate, and so dedicated to Italian independence that Fanny became truly fond of him.[4]

Her health continued excellent, and on 29th April 1810, she had an easy time giving birth to a fine boy. He was named Thomas, after his father, and given the middle name of Adolphus, honouring the uncle whose heir he would some day be.

Motherhood seemed as easy and enjoyable to Fanny as pregnancy. When the baby was about three months old she took him for a long summer visit to her father and stepmother at Heckfield. It was lovely to see how pleased the vicar was by his first grandchild. Inventive as always, the Reverend Milton devised a variety of tests to exhibit the infant's extraordinary intelligence. Fanny wrote to Thomas Anthony, 'Were I not *too wise* to be vain, I would certainly become so here. I screw my features into all possible forms, that I may not look as delighted as I feel.'

This was the first separation Fanny and Thomas Anthony had known since their marriage. They wrote frequently to each other as Thomas Anthony travelled to various assizes, and these letters were quite different from the stilted exchange of their courtship, reflecting a new intimacy and tenderness. 'God bless you, my dearest Fanny, and our darling child,' Thomas Anthony wrote. 'Give him a kiss for me every morning and tell him papa sends it to him. I shall certainly expect to hear from you at Cambridge on Tuesday. . . . Once again, God bless you both, and believe me, For ever yours, T. A. Trollope.' He concluded another letter by writing, '*Adieu! Aime-moi bien. Aime-moi toujours. Adieu! Mon âme est toute pleine de toi.*' And Fanny answered, 'Love you always? I believe I must, for I cannot help it, even tho' you do scold me when I don't deserve it.' In another letter, after giving him the latest news about young Tom, she wrote, 'Adieu, my very dear husband (I was going to write *dearest* but recollected that your *correctness* would laugh at me.) Adieu—I will not dictate the moment for your writing, but I shall wish & wish & wish & wish, till another comes. Yours wholly and for ever, F. Trollope.'[5]

Thomas Anthony joined her at Heckfield in August at the beginning of the 'long vacation' for barristers. Now it was his turn to try to conceal pride in the remarkable baby and to enjoy the quiet rhythms of summer in the country. By the time the little family returned to London, Fanny was pregnant again.

Once more she had an easy pregnancy, as easy as the six that would follow. It was 1811 when her second son, Henry, was born, also the year Parliament finally accepted the fact that old George III was no longer capable of ruling and reluctantly appointed his son Prince Regent. The forty-nine-year-old Prince was no longer the public charmer that he had been. In Fanny's drawing room the talk was critical of his self-indulgence and bloated figure, but those who had been to Brighton were forced to admire the fantastic *chinoiserie* of the palace he was building there.

The year was 1812—and the talk was about the move Napoleon's army was making towards Russia, but even more about the fantastic success of a long poem by George Gordon, Lord Byron, called *Childe Harold's Pilgrimage*. Fanny had something to say about both topics but most enjoyed praising Byron's genius. That year she gave birth to her third son, a delicate infant who was named Arthur.

The first break in the happy births came in 1813 when Fanny had a girl child who died the same day. Thomas Anthony recorded the birth and death in the family Bible, and he and Fanny rarely referred to the loss afterwards.

In 1814 the talk was of the triumph of England and her allies on the Continent and the abdication of Napoleon as Emperor of France. Fanny hardly paid any attention to the fact that she was pregnant again. On 24th April 1815, when attention was focused on Napoleon's escape from his exile on Elba and his attempts to regain power in France, Fanny gave birth to her fourth son, a sturdy boy, who was given his father's second name, Anthony. A few months later the year of Anthony's birth became forever memorable as the year of Waterloo, when Napoleon was finally defeated. A year later Fanny bore a daughter whom they named Cecilia, and in 1818 she had another daughter, Emily.

Until 1816 and Cecilia's birth, the pattern of life for the Trollopes remained rather constant. Fanny hired a reliable, if somewhat dour, nursemaid named Farmer and enjoyed her children, when she had time, in her own unworried way. During the hour before bedtime she often sang to them, lively songs to which they could dance or skip about. They all remembered one raffish song, the words of which had no meaning to them at the time.

> A captain bold of Halifax
> Who lived in country quarters
> Seduced a maid who hanged herself
> One Monday in her garters . . .
> Oh, Miss Bailey, unfortunate Miss Bailey.

It had an excellent beat for dancing.

When Thomas was four, Fanny invented a splendid game for him and a neighbour's daughter who was just his age. She got some bone cubes printed on each side with letters of the alphabet. She would toss these out on the nursery floor and offer a prize to the child who could first find and bring to her a requested letter—'Big A, little a, bouncing B. . . .'

Thomas Anthony had more rigorous plans for his children's education. Thomas Adolphus was not yet six when his father presented him with an Eton Latin grammar and told him to learn the first page and be ready for a recitation the next morning.

Fanny winced in sympathy when she came into the back drawing room before breakfast and saw the small boy kneeling before the book, which lay on the sofa, his face contorted with effort as he struggled with the strange combination of letters. But she made no protest—Thomas Anthony was the learned parent. Perhaps this was the way boys had to be prepared to enter the hallowed halls of Winchester. Soon young Henry was being handed the same difficult assignments, and Thomas Anthony had no tricks to make the learning easier. He simply expected performance, and when either of the boys stumbled or made an error, he reached out a hand and pulled the offender's hair. He may have thought he was adding incentive when he arranged to have the boys meet him each afternoon when he left his chambers in Lincoln's Inn and then walk home with him. They hurried and hopped along to keep up with his strides and only had some brief respite when he paused to point out the homes of various judges and barristers who lived in the Bloomsbury area. Before the walk was over, however, they were expected to recite a Latin verse written to an English text that their father had given them in the morning, and that part of the walk was more taxing.

On the other hand, young Thomas and Henry were allowed an extraordinary amount of freedom during the day. While Nurse Farmer was busy with the infants in the nursery, and Fanny was supervising the household or entertaining or out somewhere being entertained, Tom and Henry rambled through London like small gypsies. Their favourite haunt was Piccadilly and the White Horse Cellar, the departure point for mail coaches starting out for destinations all over southern England. Here they found it no trouble at all to learn the names of the various 'High Flyers', 'Magnets', and 'Independents', that took off with such a fine flurry of horn blowing and clattering of hooves. Once they wandered so far as a place known as Saffron Hill, which they had learned somehow was the headquarters for the city's pickpockets. They never came to harm on these expeditions, never kept them secret from their mother, and neither she nor their father seemed to think it necessary to forbid them.

But through these years, as Fanny was being both fruitful and social, Thomas Anthony was not faring so well. Each year he seemed to have fewer clients, and the income from his profession was dwindling accordingly. The reason seemed clear enough to his colleagues and his wife also. Mr Trollope was an unusually learned man but he was also unusually insistent on his own points of view, offending both clients and colleagues with his harsh judgments and impatient dismissal of any ideas that differed from his own. Sadly, Fanny saw that, as his practice declined, he suffered more and more from headaches, sometimes so severe that he had to spend a day or two in bed.

As matters worsened, Fanny and her husband discussed the situation. They did not take up his overbearing manner. Fanny had long since learned it was useless to urge her husband to greater moderation. But they had to talk about their lessening income, Thomas Anthony's poor health, and an ever-increasing family with sons who must soon have formal schooling. Was there some move they could make to improve matters?

No one is sure whether it was Fanny or Thomas Anthony who inspired the various moves on which they soon embarked. Two of their sons wrote autobiographies in their later years, but neither of them ventured a hint as to which parent was the deciding force. After all, the sons had been children when the changes occurred.

They did remember that in 1816 Thomas Anthony Trollope took a long-term lease on three hundred acres belonging to Lord North-wick in the nearby village of Harrow, at a substantial yearly rent. There was already a farmhouse on the property, but Mr Trollope at once undertook to build a large new house on this rented land. Some time in 1818, the family moved from the house at 16 Keppel Street to the new home in Harrow.

Harrow – Loss of Inheritance – Evangelic

Harrow, of course, had its famous boys' school,
Anthony had learned from some family friends, the M
lived nearby in Bloomsbury, that residents of Harro
their sons to the school without having to pay for
Merivales were planning a move to Harrow so that th
might attend the school. With four sons who had the
schooling before they were ready for Winchester, Tho
had even more reason than they to take advantage of
  A further justification of the move was the good th
air might do Thomas Anthony's health as he drove th
forth to his chambers in the city each day. Still anoth
Thomas Anthony's plan to farm some portion of the a
acquire another source of income apart from his law
  There seemed no reason at all, however, to explain
of a large and expensive house on rented property—ex
did have a large family now, Thomas Anthony wa
with an obligation to present a decent front to the wor
did want to be able to entertain in a manner suitable to
standing and her children's futures.[1]
  And so the house was built, and Fanny was bus
nishing the house and in instructing local workme
points of laying out gardens. Thomas Anthony, who
whatever about farming, hired a bailiff and other local
began to supervise the ploughing and planting of
acreage. Whatever extravagant and unexpected outla
ved, Thomas Anthony brushed them aside, assuring
would soon have the farm making money for the
intelligent person ought to be able to make a profit fro
thought, and he fancied he was at least that. He rem

to learn the names of the various 'High Flyers', 'Magnets', and 'Independents', that took off with such a fine flurry of horn blowing and clattering of hooves. Once they wandered so far as a place known as Saffron Hill, which they had learned somehow was the headquarters for the city's pickpockets. They never came to harm on these expeditions, never kept them secret from their mother, and neither she nor their father seemed to think it necessary to forbid them.

But through these years, as Fanny was being both fruitful and social, Thomas Anthony was not faring so well. Each year he seemed to have fewer clients, and the income from his profession was dwindling accordingly. The reason seemed clear enough to his colleagues and his wife also. Mr Trollope was an unusually learned man but he was also unusually insistent on his own points of view, offending both clients and colleagues with his harsh judgments and impatient dismissal of any ideas that differed from his own. Sadly, Fanny saw that, as his practice declined, he suffered more and more from headaches, sometimes so severe that he had to spend a day or two in bed.

As matters worsened, Fanny and her husband discussed the situation. They did not take up his overbearing manner. Fanny had long since learned it was useless to urge her husband to greater moderation. But they had to talk about their lessening income, Thomas Anthony's poor health, and an ever-increasing family with sons who must soon have formal schooling. Was there some move they could make to improve matters?

No one is sure whether it was Fanny or Thomas Anthony who inspired the various moves on which they soon embarked. Two of their sons wrote autobiographies in their later years, but neither of them ventured a hint as to which parent was the deciding force. After all, the sons had been children when the changes occurred.

They did remember that in 1816 Thomas Anthony Trollope took a long-term lease on three hundred acres belonging to Lord Northwick in the nearby village of Harrow, at a substantial yearly rent. There was already a farmhouse on the property, but Mr Trollope at once undertook to build a large new house on this rented land. Some time in 1818, the family moved from the house at 16 Keppel Street to the new home in Harrow.

Harrow – Loss of Inheritance – Evangelicals – Grief

Harrow, of course, had its famous boys' school, and Thomas Anthony had learned from some family friends, the Merivales, who lived nearby in Bloomsbury, that residents of Harrow could send their sons to the school without having to pay for tuition. The Merivales were planning a move to Harrow so that their three sons might attend the school. With four sons who had the need of some schooling before they were ready for Winchester, Thomas Anthony had even more reason than they to take advantage of this saving.

A further justification of the move was the good that the country air might do Thomas Anthony's health as he drove the gig back and forth to his chambers in the city each day. Still another reason was Thomas Anthony's plan to farm some portion of the acreage and so acquire another source of income apart from his law practice.

There seemed no reason at all, however, to explain the building of a large and expensive house on rented property—except that they did have a large family now, Thomas Anthony was a gentleman with an obligation to present a decent front to the world, and Fanny did want to be able to entertain in a manner suitable to her husband's standing and her children's futures.[1]

And so the house was built, and Fanny was busy both in furnishing the house and in instructing local workmen on the finer points of laying out gardens. Thomas Anthony, who knew nothing whatever about farming, hired a bailiff and other local labourers and began to supervise the ploughing and planting of some of the acreage. Whatever extravagant and unexpected outlays were involved, Thomas Anthony brushed them aside, assuring Fanny that he would soon have the farm making money for them. Any half-intelligent person ought to be able to make a profit from farming, he thought, and he fancied he was at least that. He reminded her also that some day in the future their inheritance from Uncle Adolphus would more than take care of any debts they incurred as they got the house and farm into working order.

They decided to call their new home Julians. It may have been a gesture of deference to Uncle Adolphus, squire of the original Julians in Hertfordshire. It could have been Thomas Anthony in a defiant mood, signalling to his uncle that he could have a Julians of his own without waiting to inherit one.

Whatever inspired the name, the house was definitely Julians, and the family was in residence there before the great blow fell. In 1817 they were surprised to hear of Aunt Meetkerke's death, sent proper condolences to Uncle Adolphus, and exchanged a few sympathetic remarks about the loneliness the old man would know as a widower. And then, a year later, came a letter with the news that Uncle Adolphus had married again, this time a very young woman. And still they were not prepared for the news that came less than a year after that. Uncle Adolphus was the father of a son. He had an heir.

With this announcement, Thomas Anthony and Fanny suddenly saw the promise of future security vanish. The inheritance by which they had justified one expense after another was not to be theirs after all. Looking at young Tom, Fanny recalled the time several years previously when she and Thomas Anthony had taken the little boy to visit his great-uncle and the child had been introduced to everyone on the estate as the future master of Julians. So, not only she and Thomas Anthony but Tom, too, were losers due to this wholly unexpected activity of Uncle Adolphus.

Thomas Anthony took the loss with astonishing calm. He soothed Fanny and ignored her accusations that it was all his fault for arguing politics with Uncle Adolphus. Plainly, whether Thomas Anthony had been on good terms or bad with his uncle, that had nothing to do with a healthy widower's decision to marry again and have a family. Again and again Thomas Anthony assured Fanny that the loss of their expectations from him need make no difference of consequence. They had been living all this while on Thomas Anthony's income from his profession and from various holdings and properties. They would continue to do so now, with the added income from farming. Fanny soon allowed herself to be persuaded.

In this new home she had found friends as quickly as she always did, and so, in addition to old friends who drove out from the city to spend a day, a weekend, or a week, she was entertaining local residents. A family named Grant lived in the nearest house to Julians, and the young Trollopes and the young Grants were soon on easy terms, dropping in at each other's homes without formality. Sir Francis and Lady Milman, who lived in the nearby village of Pinner, were frequent visitors.

And then there were the Drurys. The Drurys were the chief figures at the school that had helped lure the Trollopes to Harrow. Dr Drury, the patriarch of the clan, had recently relinquished the post of headmaster to a Dr Butler. But Dr Drury's brother Mark was still the second master; Harry, a son, who had been tutor and friend to Lord Byron during his years at Harrow-on-the-Hill, was another master; and William, son of Mark, was still another. They too were often at Julians.

A frequent subject of comment (when he was not present in person) was the local vicar, the Reverend J. W. Cunningham. The Drurys, High Churchmen all, were dismayed by the fact that the Reverend Cunningham was an ostentatiously Low Church evangelical. A few years before, he had written a book called *The Velvet Cushion*, which became extremely popular with Low Church members and had also won him the nickname of Velvet Cunningham among those who disliked it. The Drurys not only disliked the book but the vicar as well and found his manners so excessively smooth and ingratiating that the nickname Velvet seemed quite apt. They amused themselves with stories about his hypocritical behaviour and liked to wonder how he had achieved the Harrow living.

'It is Velvet's contention that he was awarded the living because Lord Northwick was so much impressed by one of his sermons,' one of the Drurys informed Fanny. 'Which leads one to wonder', said another, rolling his eyes, 'just when in his life Lord Northwick ever even sat through a sermon, much less listened.'

Fanny, who had been brought up in the Heckfield vicarage where the traditional doctrine and rituals of the church were as quietly taken for granted as bread and butter, was also offended by the emotionalism of Low Church practices and happily contributed her own observations on Velvet, agreeing with the Drurys that his father must have bought the living for him.

The climax of the '*affaire* Velvet' came in 1822, when Lord Byron, now a famous, or infamous, exile on the Continent, remembered Harrow-on-the-Hill at a sad crisis in his life. His daughter, Allegra, the offspring of his brief liaison with Claire Clairmont, had died in a Swiss boarding school at the age of five. Casting about for a last resting place for the child, Byron remembered Harrow and the old churchyard there where he had dreamed away some hours during his youth. He had the small body sent to Harrow for interment, along with the inscription he wished to have on the marble tablet over her grave and instructions that the funeral should be as private as possible.

The Drurys, in their capacity as churchwardens, met with the Reverend Cunningham and other vestrymen to consider the request and decided it would have a bad moral effect on Harrow schoolboys for an illegitimate child to be buried in their churchyard. The best the group could offer Lord Byron was an unmarked grave in an unconsecrated portion of the cemetery.

The Drurys brought the news to Fanny at Julians, wheezing and snorting with laughter. Their prize item of gossip was the fact that Velvet Cunningham, after the vote, had taken Harry aside to make sure that when Harry informed Lord Byron of the group's decision, he would also convey the Reverend Cunningham's greeting and his great admiration for Byron's latest poem, *Cain*. And how was that, they asked, for Low Church hypocrisy and toadying?

Fanny, caught up in the quiz, was inspired to write a long, satirical poem in the *ottava rima* style of Byron's *Don Juan*, relating the whole sad, ridiculous story.

> He saw her sicken and he watched her die.
> The soft small hands' last pressure was his own.
> His the last glance of meaning from her eye,
> And his to clasp her when the spark was flown.

Actually, the child had been in boarding school when she died, and Byron had not seen her for some months. Never mind. Fanny's

circle at Harrow was charmed by the poem and laughed with
pleasure at her descriptions of each of them, such as:

> Black letter Harry deep in classic lore,
>   whose ample front speaks frankness and good sense . . .

They were gleeful when she introduced 'the mild-eyed vicar' and
had him speaking his fatuous lines:

> And should you, Mr. Drury, chance to write
>   To your accomplished friend, I wish that my
> Great admiration of the genius shewn
>   In that performance should to him be known.[2]

The poem circulated among all the High Church folk in Harrow,
causing much amusement and winning Fanny a reputation for being
clever with her pen. Harry Drury was so pleased by it that he
rewarded Fanny with one of his own treasures, a manuscript page
on which Lord Byron had copied out one of his poems for his old
tutor and friend, signed with his autograph.

Involved in such diversions and seeing the Drurys regularly,
Fanny seemed unaware that her sons were less than happy in the
school where the Drurys taught. Young Thomas began trudging up
the hill from Julians to the school in 1818 and Henry joined him a
year later. But neither their mother nor their father, pleased that
the school was tuition-free to residents, had any clear idea of what
had happened to the institution that John Lyons had founded
centuries before as a free facility for the boys of Harrow. Over the
years the school had won such a reputation that wealthy and aristocratic families all over England began to send their sons to Harrow,
paying the fees required of non-residents. By 1818 it was chiefly a
school for paying boarders. Tom, and then Henry, were among a
handful of town boys who were scorned and bullied as 'charity
cases'.

Both Tom and Henry suffered as only the ostracized young can
suffer. They had known much freedom in London when they were
not struggling with the Latin lessons demanded by their father.

Here, in the presumed freedom of the country, they felt imprisoned. Too young for regular classes, they sat behind one master or another while he conducted scheduled lessons and then were given a bit of tutoring when the classes changed. During recess hours they crept about the edges of the playing field until it was time to make their way down the road to Julians.

Tom tried to tell his mother, usually so sympathetic, of his misery, but she turned a deaf ear. After all, the school was one of the reasons that the family was at Harrow. Tom was probably imagining things. When both Tom and Henry were taken ill in the spring with typhoid, Tom raved in his delirium of masters coming in through the windows, and of cruel boys lying in wait to punch him or trip him. But when he and Henry were safely recovered, Fanny laughed aside the revelations and sent both boys back to Harrow-on-the-Hill.

Thomas only had to endure two years of it. He had been registered at his father's old school at Winchester since his infancy and was scheduled to enter it when he was ten. That happy birthday came in 1820, and shortly after its celebration Tom hopped into the gig beside his father to be driven the sixty miles to Winchester. They had a cheerful trip. In a mellow, nostalgic mood, Thomas Anthony reminisced about the various landmarks they passed on their way. Still warmed by the same glow, he waited until Tom had passed the necessary formalities for entrance, then bade him good-bye and returned to Julians well pleased.

As it turned out, Tom also was soon well pleased. The boy liked the ancient buildings of William of Wykeham's school. He liked the medieval rituals of bells, chapels, prefects of this, that, and the other, the meals of mutton, potatoes, and beer. ('William of Wykeham, I think, knew nothing of tea!' the masters said sternly when any boys were discovered partaking of that worldly beverage.) He even liked the rituals of 'scourging', which were so formalized—gown lifted a specified number of inches, a specified number of whacks routinely administered—that the punished boy knew neither pain nor shame. Above all, at Winchester scholarship students were the élite rather than the underdogs. So Thomas Adolphus flourished at Winchester, and, a year later, Henry was also released from Harrow-on-the-Hill and came to join him.[3]

By then, the two younger Trollope boys were setting forth each morning to face the difficulties at Harrow that their older brothers had known. Arthur, always less robust than the other boys, was ten before Fanny thought him ready for formal schooling, but she had no qualms about sending eight-year-old Anthony up the hill along with him. Anthony was a strong, knockabout child, and his mother thought school discipline would be good for him.

What Fanny never seemed aware of in her youngest son was the sensitivity that lay under his rackety behaviour. To her, Tom, her oldest, was the sensitive one, responding to her moods, laughing with her, making solemn comments from time to time and showing withal the same equable nature as that of her father, the vicar of Heckfield. Anthony was something else again, given to sudden bursts of physical activity alternating with sullen bouts of retreat. She tried, or at least she thought she tried to reach him. Tom, in later years, would have some notion that Anthony had been the 'Benjamin' of the family in his childhood. But Anthony had no such memories of being cherished. He thought of himself always as the odd child out, too young to share the comradeship of Tom and Henry, too energetic for Arthur, too rough for his little sisters, and somehow never really noticed by his mother. As a result he suffered more than Tom had from the bullying he met at school, and spoke of it to no one. His mother only saw that he scuffed his way up and down the hill attracting dirt like a magnet. His shoes were always dusty or muddy, depending on the weather, his fingers and shirt smudged with ink, his hair tousled.

'How was the day, Tony?' she asked, and he either shrugged and slouched away or burst into laughter that sometimes seemed senseless.

Arthur's poor health was something Fanny could cope with more directly. His frequent colds, his lassitude, his general frailty convinced her that he was still not ready for school. In the spring of 1824 she took him to stay with her father and stepfather at Heckfield. Perhaps in that placid atmosphere he might grow stronger, and with his grandfather to tutor him now and then, his schooling would not suffer unduly.

For a while, Fanny's hopes of the therapeutic values of Heckfield seemed justified. Cheerful letters came from the Reverend Milton. Things were definitely *au mieux*. The grandfather was taking Arthur for walks, pretending to lean on his young strength. He was teaching the boy mathematics, and his progress was wonderful. Surely Euclid was going to be Arthur's joy all his life long. Suddenly, every hope was dashed. Arthur was briefly ill, and then—unbelievably—dead.

Fanny was stunned as she and Thomas Anthony journeyed to Heckfield to attend the last rites for their son. He had been delicate, yes, but Fanny had never dreamed his young life could be snuffed out so quickly.

Soon after they returned to Julians Fanny had word that her father had died.

She was quite numb with grief after two such losses. She thought of the unfulfilled promises of her son's young life and wanted to weep. Her father's death brought an entirely different emotion. William Milton had filled his years with cheerful activity of his own choosing, but she felt pangs of tenderness as she remembered such inventions of his as the *rotis volventibus*, a crazy vehicle consisting of a seat slung between two wheels of eight-foot diameter. She had a picture in her mind of a sunny afternoon when young Tom had climbed into the seat and sent the contraption careening across the lawn and down a slope and then of her gentle father racing to the rescue and warning his grandson that he should not set in motion forces that he could not control. She heard an echo of his voice softly murmuring *au mieux*. Both losses—the young life and the old one— were hard to accept.

And then, Fanny put her grief aside and ceased to refer to it. This abrupt rejection of sorrow was a trait she would show all her life. Her sons speculated about it in their autobiographies. Tom wrote, 'her mind refused to remain crushed any more than the grass is permanently crushed by the storm wind that blows over it. She had the innate faculty and tendency to throw sorrow off when the cause of it had passed. She owed herself to the living, and refused to allow unavailing regret for those who had been taken from her to incapacitate her for paying that debt to the utmost.'[4] Anthony, always less tender than Thomas Adolphus in writing of her, compared her to those animal mothers who are deeply concerned with any offspring that is within immediate sight but quickly forgetful of its existence when it is no longer nearby.

However one sees her—shallow and unfeeling, or committed to the living whatever her private sorrows—Frances Trollope had all her life a natural resiliency that enabled her to rebound from whatever grief, disaster, or calamity had overtaken her, showing few marks of her suffering.

Gradually, social life at Julians picked up again. By September, Fanny and Thomas Anthony were preparing to start on another of the junkets that they took every year during Thomas Anthony's 'long vacation'.

5

Paris – Frances Wright – La Fayette

Travelling pleased Fanny, and she looked forward to almost any destination. In the years since their marriage she and Thomas Anthony had made excursions all around southern England, taking in scenic spots of note and visiting relatives—his sisters, her sister, Mary, now married to a retired naval officer and living in Ottery Saint Mary (her brother Henry, also married by now, lived in Fulham, only twelve miles from Harrow, so there was no need of formal trips), cousin Fanny Bent at Exeter, and various friends scattered across the countryside. They had also on several occasions crossed the Channel and made their way to Paris. The old glories of that city combined with the new splendours conceived by Napoleon —its theatre, opera, and salons—all made it easy for Fanny to ignore such less attractive aspects of the city as the primitive sanitation, malodorous open drains, and night-time lanterns that were only dim blurs in the darkness. With Jean-Jacques Rousseau, Fanny was always ready to exult in '*un voyage à faire, et Paris au bout*'.

When they journeyed to Paris in 1821, some friends from Fanny's girlhood days were in the city to greet them. The Garnetts were originally a Bristol family, known to the Reverend Milton when he lived near that city. The friendship had continued after the Miltons moved to Heckfield, and the young Miltons had played with the young Garnetts when they came to visit. Then in 1797 the Garnetts had moved to the United States and settled in New Jersey, where they had remained until the death of Mr Garnett in 1820. His widow and three of the Garnett daughters then left the United States and settled in Paris. Years had passed since Fanny had seen them. She and her contemporaries, Frances, Julia, and Harriet, whom she had known as children, were all grown women now.

There was a great deal of catching up to do on what had happened to them all, and the Garnetts were anxious to get acquainted with Thomas Anthony. But they were also eager to introduce the Trollopes to the friends they had made in Paris, members of the English colony and some visiting Americans as well. One American whom Fanny met was the author Washington Irving, but she and he seem not to have made much impression on each other.

Frances Wright was something else again—a young Scotswoman who had already become a celebrity at the age of twenty-six and who entered a room trailing clouds of radiant conviction and self-assurance. The Garnetts had entertained her, and her younger, less assertive sister, Camilla, in New Jersey, two years previously, during the course of a dramatic journey the sisters had made to the United States.

Fanny Trollope met her now, in the Garnetts' drawing room in Paris—a tall, strikingly handsome young woman, who was as apt to wear Turkish bloomers as more usual feminine dress, and who, when she chose to speak, could often mesmerize her audience.

Fanny was captivated. Who was this young woman who spoke so casually about the play she had written when she was nineteen that had been produced with much success at a theatre in New York in the United States? And then had come back to England to write a book about her American experiences, *Views of Society and Manners in America*, which had won her the approval and friendship of that venerable philosopher Jeremy Bentham? The book had also excited the interest of that famous French liberal and revolutionary the Marquis de La Fayette. He had written to Miss Wright of his admiration and his hope that he might meet her the next time she was in Paris. And now, here she was in Paris, reporting ecstatically on her meetings with La Fayette and the instant rapport that had sprung up between her and the General.

It was not long, of course, before Fanny learned some of the background of this remarkable young woman. She and her sister had been born in Dundee, daughters of a wealthy merchant with radical interests. Both parents had died within months of each other when the children were small. Taken with her sister to England to be raised by an aunt, Frances had been moody and rebellious. Then she had come upon a history of the American Revolution, written by the Italian, Botta, and her life had been transformed. She was seized by a vision of an idealistic society that seemed to have been fought for and won in America. She read everything she could find about the United States. And the moment she came of age and into control of the fortune her parents had left her and her sister, she quickly and quietly arranged passage for herself and Camilla to that country, which seemed like a promised land. The new nation had been everything she expected, or almost. She had had her play produced. She had returned to England to write the book that was a paean of praise to the new democracy across the sea and to win the admiration not only of Jeremy Bentham but of all English liberals.

Before Fanny and Thomas Anthony left Paris, Frances Wright and her sister were off to spend some weeks as the guests of General Le Fayette at his country estate, La Grange, but Fanny had won a promise from Miss Wright to visit the Trollopes whenever she returned to England.

A month or so later, back at Julians, Fanny was delighted to hear that Frances Wright would be keeping her promise. She and Camilla arrived for a visit, and Fanny was agog to hear all that her guests had to relate about their time with La Fayette.

'Oh, it was wonderful,' Frances Wright cried in her rich, dark voice. She and the General had spent long hours together, sharing innumerable confidences. Dropping her voice, Frances Wright half-whispered, 'I know I can trust *you*, Mrs Trollope.' Fanny nodded, her eyes wide, and Frances Wright told her that La Fayette had confessed his continuing connection with Europe's revolutionary underground, the Carbonari. Even as the Wright sisters were visiting La Fayette at La Grange some Carbonari plots had been exposed, and various conspirators had fled to England. 'Now he has asked me to take messages to some of them,' Frances Wright whispered. 'And of course, anything I can do . . .'

Meanwhile, Fanny's old friend, Gen. Guglielmo Pepe was also a refugee in London, following his latest military venture, leading an unsuccessful Carbonari revolt in the kingdoms of Naples and Sicily. Fanny found it very exciting to bring Pepe and Miss Wright together so that the young woman could help him obtain some needed letters from La Fayette. She was happy also to arrange for Frances Wright to spend part of her time in London in the Trollope house at 16 Keppel Street. Such clandestine adventures were an intriguing background to Fanny's life, which hummed along with its usual myriad interests.

Fanny's friendship with Frances Wright helped inspire another holiday in Paris in 1823. This time, she and Thomas Anthony were introduced to the Marquis de La Fayette by Miss Wright and were pleased when he invited them to visit him at his château La Grange, forty miles from Paris in the department of Seine-et-Marne.

The château had a special French beauty, with five round towers lending it a look of medieval romance. The grounds were handsome in the formal French style, and both Trollopes were impressed by the princely way of life that La Fayette and his family enjoyed. Fanny wrote a letter to Tom describing the meal to which they sat down almost immediately after their arrival. What with La Fayette's two married daughters, their six children, three unmarried daughters, and various other relatives, there were twenty-one at dinner.

'Six of the General's men-servants waited at table,' Fanny wrote. 'These did not include two who had attended us from Paris. The dinner was excellent, and served in a very agreeable style, though not *à l'Anglaise*. . . . Our apartment is charming. It consists of two rooms and two closets. In the largest room is a very handsome bed in a recess, with rich crimson satin curtains, and a quilt of the same, covering the bed by day. In the smaller room is a small bed for Monsieur, if it were preferred. One closet is completely fitted up as a *cabinet de toilette*, the other to contain the valises, etc. . . . We passed the evening in two very handsome saloons.'[1]

The next day they strolled the gardens and grounds in the company of their host and various of his daughters and daughters-in-law. Thomas Anthony talked with the General about the political situation in France and elsewhere in Europe. Altogether, the visit, which lasted several days, was most satisfactory, and when the Trollopes departed, there was talk of another visit the next year.

But in late autumn of 1823, Frances Wright, back from another stay at La Grange, confided to Fanny that she and Camilla no longer felt as welcome at La Grange as they once had. The General's children had become jealous of his affection for the two sisters, particularly of his devotion to Frances. They did not like it that, when Frances was at La Grange, the General insisted that 'his dear Fan' have the room beneath his in one of the five round towers. They did not like the long hours the two of them spent together nor the notes they wrote to each other when apart, lavish with terms of endearment.

The family's reaction was somewhat understandable to Fanny Trollope. Although the Marquis de La Fayette was sixty-seven years old, he was still a vigorous man and a widower. Frances Wright was young, handsome, vital, and always ready to immerse herself in the concerns of her dear La Fayette, her mentor, her foster father. It was easy enough for an outsider to guess what the family feared. Their father was going to make some kind of fool of himself over this headstrong young Scotswoman.

Along with a disapproving family, La Fayette was facing other difficulties. Hints that he was still engaged in underground activities had begun to circulate, and although nothing was proven, he lost his seat in the Chamber of Deputies.

At this trying period in his life La Fayette received an invitation from the United States to make a ceremonial visit to that nation that he had helped bring into being. He was happy to accept the invitation and had only one concern. He wanted his 'beloved girls', Frances and Camilla, to accompany him, and Frances herself could not envision him making the journey to the country she admired so much without her. His family, on the other hand, could not envision anything so scandalous. Already people were beginning to smile and intimate some affair between the older man and Frances. La Fayette's daughters and daughters-in-law pleaded with him, wept, and had tantrums. He could not, he must not, give currency to the rumours by taking Frances Wright and her sister with him to America.

Fanny Trollope heard some of the story when Frances Wright made another of her quick visits to London in the spring. Miss Wright was sure she had thought of the perfect solution. La Fayette should legally adopt her and Camilla as his daughters. Surely that would silence gossip. Later, after Miss Wright had returned to France, Fanny was hardly surprised to hear from the Garnett sisters that this suggestion had only increased the outrage of La Fayette's family.

But this was the July of 1824, when young Arthur died so suddenly and William Milton died a few weeks later. Lost in mourning, Fanny followed the further course of events only vaguely. Somehow, everyone had calmed down. It was agreed that the General would leave for America as planned and that Frances and Camilla Wright would follow on a later boat. They would be designated as his wards.

By the time Fanny had put aside her grief and was planning the yearly holiday with Thomas Anthony, La Fayette was in America, delaying some lavish ceremonials in his honour so that he could meet the Wright sisters when their ship dropped anchor in New York harbour. Obviously, the Trollopes would not be visiting La Grange this year, and they decided on an excursion to the Isle of Wight.

They took with them their own domestic concerns. Thomas Anthony was disturbed by young Henry's lack of progress at Winchester. He was not adjusting to Wykeham standards and demands the way Tom was. His father had written him frequent letters, exhorting him to use his time to better advantage, reminding him that his future depended on his doing well at Winchester. Henry's responses were short and rebellious. Fanny tried to defend Henry and suggested that he might do better if Thomas Anthony were a little easier on him. 'What? What?' Thomas Anthony flicked the whip at the horse and darted a suspicious glance at Fanny. 'He has to be kept up to the mark.' Fanny sighed and said no more on that subject. Later they talked about young Anthony. Thomas Anthony wondered why he also was doing poorly at school, but Fanny had no answer.

There was a constant underlying worry about money as well. Thomas Anthony frowned before making any expenditure for food or lodging. At such times, Fanny frowned also, not sure how realistic her husband's concerns were. He had said there was no need to worry when they lost hope of the inheritance from Uncle Adolphus.

But now he spoke harshly of losses rather than profits from his farming activities on the Julians acres, of the terrible strain the rent on that property entailed, of his miniscule income from his practice as a barrister. Were they really in financial difficulties? Fanny did not know what to believe.

They returned to Julians and resumed life as before. Fanny continued to entertain and make trips to London. Some days Thomas Anthony drove to his chambers in Lincoln's Inn to gloom over his books there and what few cases had been referred to him. Other days he stayed home. There was little he could do about the farm during the winter months except to mull over the unsatisfactory accounts. More often he stayed home suffering another of his sick headaches, which he treated with ever larger doses of calomel.

During the winter Fanny mentioned her worries about young Anthony to one or another of the Drurys, who were still frequent visitors at Julians. At some point one of them recalled that a relative kept a small boys' school at Sunbury, on the Thames. Perhaps, he suggested, Tony might do better in that less demanding situation. Fanny talked it over with Thomas Anthony, and in the spring of 1825 ten-year-old Tony was removed from Harrow-on-the-Hill, and his father drove him to Sunbury to enter him in the school there.

Thomas Anthony spoke little on the journey. Young Anthony was silent also, brooding on this new evidence that he was unwanted at home, where he could be at least a witness to the laughter and good cheer that seemed to surround his mother. It never occurred to him that his mother and father might be trying to make his life happier and less lonely now that both Tom and Henry were at Winchester and Arthur was gone.

As it turned out, Anthony's forebodings were truer than his parents' hopes. Before he had been very long at Sunbury, he learned that his father was slow in paying his tuition fees. A few months later he was innocently caught up in a school scandal. Four boys were summoned before the headmaster and accused of perversion, and Anthony was one of the four. Anthony had no idea of what crime he was supposedly guilty when the headmaster expressed his shock and pronounced punishment. He stood numb and dumb, and the other boys made no effort to exonerate him. The headmaster made no enquiries. Anthony came from an aristocratic school where such vices presumably flourished, and so he was punished with the others and stumbled about his daily lessons, wondering what it was he was supposed to have done, and would he have done it if he had known, and would those others have been his friends if he had.[2]

Mercifully, perhaps, the headmaster sent no message about Anthony's disgrace to his parents. He did send messages about the unpaid tuition, and Fanny fretted about those bills.

What *was* their financial situation? Were she and Thomas Anthony really poor? If so, how could they continue the upkeep on Julians? How could Thomas Anthony keep investing in new farming experiments? How could they finance their yearly holidays?

It did no good to ask her husband. He brushed her questions aside angrily. None of it was her concern. He would take care of things. Fanny really had no choice but to continue her usual course of hospitality, dinner parties, tea parties, and trips to London while she wondered why school bills for the boys were not paid and why Lord Northwick was getting more and more impatient about delayed payments on the rent for Julians. What else could a woman do but trust her husband in such matters?

6

An Unhappy Man – Poverty – Decisions

'He was not a man to make himself popular in any position. I have said that he was moody and disappointed. He was even worse than this; he was morose, sometimes almost to insanity. There had been days in which even his wife had found it impossible to deal with him otherwise than as with an acknowledged lunatic.'[1]

It was a portrait sketched years later by Anthony Trollope after he had become a novelist and was describing a character in *The Last Chronicle of Barset*, a clergyman named Crawley. Allowing for the usual fictional disguises, it is easy to believe that the Reverend Crawley was as close as Anthony came to picturing his father in his novels. He wrote of how the curate, for all his moodiness, was held in high esteem among the poorest of his parishioners. 'They knew that he lived hardly, as they lived; that he worked hard, as they worked . . . and there had been apparent . . . a manifest struggle to do his duty in spite of the world's ill-usage.'

Thomas Anthony Trollope's eldest son, Thomas Adolphus, wrote more directly about his father in his memoirs. 'He was, in a word, a highly respected, but not a popular or well-beloved man. Worst of all, alas! he was not popular in his own home. No one of all the family circle was happy in his presence. Assuredly he was as affectionate and anxiously solicitous a father as any children ever had. I never remember his caning, whipping, beating, or striking any one of us. But he used, during the detested Latin lessons, to sit with his arm over the back of the pupil's chair, so that his hand might be ready to inflict an instantaneous pull of the hair . . . for every blundered concord or false quantity. . . . There was also a strange sort of asceticism about him, which seemed to make enjoyment, or any employment of the hours save work, distasteful and offensive to him. Lessons for us boys were never over and done with.'[2]

Thomas Adolphus remembered also that his father was fond of reading aloud to the assembled family in the evening, 'and there was not one individual of those who heard him who would not have escaped from doing so at almost any cost. . . . I remember—oh, how well!—the nightly readings during one winter of *Sir Charles Grandison*, and the loathing disgust for that production which they occasioned.'

Fanny herself, in the thousands of words she later wrote, never described her husband, but in one of her novels there was a passage that had the ring of remembered experience. 'There is always something embarrassing in the abrupt check to laughter, by the unexpected entrance of a person, or persons, totally unfit to join in it. It is like a sudden stop put to violent motion.'³

Fanny did her best against her husband's deepening gloom. She was pleased when a well-known artist, George Hayter, who was sometimes a guest at Julians, persuaded Thomas Anthony to sit as a model for one of the lawyers in the painting he was making of the trial of Lord John Russell. The sittings were a distraction that briefly lightened Thomas Anthony's spirits. When Fanny saw him brooding over the farm accounts, she urged him to apply himself to something more productive—the study of Italian perhaps. Sighing, he took her advice, and soon Fanny was writing cheerily to Tom that both of them must keep up their study in that language, or Papa would outdistance them.

Now and then through that year of 1824 she had word of Frances and Camilla Wright and their journeys in the United States. Most of her news came in letters from Julia and Harriet Garnett. They wrote that Fanny and Cam had been with La Fayette in Philadelphia, and there Frances was meeting such well-known radicals and reformers as Robert Dale Owen and his son, Robert, Jr., currently involved in taking over a communal settlement at New Harmony, Indiana, where everyone shared both labour and rewards. She had met William Maclure, who was experimenting with a new educational system wherein students earned their board and tuition by helping maintain the school by their labour. Frances and Camilla, travelling with La Fayette, had been entertained by that famous democrat and ex-president of the United States, Thomas Jefferson, at Monticello, his home in Virginia. They wrote that, in the course of all this, Frances seemed to be increasingly concerned with the problem of slavery, the one great flaw in a country otherwise so admirable, and was filling more and more of her letters to them with conjectures as to how that evil institution might be done away with. How could slavery be ended without loss to the slave owners who had huge investments in their slave property? How could an enslaved people be prepared for liberty?

Reading about all this at Julians, Fanny was dazzled by Frances Wright's brilliance. She was, Fanny thought, little less than a genius. At the age of twenty-one she had taken command of her life and her fortune, deciding for herself how she would use her talents and her money for the benefit of humanity. How different, Fanny mused, from her own situation, where she had no clear idea at all of the family's financial circumstances, spent money with no grand plan in mind, and did little with herself except preside over sociable gatherings.

Mary Russell Mitford's venture into drama came along just then to provide a distraction. Struggling desperately to support herself, her mother, and her improvident father by her writing, Miss Mitford had decided that playwriting might be more profitable than poetry. She gave Fanny a copy of an historical drama she had written and asked for her opinion. Fanny was so impressed by the play that she wrote at once to her acquaintances in the theatrical world—Will Macready, the actor, and the producer, Milman—urging them to give their earnest consideration to Miss Mitford's play, *Rienzi*.

'Mrs. Trollope . . . is a most kind and warm-hearted person,' Miss Mitford wrote to a friend, but she was not at all sure that her efforts would be of any avail.

Worry about young Henry's lack of progress at Winchester troubled both Fanny and her husband. Reluctantly, even Thomas Anthony had to admit that his second son was no scholar, and so he and Fanny cast about for some other course for him, finally deciding to settle him in a counting house in Paris. Perhaps Fanny thought he would benefit from living for a while in that city and improve his French. In the spring of 1826, Thomas Anthony drove to Winchester and brought Henry home. Then he and Fanny travelled with the fifteen-year-old boy to Paris, found him lodgings with a clergyman, and saw him established in his new situation.

This quick trip gave Fanny an opportunity to visit with the Garnetts and hear the latest word from Frances Wright. 'You will never guess!' Julia and Harriet cried. Frances and Camilla had bid adieu to La Fayette's party, which was now returning to France, and travelled further in the southern and western states of America to look for land to buy. Land? Yes. For Frances had finally evolved what seemed to her a sensible plan for ending slavery, and she herself was going to put that plan into action on a small scale as a microcosmic example to all the citizens of the United States.

Fanny's eyes widened as Julia and Harriet told her the story. Frances Wright was translating some of the ideas of Robert Dale Owen and William Maclure to her own purposes. She was establishing a colony in one of the southern states, a place called Tennessee, where she was settling a group of slaves, bought from their owners at fair prices. There the black men and women would gradually earn back their purchase price and win their freedom while at the same time they would be receiving an education to prepare them for the responsibility of supporting themselves. She was calling this Colony Nashoba—an Indian name, the Garnetts thought—and had already settled fifteen or sixteen black men, women, and children there.

'So! What do you think of that?' the Garnetts asked. But Fanny could only shake her head, marvelling at the reach of Frances Wright's commitment to her visions.

It all seemed very remote from her troubles at Julians. That summer the rent from the Keppel Street house did not come in on time. Thomas Anthony fretted constantly about the poor outlook for this year's crops. The rent they owed Lord Northwick was a constant drain. Fanny wrote to Tom at Winchester enclosing half a crown for pocket money, 'from Papa, proof at once of poverty and kindness. Without the former it would be more, without the latter it would be nothing.'[4]

And yet, for all this worry about money and talk of poverty, Fanny and Thomas Anthony made another journey to Paris in

September to see how Henry was doing and to make another visit to General La Fayette at La Grange.

Once again they were entertained lavishly, and Thomas Anthony came out of his depression enough to enjoy his talks with La Fayette and even find some amusement in a village festival, which the whole party from La Grange attended. Fanny talked to the General about Frances Wright's new project, and La Fayette shook his head. At the moment he was more worried about 'dear Fan's' health. He had had a letter from Camilla at Nashoba reporting that Frances had been very ill with a malarial fever. She had reported that Fan was now convalescent, but he had not had a letter from Frances herself to confirm that fact. He worried, he said. And dearly as he loved the young woman, he wondered if she had not been too impulsive with this Nashoba scheme. Fanny nodded in agreement, but her awe of Frances Wright's courage was not diminished. Without someone to make such grand gestures, would there ever be any progress toward a better world?

That autumn Mary Russell Mitford's play, *Rienzi*, was finally accepted by a producer. Fanny hurried in from Julians to be on hand for the opening night in late October. After all the worry and delay, it was wonderful to see the play received with acclaim. Miss Mitford wrote to a friend the next day reporting that 'Mrs. Trollope, between joy for my triumph and sympathy with the play, has cried herself half blind.'

Caught up in the special dazzle that the theatre offered, Fanny went back to Julians to try out some private theatricals there. All her friends and acquaintances at Harrow could be involved in one way or another. Even her young daughters, Cecilia, who was now ten and Emily, who was eight, could be given some small tasks in helping to mount the production. Lively gatherings argued over what play they should try, and Molière's *Les Femmes Savantes* was finally chosen. Then there was the entertainment of deciding on the cast and the further diversion of rehearsals, collecting costumes, and improvising settings.

A new friend, a volatile young Frenchman named Auguste Hervieu, became part of the activity. He was an artist, with the romantic sort of background that pleased Fanny. The son of a colonel in Napoleon's army who had died in the retreat from Moscow, young Hervieu had involved himself in underground activities against Louis XVIII; his other major interest was studying art. After participating in an unsuccessful anti-monarchist expedition to Spain, he learned he would be subject to imprisonment if he returned to France, and so, like many others in the same situation, he had made his way to London. He was just managing to stay afloat by giving drawing lessons when Fanny met him and took him under her wing. He gave her girls drawing lessons, and Fanny urged all her friends to commission portraits or hire him to teach their children. Meanwhile, he helped in the theatricals by making sketches of settings and costumes.

With everyone happily involved, a production of *Les Femmes Savantes* was finally presented to the satisfaction of all concerned.

Sometime during those months, the grateful Auguste Hervieu made a sketch of Emily, a charming picture of a young girl seated at her desk, a school book before her, while she blows bubbles from a soap-bubble pipe. On the wall behind her hangs the motto 'Study with determined zeal'.

That spring of 1827 Winchester finally had an opening for young Anthony. His father went to Sunbury to pick him up and drive him to the school, where Tom had been enrolled long enough to become a prefect. Fanny wrote to Tom advising him of his brother's arrival. 'I daresay you will often find him idle and plaguing enough, but remember, dear Tom, that in a family like ours, *everything* gained by one is felt personally and individually by all. He is a good-hearted fellow and clings so to the idea of being Tom's pupil and sleeping in Tom's chamber, that I think you will find advice and remonstrance better taken by him than by poor Henry. Greatly comforted am I to know that Tony has a prefect brother. I well remember what I used to suffer at the idea of what my little Tom was enduring.'[5]

'Comforted' in her own mind, Fanny never learned that her 'dear Tom' was generally unheedful of her advice about treating Tony gently. Years later, Anthony wrote, 'Since I began my manhood, I and my brother Tom have been fast friends. Few brothers have had more of brotherhood. But at Winchester he was of all my foes the worst. As a part of his daily exercise he thrashed me with a big stick.'[6]

Tony's sufferings being unknown at Julians, Fanny and Thomas Anthony were concerned again about 'poor Henry'. He was not doing well in the counting house in Paris. There seemed nothing to do but bring him home again and look about for some other employment for him.

It was not a good time to have him return. His father was no longer trying to conceal his worries about money. If Fanny did not have to deal with her husband as an 'acknowledged lunatic', she did have to do something in a positive way to calm him. Very belatedly, she realized that they truly were in financial trouble. Perhaps, she thought, it was the rent they had to pay Lord Northwick each month that was crushing them. How could they find some income to offset that? She looked about her at the large, handsome house in which they lived. She remembered that farmhouse on the property, which they had dismissed as a residence some years before. It did not seem so impossible now.

She and Thomas Anthony discussed it. Neither one of them was happy at the thought of leaving Julians, but if they could let the big house at a good figure, it would help meet the payments due to Lord Northwick. With a little effort and expense they could make the old farmhouse liveable, and so they quickly agreed to try.[7]

There was some irony in the fact that the tenant they found for Julians was the old object of Fanny's mockery, the Reverend Cunningham. As the transaction took place, she was grateful chiefly for Velvet's suave social manner that eased them over any unpleasant memories. After that, she kept busy supervising the removal of family furniture and effects to the new residence. In a brave gesture of maintaining continuity, she and Thomas Anthony decided to call this house Julians Hill.

The old farmhouse was not unattractive in a rustic way. It stood on a gentle rise and was backed by a few old trees. With the addition of some bay windows for the drawing room and after some general repairs had been made, it was not impossible at all, but it did seem somewhat shabby, old-fashioned, and cramped after the space and convenience of Julians.

Fanny, Thomas Anthony, Henry, and the little girls were just settling in at Julians Hill when Frances Wright returned to England. Soon she got in touch with her old friend, Mrs Trollope, and soon after that, she rode out from London to visit her at Harrow.

Fanny was delighted to see the young woman again. However ill she might have been in America, Frances Wright had regained all her vitality, and she glowed as she talked of the progress being made at Nashoba. Yes, she had left Camilla there, along with a young Quaker, Richeson Whitby, who had been recruited from New Harmony, and a wonderfully intelligent, dedicated Scotsman, James Richardson, whom Frances had met in Memphis. Richardson had been educated as a doctor, Frances Wright told Fanny, and it was undoubtedly due to his care of her that she had recovered from her nearly fatal bout of malaria. Now this fine man was acting as general supervisor of her little colony in her absence, planning and overseeing the ploughing, planting, and tending of crops and looking after the welfare and education of the black settlers.

She had returned to England hoping to interest some intelligent, cultured people in joining her at Nashoba. She envisioned an integrated community where the artificial barriers of race would no longer divide blacks and whites. Her eyes shone, her hands gestured, as she described a colony where whites and blacks lived together in a beautiful natural setting, each race learning from the other. To illustrate what she meant, she spoke of a talented mulatto woman, Charlotte Larieu—'Mamselle Lolette', they called her—who had joined the colony at Nashoba to teach French. Mamselle Lolotte's daughter Josephine was there as well and Frances had rarely seen a more beautiful and intelligent young woman. Ah, if Mrs Trollope could only see her herself.

Impulsively, Fanny cried, 'Why not?'[8]

At first, Frances Wright ignored the interruption, but Fanny insisted. 'Why shouldn't I be one of those to join you at Nashoba? And Henry too! Surely you must have some useful employment there for a young man of his age. It might be just the answer for him.'

Now Frances Wright paused and looked at Fanny. She laughed a little. 'Oh, no,' she said. 'No, I don't think so. Not for you.'

'But why?' said Fanny. 'Why ever not?'

Miss Wright was a visionary with a great talent for blinding herself to any aspect of reality that ran counter to her dreams. Among others whom she had approached in England about the possibility of joining her at Nashoba was Mary Shelley, the widow of the poet, who was considering the idea. But Mary was a radical, born of a radical mother, reared in a home that seethed with radical ideas. She had run off with Percy Bysshe Shelley, after all, a man who seemed, half the time, to live in another dimension. Miss Wright was able to picture Mary Shelley at Nashoba, but looking at Fanny Trollope, she shook her head.

But the impulse, the notion, the idea had taken hold of Fanny's imagination. She wanted to do something more with her life than she had done so far, and she wanted to see Henry settled in some way. She had a vague feeling that some really drastic change was needed to improve life for her husband, herself, and her family. An upheaval like a move to America might be just the thing. Besides, she loved to travel to new places, and what could be newer than the New World. Fanny brushed aside Frances Wright's protests and broached the idea to Thomas Anthony.

As always, he frowned when presented with an idea that he had not originated. What did a colony to redeem slaves in a foreign land have to do with Fanny or him or Henry? It was absurd, idiotic. Besides, what would it cost? There would be the passage and travelling expenses. Miss Wright might want an investment in her colony. And so on and so on.

But Thomas Anthony also felt the need for a drastic change of pattern. The farms were still not doing well. The move to Julians Hill had simply been a step downwards and no solution to the basic problem of a larger, more stable income.

It occurred to him that there were surely commercial possibilities in the New World, a developing nation. Some sort of emporium to retail needed British goods might do well in some frontier area. And once such an enterprise had been established, Henry could be put in charge of it, and they would have an answer to his future. He would be settled, and they could all look forward to the profits that would come rolling in for the trifling effort of shipping the goods.

Fanny seized on the idea, with no thought for the fact that her husband had as little experience in commercial retailing as he had had for farming. Why not? she said. It might be the very thing to turn the tide in their fortunes. She and Henry could spend some months in Nashoba, both of them finding useful occupations in the colony. Then, leaving him there, she could journey on, find a proper location for a commercial enterprise, after which Thomas Anthony could join them to make the final arrangements.

Thomas Anthony interrogated Frances Wright, asking what she had observed on her travels to the west. Were there towns, villages, outposts where an outlet for British goods would be welcomed?

Miss Wright was affronted at having to defend the new nation that meant so much to her. Of course there were towns and villages to the west—even booming cities, like Cincinnati, on the Ohio River, which had sprung up in the wilderness some thirty years before and which was now growing rapidly. She assumed such cities would welcome British merchandise. Every sort of enterprise flourished in places like Cincinnati. However, she said, she did not want to encourage Mr Trollope to invest in such a distant land.

'But you have invested,' he responded. 'Invested a great deal of your capital in a simply altruistic venture in a foreign land.'

'Well, yes, but that is different,' Frances Wright said in exasperation. She tried to explain that she was not seeking financial returns from her investment, simply the freeing of certain slaves and the proof that her scheme for ending slavery was sensible and workable.

'But a commercial venture in a town like Cincinnati might succeed?' Thomas Anthony insisted. And Frances Wright could only agree that it might.

She spent more of her time trying to convince Mrs Trollope that a trip to the United States was ill-advised, too rigorous, too expensive, and its outcome too unpredictable. When she had to end her visit at Julians Hill for various appointments in London, Frances Wright hoped the matter had been settled.

She simply did not realize the tremendous personal impact she had made on Fanny. Shortly after Miss Wright's departure Fanny wrote to Julia Garnett. 'Never was there I am persuaded such a being as Fanny Wright—no never. Some of my friends declare that if worship may be offered it must be to her—That she is at once all that woman should be, and something more than woman ever was. . . . Will it be possible to let this "angel" depart without vowing to follow her? I think not. I feel greatly inclined to say "where her country is, there shall be my country"—.'[9]

Frances Wright came back to Julians Hill after various excursions to find that all her counsel had been disregarded. Fanny and Thomas Anthony had decided that Fanny should go to America with Miss Wright, taking with her Henry and the two girls, Cecilia and Emily. Miss Wright saw she could do nothing to dissuade them and simply nodded at the proposal that Auguste Hervieu, the young French artist, should also be part of the group. He could be the drawing master at Nashoba, Fanny suggested. Fanny also arranged to take her maid, Esther, and one of her husband's farm employees, William Abbot—it would be inconceivable to travel without servants.

Once the decision had been made, the departure date approached with astonishing speed. Fanny packed trunks with clothes, necessities, and books for herself and the children. On 4th November 1827, the party assembled at the Thames River landing to board the sailing ship *Edward* for the voyage to America. Mr Trollope would follow them within the year.

And then the wind came up, the sails filled. Fanny Trollope and her children were off, following that 'angel', Frances Wright, to the open sea and then—America.

PART TWO

American Manners
1827–1831

7

New Orleans – Mississippi Steamboats – Memphis

It was 1827, and Frances Milton Trollope, aged forty-seven, had very little notion of the country to which she was going.

The one-time colonies of England had been in revolt when she was born. They had achieved their independence as thirteen states and written their constitution when she was a child, but rarely did the talk at the Heckfield vicarage centre on the new republic across the seas.

Later, of course, Fanny became familiar with some of the names in the American pantheon—George Washington, John Adams, Thomas Jefferson, James Monroe. She may have heard vaguely of something called the Louisiana Purchase, which had tripled the size of the nation and opened a vast wilderness to settlement for all who were strong, daring, or desperate enough to try their luck there, but it had little meaning for her. Neither did she know much about the War of 1812, which to Americans was a heroic testing of young David against a mighty Goliath but which in England was simply an irritating distraction from the main business of subduing Napoleon.

She knew nothing of the American fever to grow, to stretch out, to hack down forests and then rush on to the next hurdle in a great effort to conquer the wilderness. The country in which she lived had been tamed centuries and centuries before. Forests and heaths and moors might remain, but they were almost civilized.

What notions she did have about the land to which she was travelling had come chiefly from Frances Wright. According to her *Views of Society and Manners in America*, there had never been such even-tempered people as those in the United States. 'Cheerful—clean—neat—full of life and energy of youth—mild laws of punishment—integrity of Congress—confidence of the people in that integrity. . . .' Miss Wright's book had been filled with such phrases.

Describing her approach to New York City in 1818, Frances Wright had rhapsodized about 'The purity of the air, the brilliancy of the unspotted heavens, the crowd of moving vessels, shooting in various directions, up and down and across the bay and the far-stretching Hudson. . . . We approached these shores under a fervid sun, but the air, though of a higher temperature than I had ever before experienced, was so entirely free of vapour, that I thought it was for the first time in my life that I had drawn a clear breath.'[1]

She wrote of her surprise on disembarking from her ship. There were no needy applicants for alms. 'Instead, much cheerful help from denizens of the quay. . . . They were rendering civilities, not services, and a kind "thank ye" was all that should be tendered in return.'

If she had any reservations, they were mild. She did write of Americans that there was 'nothing of the poet in them, nor of *bel esprit*'. She also admitted that in taverns and inns there was 'some indifference of the proprietors and servants' to the welfare of the guests, but she hastened to add that there was no insolence.

To all of this, which Fanny Trollope had absorbed both from the book and her conversation with Frances Wright, was added the glamour of a stage whereon people acted in new and honest ways, refusing the hypocrisy of the past. There was the matter of sexual honesty, for instance.

'Sexual honesty?' Fanny had echoed when Frances Wright brought up the subject at Julians Hill before their departure.

Yes, replied Frances Wright. Surely Mrs Trollope was aware of how much dishonesty surrounded the whole matter of sexual activity, the furtive manner in which affairs were conducted and yet the hypocritical gossip and laughter by which they were acknowledged. Miss Wright decried this sort of behaviour and declared that it would not exist at Nashoba.

Some recent communications from Nashoba and other parts of the United States had made the topic especially pertinent. Miss Wright's admired friend, James Richardson, whom she had left in charge during her absence, had gathered the colonists together one morning to inform them that, the night before, he and Mamselle Josephine had begun to live together. He wanted to point up both the absolute equality of the races at Nashoba and the equality of the sexes, whereby a mutual admission of affection sanctified a relationship more truly than any legal decree.

Frances Wright had had word of this because James Richardson had been impelled to report the incident to Benjamin Lundy, the publisher of an abolitionist newspaper, *The Genius of Universal Emancipation*. Mr Lundy had published Richardson's letter as an evidence of advanced and emancipated behaviour, and there had been a predictable reaction of outrage as other, less radical newspapers picked up the letter and published it for the titillation of their conservative readers.

'Well,' said Fanny Trollope, 'well indeed.' Half-mesmerized by Frances Wright's eloquence as always, she found it impossible to say that she approved of sexual hypocrisy. On the other hand, did she really approve of James Richardson's bold public announcement?

If Frances Wright decided to be candid about this situation at Nashoba in a final attempt to dissuade Fanny from accompanying her there, her effort failed. Fanny, who liked to think of herself as a liberal, open to all advanced ideas, was soon able to declare her entire sympathy with James Richardson and Mamselle Josephine and her dismay at the narrow-minded people who were trying to make a *cause célèbre* of an honest avowal of activities in which they also indulged but tried to hide.

One result of the James Richardson revelations was that Frances Wright spent a good portion of her time on the voyage to America in writing a dramatic defence of sexual relations based on personal commitment rather than social contracts. Listening to Miss Wright read some of her telling passages as the ship rose and fell over the swells of the Atlantic, Fanny had found it all logically indisputable, bathed in the brilliant sunrise light of the new land that they were approaching. She might make sure that Cecilia and Emily were occupied with their books, that Auguste Hervieu and Henry were busy walking around the decks or essaying to climb some of the lower masts, but she herself could understand these larger, grander views of life that Frances Wright was expounding.

The first signs of approaching land came on Christmas Day 1827, when they saw the blue waters of the Gulf of Mexico charged with an influx of muddy brown from the Mississippi River. After seven weeks at sea, they all found this a welcome sight and hung over the rails, watching for the landfall. Soon they were staring at long-legged pelicans standing on mud flats that rose a little above the water. Then a pilot boat came to guide the larger vessel over the bar.

Fanny's delight turned to bewilderment. 'I never', she wrote later, 'beheld a scene so utterly desolate as this entrance of the Mississippi.'[2] The mast of a vessel long since wrecked rose up from one of the flats. Bulrushes of enormous growth became visible. They passed a cluster of huts, inhabited by pilots and fishermen, and then travelled on between mudbanks and bulrushes, hour after hour, for it required two days to manage the passage from the river's mouth to the port of New Orleans.

Frances Wright had not tried to romanticize that city to her companions. On her first visit to New Orleans, two years before, she had seen it as 'a Babilon of the Revelations, where reigneth the great Western Slavery mud & mosquitos.'[3] But Fanny's enthusiasm rose again when they finally landed. There they were, on the 'soil of a new land, of a new continent, of a new world', and she looked about eagerly as they followed Miss Wright to the lodgings she had chosen for them.

By and large, the town itself seemed not so strange to Fanny, the houses, the cathedral, and the plaza all reminding her of a French provincial village. But the trees, the flowers, the vegetation were foreign and exciting. How delightful and unsettling to see orange trees in fruit and flower, green peas and red peppers on the vine in late December. How odd to be so warm and know that it was Christmastime.

A strange thrill ran through Fanny when she saw the first black people of her experience. She and the children left the hotel as soon as they had settled their luggage to go out and walk around. And there was a young black woman, sweeping the steps of a house. A slave! The first slave they had ever seen! Venturing to speak to her, Fanny felt she could hardly address her with sufficient gentleness, and she was astonished by the girl's gay and civil response. When

Fanny asked about the red pepper pods and the girl hurried to give her several, Fanny was fearful that she would be punished by a hard mistress for her generosity. 'How very childish does ignorance make us!' she wrote later, 'and how very ignorant we are upon almost every subject, where hear-say evidence is all we can get.'[4]

During the few days they spent in New Orleans, Fanny continued to invent romantic miseries for every black woman, man, and child she saw. She heard about the great division in New Orleans society between the Creole families and those strangely indulged, pampered, and totally ostracized young women known as quadroons. As Fanny understood it, these girls, the acknowledged daughters of American or Creole fathers, were given every advantage in their upbringing, every luxury in their surroundings, and often became most attractive and alluring women. But custom denied them admission to regular society, and it was not possible for them legally to marry into that group. Young men of standing frequently formed liaisons, sometimes of lifelong duration, with these young women, but never could the quadroons hope for any legal recognition. This was all bizarre and fascinating to Fanny, who tucked the information away, quite unaware that one day she would use it in plotting a romantic novel.

She observed a situation more in accord with her expectations of America, that noble republic, when she visited a milliner's shop. Here the young woman who waited on her and who was also the owner of the shop was indubitably a lady. This was more like the overturning of Old World standards that Fanny had anticipated. A lady could easily own and manage a commercial establishment in America, and serve customers as well, without losing any of her dignity or standing. It augured well for that commercial enterprise that Thomas Anthony Trollope and his wife might establish in the United States one day.

In the same shop she also met Frances Wright's friend, the venerable William Maclure, who had such new and sensible ideas about education. He had recently taken over the socialist colony at New Harmony, Indiana, from Robert Owen, where he was establishing his ideal school. Fanny talked with him briefly about the progress of his experiment and was suitably impressed.

But she, and all her group, were looking forward beyond anything else to Miss Wright's Nashoba, their own destination. A day or so later, Fanny, Henry, Cecilia and Emily, Auguste Hervieu, the manservant and the maidservant followed Frances Wright to the wharves to board the steamboat that would carry them northward up the Mississippi towards her colony near Memphis.

The *Belvidere* was one of many steamboats clustered at the New Orleans wharves, and Fanny thought that in America, land of great rivers, steamboats were like the stage coaches and fly wagons of England and Europe, but splendid and well-appointed like no conveyances she had ever seen before.

Alas! the first impressions of a handsome apartment, fitted with neat little cots under a double line of windows, and of a smaller compartment, also windowed and carpeted, were soon swept away by less attractive sensations.

'Let no one who wishes to receive agreeable impressions of American manners, commence their travels in a Mississippi steam boat,' she wrote later, 'for myself, it is with all sincerity I declare, that I would infinitely prefer sharing the apartment of a party of well-conditioned pigs to the being confined to its cabin.'

What most horrified Fanny, her children, and Auguste Hervieu, was something she really hated to name, it was so 'deeply repugnant to English feelings'. But there it was, all around them, 'the incessant, remorseless spitting of Americans'.

The handsome apartment was, she discovered, the gentlemen's cabin, and they had exclusive use of it except at mealtimes, when breakfast, dinner, and supper were laid there, and ladies were permitted to enter to take their meals. But oh, the filthy carpet in that handsome apartment! Fanny and the girls felt their toes recoiling in their shoes as they walked upon it.

And then there was the matter of the 'courtesies of the table'. Fanny, accustomed all her life to a certain decorum and conversation with meals, was appalled by the table manners on a Mississippi steamboat, 'the voracious rapidity which with the viands were seized and devoured, the strange uncouth phrases and pronunciation; the loathsome spitting, from the contamination of which it was absolutely impossible to protect our dresses; the frightful manner of feeding with their knives, till the whole blade seemed to enter into the mouth; and the still more frightful manner of cleaning the teeth afterwards with a pocket knife'.

She tried to remind herself and her children that it was 'easy and invidious to ridicule the peculiarities of appearance and manner in people of a different nation from ourselves'. Nevertheless, 'it was impossible not to feel repugnance at many of the novelties that now surrounded me'.

By now Frances Wright was wholly concentrated on what lay ahead at Nashoba and had no time to explain to her fellow travellers that they were witnessing frontier manners, not those prevalent in the East. Nor did she explain why they heard almost every male in the gentlemen's cabin addressed by some title, such as General, Colonel, Major, or Judge. Miss Wright might have told them that this also was a frontier habit, a conceit unknown in the East and South.

Fanny and her group spent as much time as possible on the gallery that ran around the cabins, where they could sit and observe the passing scenery. Now and then the boat stopped to take on wood and a hundred or more men rushed up from the lower decks to carry the wood on board. These men, Fanny learned, had brought cargo down to New Orleans on flatboats, where the boats were abandoned for scrap lumber after the cargo was unloaded. They were now paying for their voyage to their homes up the river by this service.

The Trollopes sat on deck watching the unbroken flatness of the banks of the Mississippi, interested by the strange vegetation, the palmettos, the ilex, the sugar-cane fields, and here and there a cotton plantation. Then the level lines were broken by intervals of higher ground, the 'bluffs'. By this time there were fewer signs of cultivation and even fewer of human habitation. Only occasionally did they see sad clusters of huts, many of them constructed on piles so that when the river flooded the houses would not be washed away. Or they would see a single hut not far from the bank and surrounded by wilderness, where some enterprising soul made his living by cutting down trees and sawing them up into firewood for the steamboats.

Fanny was dismayed by the unhealthy look of the men, women, and children she saw around these miserable dwellings. They all seemed thin, with bluish-white complexions and knotted bones. The cows and pigs grazing near these houses seemed equally poor.

Mile by mile the scenery grew more desolate, and now and then they saw the smoky pall of a burning forest. By now the Trollopes were as eager as Miss Wright to reach the haven of Nashoba.

They were still some miles south of Memphis when the steamboat shuddered violently and was jolted to a stop.

'We've hit a snag!'

'A sawyer!'

'We're aground!'

The more knowledgeable passengers were quick to diagnose the trouble and then beguiled away the time by making wagers as to how long it would take to free the vessel. As it turned out, the boat remained immobile for a day and a half until at last another steamboat came along that was heavy enough to rescue it by throwing out grappling irons and towing it free. Everyone sighed with relief as they churned onwards. But once again they were delayed. On the day they were due to reach Memphis, a heavy rain began to fall, and it was almost midnight before the *Belvidere* had chuffed and splashed its way through the teeming waters to the wharf at the foot of the high bluff on which the little city was situated.

In the streaming night, lit up with flickering lanterns and smoky pine knots, the passengers for Memphis and Nashoba disembarked on to a rude wharf, their trunks, bags, and boxes tumbling after them. There were no stairs or steps leading to the top of the bluff, only a roughly gouged-out path to mark the way. They went slogging slowly upwards through the mud. Faithful William and Esther, carrying the most necessary bags, tried to help Fanny and the girls as they slipped and slid in the squelching ooze underfoot. Every so often one of the party fell forward on to hands and knees on the steep slope. Gloves and even a couple of shoes were lost.

But the eager Frances Wright had charged ahead up the bluff to meet friends who were awaiting her arrival, and she was there to urge on the stragglers as they panted up to level ground. At last they were shown into the best rooms of Memphis's brand new hotel. Tired, wet, and muddy, Fanny found the accommodations less than cheering. New to western America, she still had to learn that the natives were accustomed to what they called 'getting along', a phrase Fanny finally interpreted as meaning to get along with as few of the comforts of life as possible.

Everything continued strange and comfortless the next day. After the public meals on the steamboat, Fanny thought that she and her group would enjoy having dinner in their rooms at the hotel. Frances Wright quickly discouraged the idea, telling Fanny that the lady of the house would take such a request as a personal affront. Obediently, Fanny and her children went to the hotel dining room at the proper hour and found a table laid for fifty persons. Once again she was amazed by the rapidity with which everyone ate and with the lack of conversation. 'The only sounds heard were those produced by the knives and forks, with the unceasing chorus of coughing, etc.' Fanny, Frances Wright, Cecilia, and Emily were the only females present except for the hostess, 'The good women of Memphis being well content to let their lords partake of Mrs. Anderson's turkeys and venison (without their having the trouble of cooking for them) whilst they regale themselves on mush and milk at home.' She was somewhat surprised to see William, her manservant, sitting opposite her as close to the head of the table as she. Well, they were in America now, where all were deemed equal, and Fanny was more amused by the new arrangement than William, who kept his eyes lowered in his discomfiture.

They had planned to travel on to Nashoba the same day, but they were told that the rains of the day before had caused such flooding of the road into the forest that they had better delay their departure. Frances Wright was tense with impatience, but Fanny, Henry, Cecilia, Emily, and Auguste Hervieu were content to spend the afternoon rambling around the little town of Memphis. Gazing down, they saw that the town was situated so high above the Mississippi River that the river looked like a great lake. Looking the other way, they saw the forest rising like a dark wall beyond the settled area, and they found it exciting to think that soon they would be penetrating that mysterious barrier as they made their way to Nashoba.

A high-hung wagon, called a Dearborn, drawn by two horses, was waiting for them the next morning, to carry them the fifteen miles to Miss Wright's colony. Miss Wright, Fanny, and all her group climbed aboard and arranged themselves among the luggage. The black driver cracked his whip, and they were off, jolting down the road to the forest.

They had not travelled far into the forest shadows before it was clear that the flooding had not abated very much. Small water-courses ran here and there, the wider of them spanned by rude bridges formed of trunks of trees with small branches laid across them. These structures trembled in an alarming way when the horses and wagon passed over them. The travellers finally arrived at one bridge that seemed so badly weakened that their driver chose not to test it but decided to drive the wagon straight through the stream to the other side.

The horses plunged into the water, the wagon following in a rush of waves and spray. Almost at once the wheels of the Dearborn began sinking into the mud. The water was up to the bed of the wagon, the horses were thrashing and kicking about, but there was no forward motion.

The group in the wagon looked anxiously at the driver. He was smiling as he clutched the reins, trying to subdue the panicky horses. 'Well,' he said cheerfully, 'I expect you'll best be riding out upon the horses as we've got into an unhandsome fix here.'

'Riding out on the horses' entailed a great deal of backing and filling, unhitching and rebridling. They had travelled such a short distance that they decided to return to Memphis, but everyone was thoroughly soaked by the time they got there and had to dry out before the fireplace in Mrs Anderson's hotel.

But Frances Wright could endure no more delay. She comman-deered two horses and, accompanied by William, rode off towards Nashoba. Afterwards William told Mrs Trollope that they rode through places that might have daunted the boldest hunter but that 'Miss Wright took it quite easy'.

The next morning Fanny, the children, and Auguste Hervieu again boarded a Dearborn and set forth towards Nashoba. The flooding had subsided by now, but Fanny was surprised at how soon any traces of what seemed like a real road had vanished. There was instead a clearing of the trees, cut away for a passage, but leaving stumps sometimes three feet high. The Dearborn bumped and crashed among these, and Fanny, Henry, and Hervieu laughed away their bruises and comforted the little girls with praise for the skill of their driver.

'Only think', said Henry, 'how well such a driver would do steering the horses in and out of the traffic on Bond Street,' and everyone laughed at the memory of that civilized thoroughfare, crowded with carriages and lined with buildings. Between lurches and bounces they stared in wonder at the tall crowns on the trees and the entangling vines that made a maze of their passage on either side. Now and then, birds, alarmed by the racket of the horses and the wagon, flew up before them, shrieking warnings.

And then the driver was pulling into a sort of clearing and drawing the horses to a stop. They had arrived at Nashoba.

8

Nashoba

Writing later about their arrival, Fanny dropped nine dots into her manuscript to signify the inadequacy of words to convey her emotions: '. . . . . one glance sufficed to convince me that every idea I had formed of the place was as far as possible from the truth'.[1]

Frances Wright had tried to discourage her from coming, suggesting Fanny might not be fit for the new surroundings. Fanny, however, was unable to think of herself as unfit for anything. Besides, nothing Miss Wright had said had described the actual situation. She had spoken of houses, barns, planted fields, and Fanny had erected a little English village in her imagination. Instead she saw a few acres raggedly cleared, with the ever-present stumps thrusting up here and there, the ground a mess of rutted mud, and a few buildings of the most primitive description surrounded by abandoned wheelbarrows and other farm implements.

'Desolation was the only feeling,' Fanny wrote, 'the only word that presented itself: but it was not spoken.'[2]

Cheery cries of greeting were required instead, for there was young Camilla Wright, looking very pale and thin, coming towards Fanny with her arms outstretched.

'My dear Camilla, how lovely to see you again!' Except that it was frightening, rather, to see what a change had been wrought in the gentle, pretty girl since Fanny had seen her last.[3]

Then Camilla stretched out a hand to a pale young man who lingered a step or two behind her and brought him forward. 'And this is Mr Whitby—' she was saying, when Frances Wright interrupted.

'—The bridegroom,' she said. 'Only think what a surprise these two had waiting for me when I arrived yesterday. They are married!

Did the deed just a few weeks ago, while we were still at sea. Ah, my dears, you might have waited for us,' and she put her arms around Camilla and Richeson Whitby.

Married? Camilla and this pale, intense young man? Fanny blinked and tried to rise to the occasion, pushing aside thoughts of the brave pronouncements against marriage and its hypocrisy with which Miss Wright had been indoctrinating her during the last weeks.

'A surprise indeed! I am so happy for you,' she murmured, glancing from the newly married pair to Miss Wright, who seemed not at all disturbed by their defection from principle, but petted and patted them both.

But there was no time to dwell on the matter, for Frances Wright was anxious to introduce the various black men, women, and children who had been standing nearby, smiling and nodding. Fanny and her group nodded and smiled in return.

'And now you are probably wondering about James Richardson and Mamselle Josephine,' said Frances Wright. Fanny was too dazed by this time to have given a thought to them and the relationship between them that had been so publicly announced a few months before. But it seemed they had departed the colony a few months previously, their destination announced as New Orleans. Presumably they had not yet arrived in that city when Miss Wright and the Trollopes were there, or they would have met.

Frances Wright brushed aside any concern about them. She still had perfect faith in James Richardson, and she refused absolutely to believe the stories that Camilla said were circulating in Memphis and elsewhere that he had beaten and otherwise punished the black residents at Nashoba for idling at their work and failing to understand that they were labouring for their own freedom.

At this point, as Fanny, Henry, and the two little girls stood in confused silence, Auguste Hervieu created a distraction. Where, he asked, was the schoolhouse? Where was the studio in which he was to teach art?

Miss Wright waved generously. To be honest, these were not yet built but would soon be erected—over there, or perhaps there.

Auguste Hervieu flew into a tantrum, shaking his fists and asking in his broken English why he had been brought this distance, with such promises, to nothing, nothing—*rien du tout*—but wilderness.

Miss Wright was unruffled, having already decided that the young Frenchman was not good for much but his art. The scene that followed was more distressing to Fanny. She had come to rely, to a degree, on the volatile young man and felt bereft when he took one of the horses to ride at once back to Memphis, where he might at least pick up some portrait commissions or find some young people to instruct in the rudiments of drawing.

'Desolation. . . .' Fanny did not speak the word. 'I think, however, that Miss Wright was aware of the painful impression the sight of her forest home produced on me, and I doubt not that the conviction reached us both at the same moment, that we had erred in thinking that a few months passed together at this spot could be productive of pleasure to either.'[4]

Still, certain formalities were required. Reasonable excuses must be offered. Health considerations seemed the most pertinent, especially after Camilla confessed to Fanny that she had not really been well since settling in Tennessee. The heat and dampness of the summer brought on one spell of illness after another. Perhaps it was a sort of malaria. Fanny recalled the near-fatal bout with malaria that Frances Wright had suffered a year before.

And so, when she had nerved herself to speak to Miss Wright, Fanny insisted that in spite of her hopes for a long visit at Nashoba, she dared not expose her children, especially the two little girls, to a prolonged stay in such an environment.

Frances Wright nodded, accepting the excuse. 'To do her justice,' Fanny wrote later, 'I believe her mind was so exclusively occupied by the object she had then in view, that all things else were worthless, or indifferent to her. I never heard or read of any enthusiasm approaching hers, except in some few instances, in ages past, of religious fanaticism.'[5]

Before she could depart, however, she was compelled to deal with the problem of money. She had come to Nashoba expecting to stay for several months and had no cash with which to travel on. She asked Miss Wright for a loan of three hundred dollars (or perhaps this was the return of money she had invested in Nashoba). Miss

Wright understood her need but said no money could be disbursed without the approval of the board of trustees—and the board could not meet until Robert Owen, Jr., arrived. Such formalities seemed rather preposterous in the wilderness, but there was nothing to be done but wait for Mr Owen's arrival.

The days passed in a maze of discomfort. They had no milk nor any beverage except rainwater at Nashoba. Despite all the planting that had been done the previous summer they had no vegetables. There was no meat but pork and no butter or cheese. Fanny shared Frances Wright's bedroom. 'It had no ceiling, and the floor consisted of planks laid loosely upon piles that raised it some feet from the earth. The rain had access through the wooden roof, and the chimney, which was of logs slightly plastered with mud, caught fire a dozen times a day.'

Henry, Cecilia, and Emily were fretful and bored. Beyond the muddy fields the forest was too dense for them to attempt the sort of walks with which they usually beguiled idle hours. They had long since read all the books they had brought with them. Fanny racked her brain trying to think of lessons or amusements to occupy them so she would have some time free to concentrate on what was to become of them all.

She was four thousand miles from home, and completely on her own for the first time in her life. No Thomas Anthony to consult, either for better or worse. Back in England, at Julians Hill, they had talked of Cincinnati and the possibility of some commercial venture in that thriving new city. Very well. When she and the children were able to leave Nashoba, Cincinnati would be their destination— though exactly what she would do when they arrived there she could not yet envisage.

She considered the problem of Henry, her restless sixteen-year-old son. Nashoba was to have provided occupation for him, but that dream had died. She had to find some sensible activity that would fill his days. Frances Wright reminded her of William Maclure's experimental school at New Harmony, where Henry could study under various brilliant men and all at no cost. He would earn his own way by helping maintain the school. Fanny's disillusionment with Nashoba had not caused her to reject all of Frances Wright's interests and advice. She was still a genius, a young angel, and she made the school at New Harmony sound very appealing. Fanny learned that New Harmony was not far from the Ohio River, the waterway by which she and the children would be travelling to Cincinnati, and so it would be easy for Henry to make his way there.

At last Robert Owen, Jr., arrived at Nashoba. The board of trustees duly met in one of the makeshift cabins and voted Mrs Trollope three hundred dollars. Fanny was able to collect her children, her luggage, her manservant and maidservant and depart from Nashoba.

She had found no beauty in the scenery around Nashoba, nor could she conceive that it would possess any even in summer. She would recall later that the aspect of the heavens by night was 'surprisingly beautiful'. She had never seen 'moonlight so clear, so pure, so powerful'.[6] But those were her only pleasant memories of Nashoba.

9

Cincinnati – American 'Help'

They had to linger five days in Memphis waiting for a steamboat bound northwards up the Mississippi and then eastwards up the Ohio to Cincinnati. Auguste Hervieu, who had exhausted what few demands there were in the little city for his talents as a portraitist, joined them, and they whiled away the time taking walks and playing Patience. They also heard a good deal about the city towards which they were headed. Everyone to whom they spoke was eager to praise the beauty, wealth, and prosperity of Cincinnati.

As a result, Fanny was in high spirits when they finally boarded a steamboat that would carry them there. Once again, she had '*un voyage à faire, et Paris au bout*'. With happy expectations to buoy her, she refused to be bored with the wearisome scenery of the 'father of waters', 'forest—forest—forest; the only variety . . . produced by the receding of the river at some points, and its encroaching on the opposite shore'.[1] But finally they entered the Ohio, the river that the French called 'La Belle Rivière', and to Fanny and her group it seemed well named. Its waters were bright and clear, the scenery varied. Primeval forest still occupied some portion of the ground, but it was broken by frequent settlements. Sometimes they saw 'pretty dwellings with gay porticoes'. Sometimes a mountain torrent came pouring 'its silver tribute to the stream', and if only there had been occasionally 'a ruined abbey, or feudal castle, to mix the romance of real life with that of nature', Fanny thought the Ohio would be perfect.

Where the Wabash flowed into the Ohio, the steamboat halted briefly, and this seemed the logical place for Henry to disembark and make his way a few miles up the Wabash to New Harmony and Mr Maclure's school. As they parted, Fanny held his face in her hands and told him to be brave, study diligently, and that she hoped

before too many months had passed she and his father would have
established some sort of enterprise in Cincinnati. Then they would
be sending for him and—she laughed as she said it but still half-
believed it—his fortunes and theirs would be made. Then the steamboat's engines started up again. It was time for Fanny to hurry
back on board and to wave and watch as the figure of her son grew
smaller and the boat churned on towards Louisville.

The boat stopped for several hours at that city, allowing Fanny,
Hervieu, and the little girls an opportunity to roam about its streets
and observe the few sights it had. By and large, Fanny thought it a
pleasant place, prettily situated in beautiful rolling country, but she
was dismayed to learn that here also a 'bad fever' raged in the warm
season, just as it did farther south along the Mississippi. Then they
were back on board again, and the voyage continued.

They reached Cincinnati on 10th February 1828. Disembarking,
they saw a city 'finely situated on the south side of a hill that rises
gently from the water's edge', but it hardly struck any of them as
the remarkable city that had been promised. It wanted 'domes,
towers, and steeples', even though it did have a noble landing
place, extending for more than a quarter of a mile along the
river.

They made their way to the Washington Hotel and were pleased
to learn they had arrived just in time for dinner. But when the dining
room door was opened, Fanny recoiled at the sight of 'sixty or
seventy men already at the table'. Finally they took their meal with
the women of the innkeeper's family and then went forth to look for
what Fanny now wanted most—a roof of her own for herself and her
children.

The real estate agent to whom she was referred sent her off with
a small boy as a guide. Fanny, with Cecilia and Emily trudging along
beside her, and Hervieu in the rear, followed the lad on the planks
that served for pavements up one street and down another. For a
while, Fanny was bemused by the curious layout of the town. It
seemed to be built chiefly in squares, each consisting of a block of
buildings fronting north, east, west, and south, and intersected by
alleys, which gave each building a back entrance.

After they had walked for some time, however, seemingly to no avail, Fanny asked the boy just where the houses were that they were to examine.

'I am looking for bills,'* the boy replied.

'Well,' said Fanny. 'I can do that myself. Perhaps we do not need you.'

At this the lad protested and asked that he be given just a little more time. Now as they proceeded, the boy ran up to the front door of every house they passed and knocked, and if someone opened the door, he asked if the house was to let.

Fanny only had to watch this manœuvre two or three times before she stopped their guide. 'I can also do that myself,' she said. 'Be off with you. We do not need your services.'

But now the boy stood his ground and, scowling up at her, said, 'In that case, ye'll pay me a dollar for my services.'

Fanny rolled her eyes towards Hervieu in wonder and exasperation but it seemed simpler to pay the boy than argue. The lad took off, and Fanny, Hervieu, and the girls continued on their own.

After trudging up and down a few more squares or blocks, they were delighted to find a small house that did have a To Let sign. Fanny knocked on the door, learned that it was furnished and available immediately, and was so relieved that she scarcely examined it before arranging to lease it.

Once they returned to the hotel, she, Hervieu, and the girls wanted nothing more than a quiet supper in their own rooms. Fanny had the good luck to make the request for this from a good-humoured Irishwoman.

'Ooh, my honey, ye'll be from the old country,' the woman said. 'I'll see you will have your tay all to yourselves, honey.'

But the 'tay', accompanied by such American tidbits as hung beef and sundry sweetmeats of brown sugar, had scarcely been delivered when there was a knock on the door and the landlord appeared.

'Are any of you ill?' he asked.

'No, thank you, sir; we are all quite well,' Fanny replied.

'Then, madam, I must tell you that I cannot accommodate you on these terms; we have no family tea-drinkings here, and you must live either with me or my wife, or not at all in my house.'

* That is, signs saying To Let.

Startled by the landlord's tone, Fanny tried to apologize. She was sorry if she had offended, but she and her family were strangers and not accustomed to the manners of the country.

The landlord was not appeased. 'Our manners are very good manners, and we don't wish any changes from England,' he said, and went out, slamming the door behind him.

To Fanny, who had spent the last two months observing American manners, it was something of a jolt to discover that her manners were also being observed and not approved. She was pleased that by the next day she and her party would be in a home of their own.

Unfortunately, she had been in such a hurry to rent a house that she had neglected to check certain basic facilities. William and Esther had transported the luggage to the house and the little girls were unpacking when Fanny discovered there was no pump for water, no cistern, no drain of any kind. Nor could she or Esther discover where they were supposed to put the garbage. She sent for the landlord of the house to ask about these matters, especially the garbage. For the first time Fanny heard herself addressed in a way that would soon become familiar—she was called 'old woman', or 'English old woman'.

'Your help', said the landlord, 'will just have to fix them all in the middle of the street, but you must mind, old woman, that it is the middle. I expect you don't know as we have got a law what forbids throwing such things at the sides of the streets; they must just all be cast right into the middle, and the pigs soon takes them off.'

By this time Fanny had observed that pigs roamed the streets of Cincinnati, and she had guessed the service they rendered. Thin-backed and dirty, they rooted up and down through every quarter of the city, disposing of the more edible garbage while fattening themselves for their eventual end in one of the many slaughterhouses around the town. Fanny could only accept it as another evidence of American manners, and as she travelled more extensively, she learned that Cincinnati was not the only city to use pigs as garbage collectors; even in New York City the creatures were let loose in the same way.

She was still determined to be pleased by Cincinnati. Nashoba had failed her; Cincinnati must not. As soon as she had a free space to lay out inkstand and paper, she wrote a long letter to Thomas Anthony, relating the circumstances that had brought her and the children to Cincinnati so much earlier than they had planned, telling him of her urgent need for money, and asking how soon he could join her in America to assist in establishing some commercial venture that would bring them security.

She entrusted the vital letter to the erratic postal service with a prayer. It had to travel by steamboat eastwards to make connexion sometime, somewhere, with a ship bound for England. She sighed as she wondered how long it would be before she could expect an answer, and then turned to the next order of business. She needed another servant, a cook.

Now she discovered she must watch her language as well as her manners in America, where it was 'more than petty treason to the Republic to call a free citizen a *servant*'. She learned quickly that in asking her neighbours if they knew of any such workers, she must ask of getting 'help'. After her request had been thus offered, she was pleased when a strong young woman came to the door and announced, 'I be come to help you'.

Fanny asked what her wages were by the year, and this was another mistake, 'Oh Gimini!' the young woman replied, laughing, 'you be a downright Englisher, sure enough. I should like to see a young lady engage by the year in America! I hope I shall get a husband before many months, or I expect I shall be an outright old maid, for I be most seventeen already; besides, mayhap I may want to go to school. You must just give me a dollar and a half a week, and mother's slave, Phillis, must come over once a week, I expect, from the other side of the water to help me clean.'

Such a speech, and other conversations she was having in Cincinnati, were so novel to Fanny that she began to write them down in order to quote them in letters to friends at home. Without such documentation she was sure that such people as Lady Dyer, Mary Russell Mitford, and the Grants would never believe her.

New revelations came with each passing day. The young woman who was to 'help' had only one dress, a gaudy affair that Fanny thought unsuitable for housework. Fanny gave her some money to purchase material for a work dress and then made it up for her. The girl smiled as she put it on and seemed pleased but offered no word of thanks. Soon she was asking Fanny, Cecilia, and Emily to lend her various articles of dress. When they declined to do so, she frowned. 'Well, I never seed such grumpy folks as you be; there is several young ladies of my acquaintance what goes to live out now and then with the old women about the town, and they and their gurls always lends them what they asks for; I guess you Inglish thinks we should poison your things, just as bad as if we was Negurs.' The last straw came when Fanny refused to lend the girl money to buy a silk dress for a dance. She left saying, 'Then 'tis not worth my while to stay any longer.'

The next one to come 'help' was a pretty young girl, and Fanny thought her natural disposition was gentle and kind, but 'her gentleness turned to morbid sensitiveness, by having heard a thousand and a thousand times that she was as good as any other lady, that all men were equal, and women too, and that it was a sin and a shame for a free-born American to be treated like a servant.' When this young woman learned that Fanny expected her to dine in the kitchen, she was deeply offended. 'I guess that's 'cause you don't think I'm good enough to eat with you. You'll find that won't do here.' Fanny tried to conciliate her, paid her high wages, and gave her various items of clothing. But soon enough the girl appeared one morning and said 'I must go'. 'When shall you return, Charlotte?' asked Fanny. 'I expect you'll see no more of me,' said Charlotte and departed.

Fanny's next experience with Cincinnati 'help' seemed more promising. A young woman named Nancy Fletcher appeared, and her manner seemed so frank that she quite won Fanny's confidence. She told a story of childhood misery, a cruel stepmother and cheating brothers, but said that her whole life had changed since she had 'got religion'. She asked only to be allowed to go to meetings two nights a week besides Sundays, and Fanny was happy to grant such a modest request. In the weeks that followed Fanny sometimes heard her return very late at night indeed, but when questioned, Nancy always spoke rapturously of the many souls that had been saved at the meeting that night. It was only after she had fallen ill and Fanny had nursed her to recovery and then sent her off to her family for further convalescence that a neighbour came to Fanny to inform her

that Nancy Fletcher was 'the most abandoned woman in the town
. . . she boasts of having the power of entering your house at any hour
of the night'. When Nancy Fletcher returned and was confronted
with this information, she merely shrugged and said, 'I must just
put up my things'.

Later, when she wrote of her life in America, Fanny apologized for
saying so much concerning her difficulties with domestic help but
felt they were characteristic of America and so must be included
along with spitting and other disagreeable topics. Trying to give
things some balance, she recalled the excellence of the Cincinnati
market, which she thought unsurpassed for 'excellence, abundance,
and cheapness', except for fruits, which did not seem as fine to her
as those of England. She had been surprised to find that there were
no individual butcher shops or fishmongers. Meat and fish both had
to be bought at the central market. This opened so early and customers appeared so promptly that it was necessary to be there by seven
at the latest, for things were pretty well picked over by eight o'clock.
Still, if Fanny was there in time, she found excellent beef, 'and the
highest price when we were there, four cents (about two-pence) the
pound'. The mutton and veal did not seem quite so fine, but Fanny
liked the poultry, 'fowls or full-sized chickens, ready for table,
twelve cents, but much less if bought alive'. When summer came,
she and all her family were delighted by the tomatoes, 'that great
luxury of the American table'.

But long before summer came, with its luxurious tomatoes and
sweet garden lettuce, long before she had settled the vexing problem
of 'help', Fanny had had a letter from Henry at New Harmony. He
was sick, he was miserable, the school was not at all what they had
expected. Please could he join her in Cincinnati?

Already the three hundred dollars that Fanny had obtained from
the Nashoba Board of Trustees was exhausted. Apologetically, she
was turning to Auguste Hervieu for money to tide her over until a
money order came from Mr Trollope. Fortunately, the young artist
had quickly picked up some portrait commissions in Cincinnati and
made the acquaintance of a German artist, Frederick Eckstein, who
had established an art school, grandly named The Academy of Fine

Arts. Eckstein was eager to have Hervieu join him as an assistant. So Hervieu had money in his pocket and prospects for the future and was glad to share what he had with the woman who had been so kind to him.

Money for his fare was sent off to Henry. A week or so later he arrived, looking feverish and ill. His mother's first concern was to put him to bed and summon a doctor. She was surprised to find Dr William Price here, an advanced thinker who had spent some time at New Harmony and knew Frances Wright. But it was reassuring that Dr Price was not alarmed by Henry's condition and prescribed only a little calomel and rest.

Gradually, as he recovered, Henry told his mother the story. Dr Maclure, who was supposed to have been supervising the academic aspects of the school at New Harmony, had left for Mexico before Henry arrived there. He had put the school under the authority of a Frenchwoman, his long-time companion and assistant. With Maclure away, this woman had generally abandoned the programme of alternating the students' time between study and labour. Henry found himself spending most of his days working in the kitchen, the farmyard, or the fields. Sometimes he was delegated to feed and water the livestock. Other times he was peeling potatoes, baking bread, or cleaning the various buildings connected with the school. No lessons at all? asked his dismayed mother. Well, Henry replied, there had been a teacher of geology, who had made that subject seem quite interesting, but he had had little time to pursue it. He had worked and then become sick. He pressed his mother's hand, thanking her for rescuing him. Most of the students at New Harmony had no hope of escape. Their parents had enrolled them there in the first place because they were too poor to keep them at home.

Fanny murmured sympathy, thought of her own financial straits, and felt a clutch of fear as another American dream crumbled. First Nashoba—then New Harmony—were her hopes about Cincinnati also to be doomed?

For a while it seemed they must be. No letters and no money came from Thomas Anthony. Fanny was now relying completely on Auguste Hervieu for daily expenses. But Hervieu also was finding some American ways difficult. He joined Eckstein at his academy and was appalled by the lack of order in the school. The students chattered constantly and ran about the studio. Hervieu protested to Eckstein saying that it was impossible to teach unless some discipline was imposed.

Eckstein shook his head. 'Very goot, very goot in Europe,' he said, 'but American boys and girls vill not bear it, dey vill just vat day please.' At this the impetuous Hervieu flung up his hands and said he was through—*fini*—and took his leave.

Henry had become aware of the family's financial plight by now and was seized with the desire to do something to help. He was not strong enough for much activity, but surely he was strong enough to teach. He had never been a scholar, but surely, grounded in Latin since his earliest years, he might be able to give lessons in that subject. He inserted an advertisement in the *Cincinnati Gazette*. 'Mr Henry Trollope, having received a completely classical education, at the royal college of Winchester (England), would be happy to give lessons in the Latin language to gentlemen at their own houses. . . . Terms: Fifty cents for lessons of one hour.'[2]

He waited hopefully, but there were no answers.

About then, when it seemed there was nothing for Fanny to do in Cincinnati but wait for a letter that never came, she visited Cincinnati's Western Museum, met its curator, Joseph Dorfeuille, and found one outlet for her frustrated energies, employment of a kind for Henry, and work for Hervieu.

10

Dorfeuille's 'Hell' – Lectures – 'Dropping In' – Revivals

Fanny had looked for some cultural amenities in Cincinnati ever since arriving in what seemed to her a '*triste* little town'. No concerts ever seemed to be given. No art galleries existed. There were no public balls. Cincinnati did boast one theatre, but when Fanny attended a performance, she found few women present. She learned that 'the larger proportion of females deem it an offence against religion to witness the representation of a play'. And she had been outraged by the behaviour of the men in the audience. Some sat with their heels on the backs of the seats in front of them. Others perched on the balcony railings with their backs to the stage, engaged in conversation with their companions regardless of the drama onstage. Some kept their hats on, while others took off their shirts for comfort, and there was always a good deal of spitting going on. Fanny was even more distressed by such an audience because it seemed to her that the actor-manager and his wife, a Mr and Mrs Drake, were talented performers. She visited them after the entertainment to congratulate them and commiserate with them for the lack of appreciation they were accorded.

After such experiences she did not expect too much from the Western Museum, one of two little museums in the centre of the city. However, she found an interesting collection of Indian antiquities, rock specimens, and other local wonders. Mr Dorfeuille, the curator, was touched by her appreciation. Few Cincinnatians cared much about the exhibits, he told her. In fact, just to keep the museum open he had installed some wax figures, supposed to be crowd pleasers, on the second floor.

Fanny and Hervieu, and probably Henry as well, trudged up to the second floor and surveyed the wax figures: a 'Human Monster and Cannibal'; 'a representation of the death of Washington, with four figures'; and a figure of the Indian chief, Tecumseh, in full regalia.

Alas, Mr Dorfeuille confessed, even these attractions were not bringing him many visitors. He had ordered them at great cost from the east. There had been further cost when they arrived damaged and he had to hire someone to repair them. He called to a young man busy in another part of the room. 'Hiram, come meet some people from England.' Fanny and her group were introduced to Hiram Powers, a tall, lanky, bright-eyed youth, only a little older than Henry. Mr Dorfeuille said that Hiram Powers could do almost anything, repair clocks, make sculptures from life, even tune organs. But in spite of all his skill in repairing the figures, the museum was still losing money.

Perhaps, Fanny suggested, what was needed was a real novelty. Wax figures of Indians and of George Washington were all very well but not very unusual. Suppose Mr Dorfeuille should offer something really astonishing. Perhaps—oh, a sybil or an oracle—who could answer questions from all who approached.

Mr. Dorfeuille stared. Well, yes, he began, but. . . . But Fanny's theatrical instincts were aroused. He need not call it an oracle if that seemed too difficult. He could just have someone—call her an invisible girl, if he liked, speaking from some hidden source in a strange and eerie setting. Painted transparencies lit from behind would create the effect. And here was Mr Hervieu, a famous artist from France, who could paint the transparencies. As for the invisible voice—why not young Henry? He could give his voice a girlish lightness. He was quick and able to improvise not only in English but in Latin or French as well, if that would add to the mystification. Mr Dorfeuille hesitated only a moment. Yes, he agreed. It was worth a try.

Fanny enjoyed herself thoroughly as she directed proceedings during the next few weeks. Hervieu painted transparencies frantically. Henry practiced speaking like a sybil, and Hiram Powers created a chamber with a proper hidden position for the oracle and rigged up the trumpet through which the answers would be delivered.

Advertisements in the local newspapers heralded the opening.

'The Invisible Girl, at the Western Museum . . . is now ready to deliver her RESPONSES to visitors. The chamber prepared for the audience is fitted up as one of those theatres of probation in the *Egyptian Mysteries*, in which the candidate for initiation was subjected to her incipient trials. The light is admitted through *transparencies* painted by MR. HERVIEU.'[1]

The new attraction was a sensation beyond anyone's hopes. The Western Museum, once so deserted, was soon filled with mystified patrons, eager to try the Invisible Girl with their questions, all of which were answered promptly if they were not 'improper or immodest'. Inspired by Fanny's enthusiasm, Hiram Powers had also modelled a tableau of 'Hecate and the three weird sisters', as well as a group of *banditti*, to add to the spectacular effects.

Mr Dorfeuille might have kept the museum busy all summer with 'The Invisible Girl'. He closed it after eight weeks, with a public notice of thanks to the citizens for their approval, only because Fanny had come up with an even more sensational idea. Next they would offer a representation of Dante's 'Infernal Regions', no less. Fanny had been familiar with Dante's *Divine Comedy* since girlhood. Now, with Hervieu to paint transparencies and the talented Hiram Powers to model figures, she found it great fun to tell them about the scenes they should illustrate. All during the last weeks when the Invisible Girl was answering questions, Hiram had been creating a colossal figure of Minos, the Judge of Hell; a frozen lake from which emerged the heads of doomed earthlings; various monsters; imps and birds and animals of evil omen. For the background, Hervieu painted visions of Purgatory and Paradise, full of symbols of hope, but the emphasis was on the terrifying images in the Inferno, created by Hiram Powers.

Fanny travelled with her own copy of Dante. She made her own free translations of various passages and these were printed and posted at proper intervals to explain the scenes. She and Hiram arranged for sound effects as well, shrieks and groans that would rise from the Inferno when the backstage lamps were extinguished from time to time.

Newspaper advertisements announcing this spectacle drew crowds even larger than 'The Invisible Girl'. The crush was so great, with people pushing in to touch the hellish creatures, that Hiram Powers had to set up an electrified fencing around the exhibits. Fanny wrote a portentous warning against pressing too near to the mysteries. Hiram painted the warning in flame-coloured letters and posted it prominently. Even so, the curious or venturesome risked the consequences, and when they got a sharp electric shock it only added to the attraction of 'The Infernal Regions'.

How much Fanny, Henry, and Hervieu shared in the profits from this highly successful venture is not on record. But late in May, Fanny rented a larger, more comfortable house in a suburb called Mohawk, a mile or so from the centre of town, and moved her family there. There was a wooded slope behind the house. The river ran not far in front of it. Altogether it was in a much pleasanter site for the daily walks on which Fanny insisted.

Finally, in June, a letter came from Thomas Anthony. He wrote that he planned to join Fanny in Cincinnati by the middle or end of summer. He also enclosed a money order. Overjoyed by the news and the money, Fanny hurried to buy some of the necessities that had been beyond her means for so long—new shoes for Cecilia and Emily, fabrics to make them new gowns.

Cincinnati had at last become possible. Along with the excitement of reviving the Western Museum, she had found various friends, apart from the grateful Mr Dorfeuille and the clever Hiram. Dr Price had become an amusing friend, a cheerful agnostic in a community that seemed to revolve around churchgoing. His wife and pretty daughters, more conventional in their views, had also become friends, and the Prices and the Trollopes visited back and forth. Timothy Flint, minister, novelist, and currently editor of the *Western Monthly Review*, was another Cincinnatian whose conversation was refreshing to Fanny. He had such 'first-rate powers of satire and even of sarcasm'. She enjoyed his family as well and especially admired his beautiful and talented young daughter.

Stimulated by her activities on behalf of the museum. Fanny now had a vision of the sort of commercial enterprise she and Thomas Anthony might establish in Cincinatti that would not only benefit them financially but be of real value to the city's residents.[2] From the moment of her arrival she had been disturbed by what seemed to her 'a total and universal want of manners, both in males and females'.[3] In general, the people to whom she talked seemed sensible enough, but excepting those she now counted as friends, she felt there was 'no charm, no grace in their conversation'. What Cincinnati lacked, she felt, were places that encouraged an appreciation of the small refinements and elegancies of life. There were no smart shops, no coffee or tea houses where females could meet in attractive surroundings. There were no public gardens or other pleasant areas where males and females alike could meet and speak of something else than sermons or hog butchering.

Her vision was of a centre that would provide all those necessary refinements under one roof. It would have shops, of course. But why not also a tea-room? An ice-cream parlour? An art gallery? Perhaps a room where stock-exchange figures were quoted and gentlemen could sip juleps as they checked the market? Certainly a concert hall that could also function as a lecture hall. Fanny had early discovered how important lectures were to Cincinnati residents, the next most popular public functions after church services. She had gone to several lectures herself in the absence of other entertainment and had been mildly amused by a series of talks by a phrenologist, an interpreter of that popular new pseudoscience that purported to read and analyse character by the conformations of the head.

She was considering further possibilities for a real cultural centre when she saw the announcement of another lecturer soon to appear. Frances Wright was coming to speak in Cincinnati! Fanny had not heard from Miss Wright for some time, but if she was surprised that the young woman was now adding lecturing to her many activities, the other residents of the city were astounded.

Miss Wright was known by name and reputation to almost everyone. The outrageous nature of her experimental colony and the scandals that had come out of it had made her a general subject of gossip. But that 'a lady of fortune, family, and education, whose youth has been passed in the most refined circles of private life', should present herself before the public as a speaker 'in America, where women are guarded by a sevenfold shield of habitual insignificance',[4] strained credulity. As a result, almost everyone planned to attend her lecture, see her in person, and be scandalized.

There was such a stir about the event that Fanny considered not going for fear of the crowd that would be present. But Mrs Price told her the doctor was making up a party for the occasion and insisted that Fanny join the group.

The courthouse where the lecture was to be given was as crowded as Fanny had feared, but Dr Price found good seats and soon Fanny was glad that she had come. The familiar figure of Frances Wright appeared on the platform. 'Her tall and majestic figure, the deep and almost solemn expression of her eyes, the simple contour of her finely formed head, unadorned, excepting by its own natural ringlets; her garment of plain white muslin . . . all contributed to produce an effect, unlike anything I had ever seen before, or ever expect to see again.'[5]

And how Frances Wright could talk! Fanny glanced around the auditorium to see how the Cincinnati citizens were reacting to the eloquence of this woman they had come to jeer. She saw them gradually yielding to Frances Wright's spell, becoming quiet, attentive, and, at the end, uproarious in their applause. It helped, of course, that for her first lecture Miss Wright had not chosen to discuss such controversial topics as free love or abolition but spoke instead on the nature of true knowledge and said little with which anyone could disagree.

After the lecture it was impossible that Fanny should not accompany the Prices to seek out Miss Wright. Impossible for Fanny not to insist that Frances Wright should come and stay at Mohawk cottage. And after dinner there were many questions to ask. Why had she left the settlement to go lecturing? How were Camilla and her husband? What was happening at Nashoba?

Nashoba? Frances Wright waved a hand dismissingly. She had decided to disband Nashoba. Fanny stared. What had happened within the span of six months to cause her to give up on the dream that had obsessed her so long? Frances Wright was very cool and objective about it. Four years of experience had forced her to realize that the slaves she had gathered together could not produce enough by their labour to provide food and clothing for themselves, much less lay by any surplus funds for their emancipation. They were also a constant source of anxiety to her and a steady financial drain. Naturally, she was not going to abandon these black men, women, and children for whom she had assumed responsibility. Her plan was to free them all and them arrange for their passage to Haiti, where she would place them under the protection of the governor.

Fanny could only nod. Miss Wright could make everything seem possible—if one dream had died, there was still a new dream ahead. What America needed now, Frances Wright said, was a wider education of the public. That was why she had lectured in Cincinnati and she was planning an extended lecture tour eastwards along the Ohio River to New York and Philadelphia later in the year. Before embarking on that tour, however, she was going to be in New Harmony for a while, helping to edit its newspaper. A brilliant Frenchman, Guillaume Sylvan Phiquepal D'Arusmont, had joined the group there. Miss Wright's eyes were shining as she enlarged on the way he and she might work together so that the missionary aims of that utopia might become more successful.

It was no longer possible for Frances Wright to mesmerize Fanny Trollope as she once had done. Fanny had heard once too often the nation's favourite axiom that Frances Wright was also fond of repeating: 'All men are born free and equal.' Whatever Fanny had thought before leaving England, after six months in Cincinnati she was convinced it was a doctrine against which common sense revolted, 'a false and futile axiom, which has done, is doing, and will do so much harm to this fine country'. She knew the phrase was attributed to Thomas Jefferson and that 'few names are held in higher estimation in America than that of Jefferson'. Still, she had heard appalling stories about him in Cincinnati. People spoke with tolerant amusement of the children he had fathered on his female slaves, about his pleasure in being waited on at table by one of his own 'slavish offspring', and his lack of concern when one of them attempted to escape. 'Let the rogues get off, if they can; I will not hinder them.'[6]

Fanny never troubled to try to find out how much of this gossip had basis in fact. She was content to consider the author of the doctrine as a hypocrite, 'an unprincipled tyrant, and most heartless libertine'.

But however she viewed Thomas Jefferson and his contribution to the democratic dream and however deluded she thought Miss Wright to be, she was still impressed by the young woman's intensity and commitment. And so they parted friends, Frances Wright, her eyes for ever on some ideal, and Frances Trollope, not without ideals, but her eyes more sharply fixed on what was right in front of them, noting, more often than not, what was absurd, ridiculous, or hypocritical.

During that summer of 1828 she began making notes on some of her experiences that seemed uniquely absurd and American. The idea of working these notes up some day into a book may have begun to glimmer in her mind. There was, for instance, the American custom of neighbours who 'dropped in' now and then. Male or female, the visitor opened the door, walked in, and nodded.

'How do you do?' Fanny would say.

'Tolerable, I thank ye, how be you?' was the usual response.

Recalling these visits, Fanny wrote, 'If it was a female she took off her hat; if a male, he kept it on, and then taking the first chair in their way, they would retain it for an hour together, without uttering another word; at length, rising abruptly, they would again shake hands, with, "Well, now I must be going, I guess," and so take themselves off, apparently well contented with the encounter.'

Fanny soon learned that it was customary for the person being visited to continue with whatever he or she had been doing without discomposure, but she could never attain this detachment. If she had been reading or writing, she felt she must drop that employment and carry on a rational discourse. After several such visitations, she made a record of one in which her caller had been a milkman:

'Well, now, so you be from the old country? Ay, you'll see sights here, I guess.'

'I hope I shall see many.'

'That's a fact. I expect your little place of an island don't grow such dreadful fine corn as you sees here?'

'It grows no corn at all, sir.'

'Possible! no wonder, then, that we reads such awful stories in the paper of your poor people being starved to death.'

'We have wheat, however.'

'Ay, for your rich folks, but I calculate the poor seldom gets a belly full.'

'You have certainly much greater abundance here.'

'I expect so. Why they do say, that if a poor body contrives to be smart enough to scrape together a few dollars, that your King George always comes down upon 'em, and takes it all away. Don't he?'

'I do not remember hearing of such a transaction.'

'I guess they be pretty close about it. Your papers ben't like ourn, I reckon? Now we says and prints just what we likes.'

'You spend a good deal of time in reading the newspapers.'

'And I'd like you to tell me how we can spend it better. How should freemen spend their time, but looking after their government, and watching that them fellers as we gives office to does their duty, and gives themselves no airs?'

'But I sometimes think, sir, that your fences might be in more thorough repair, and your roads in better order, if less time was spent in politics.'

'The Lord! to see how little you knows of a free country? Why, what's the smoothness of a road, put against the freedom of a free-born American? And what does a broken zig-zag signify, comparable to knowing that the men what we have been pleased to send up to Congress, speaks handsome and straight, as we chooses they should?'

'It is from a sense of duty, then, that you all go to the liquor store to read the papers?'

'To be sure it is, and he'd be no true-born American as didn't. I don't say that the father of a family should always be after liquor, but I do say that I'd rather have my son drunk three times in a week, than not look after the affairs of his country.'[7]

To Fanny, the words *freeman* and *freeborn American* seemed to occur in every other sentence in Cincinnati. She was accustomed now to being referred to as 'the English old woman', but she did laugh when she observed that in mentioning each other her neighbours constantly employed the term *lady*. Instead of saying 'Mrs So-and so', they spoke of 'the lady over the way that takes in washing', or of 'that there lady, out by the gully, what is making dip-candles'.

Fanny laughed. She shook her head. She thought how rarely she heard a nicely turned sentence in this country where everyone was so proud of being free and equal. And she thought some more about her dream project, a centre of refinement both in goods and entertainment. And she longed for the arrival of her husband so that she could lay her plan before him and get his views and approval.

The summer wore on with the oppressive, humid heat of a river valley. Sometimes the Trollopes gathered up books, sketch pads, and a picnic basket and made their way along the riverbank to find a pleasant spot to lounge and sketch and read. This was rather shocking to the more puritanical observers, who felt it was somehow immoral for young women to sit on the ground in the company of young men. Aware of the disapproval their behaviour engendered, the Trollopes nevertheless continued their excursions.

But now as Fanny looked vainly each day for her husband's arrival she was almost compulsive in observing whatever curious aspects of American life presented themselves.

A revival? She had no idea what the term meant when she first heard it and was bewildered by remarks such as, 'The revival will be very full,' or, 'We shall be constantly engaged during the revival'. At length she discovered that 'the unnational church of America required to be roused, at regular intervals, to greater energy and exertion. At these seasons the most enthusiastic of the clergy travel the country, and enter the cities and towns by scores, or by hundreds, as the accommodations of the place may admit, and for a week or fortnight, or, if the population be large, for a month they preach and pray all day, and often for a considerable portion of the night, in the various churches and chapels of the place.'[8] These itinerant clergymen were of all persuasions, except the Episcopalian, Catholic, Unitarian, and Quaker, and they were mostly lodged in the houses of their respective followers.

Fanny could not help but be amused by the similarity between the 'feelings of a first-rate Presbyterian or Methodist lady, fortunate enough to have secured a favourite itinerant for her meeting, and those of a first-rate London Blue, equally blest in the presence of a fashionable poet.'[9]

Her amusement vanished when she finally attended an evening meeting at a crowded church. All her senses of propriety were offended by the minister and his extravagant vehemence. A student of Dante's *Inferno* herself, an eager contributor to Mr Dorfeuille's hellish exhibits, she was nevertheless appalled by the minister's dramatic exposition of the hell that awaited the sinners among his listeners. To Fanny, Dante's hell was redeemed by symbolism and poetry, Mr Dorfeuille's 'Hell' was a big joke, but this minister was really trying to terrify his audience with the immediacy of fire and brimstone. He worked deliberately on the volatile emotions of the younger members of the congregation, the young women in particular. When the minister, sweating from his efforts, finally concluded, the young creatures who had been most affected fell on their knees to the floor, sank forward on their faces, and uttered violent cries and shrieks, 'Oh, Lord! Oh, Lord Jesus!' 'Help me, Jesus!' and so on.

Fanny's distaste for personal and overfamiliar religious rituals dated back to her original dislike of the unctuous Velvet Cunningham, still resident, so far as she knew, of Julians. Her revulsion in this hot, crowded foreign setting was even more extreme. 'It is thus the ladies of Cincinnati amuse themselves: to attend the theatre is forbidden, to play cards is unlawful; but they work hard in their families, and must have some relaxation. For myself, I confess that I think the coarsest comedy ever written would be a less detestable exhibition for the eyes of youth and innocence than such a scene.'[10]

Gradually, the weather grew cooler, but this waning of summer made Fanny almost despair of Thomas Anthony. If he did not come soon, he might delay his Atlantic passage until spring, and she did not know how she could endure so many more months of uncertainty in a strange land.

And then one evening late in September when the family was relaxing on the piazza after dinner, they saw two figures carrying bags walking up the road towards the house. Fanny stood in a sort of quivering presentiment. One by one the others also stood. Soon it was clear that one of the figures was Mr Trollope. Fanny raced down the steps and along the path towards him. Then she saw the second figure more clearly. A well-built stripling of eighteen, stocky, sturdy, unmistakable—her eldest son, Thomas Adolphus.

Fanny flung herself upon both of them. Her husband had come at last. The waiting of so many months was over. And her heart warmed at the sight of Tom. She never admitted to a favourite child, but Tom had been the first, he had always been the easiest, the one she could talk and laugh with as she could not with any of the others.

In the dusk, Henry, Cecilia, Emily, and Auguste Hervieu hurried to gather around the newcomers, and as they all trooped into the house together, Fanny was sure that soon now the promise of the New World would be fulfilled.

11

Anthony – The Bazaar – Andrew Jackson

Thirteen-year-old Anthony, back at Winchester after a desolate summer holiday, really did not feel much surprise to hear that his father had left for America without paying his school bills. He stood stolid in his long, dirty student's gown while one of the masters told him that the school authorities were graciously allowing him to stay on at the school and continue his studies, at least for a while, but he should be warned that the same authorities had informed the town shopkeepers of young Trollope's indigent condition. He could expect no credit anywhere.

Anthony accepted it numbly. This sort of thing was always happening to him. His bills were rarely paid. He never had any pocket money. And when it came to junkets or journeys, he almost never went along. He took it quite for granted when his father was preparing for his trip to America that Mr Trollope should decide to take Tom with him—his mother would be so happy to see her oldest son again. Meanwhile, to save money, Julians Hill was being rented while Mr Trollope was gone. This presented a certain problem as to where Tony should go during his holidays. With friends like the Grants and the Milmans living near Harrow, with Fanny's brother, Henry, living at nearby Fulham, with other friends and relatives here and yon, it was odd that Anthony's father decided the boy's holidays should be spent in his chambers at Lincoln's Inn. The weeks Anthony spent there, after his father and brother had sailed, were like a haunted dream to him. In the late summer all the chambers were deserted. He roamed the echoing corridors and empty courtyards. He looked for things to read and found a fine-print edition of Shakespeare and two volumes of James Fenimore Cooper's novel *The Prairie*. When the Cooper narrative broke off abruptly at the end of the second volume and he could not find the concluding volume anywhere, he filled some hours by imagining his own ending to the story.

After that lonely interlude he had journeyed back to Winchester to the old loneliness of being without friends in a noisy crowd of his fellows. Fellows who would now scorn him as the Harrow boys had done for being without funds, never able to stand treat, not even able to tip the servants.[1]

Leaning over his books, Anthony wondered what the voyage across the Atlantic had been like for his father and Tom. He wondered what the New World was like and imagined the travels of his father and brother towards Cincinnati. He wondered about their arrival in that strange, foreign city and their meeting again with his mother, Henry, his young sisters, and Hervieu. Rejected by everyone around him, Anthony was beginning to live in a world of his imagination, watching the behaviour of those around him in a fascinated but detached way, inventing their behaviour when they were absent from his sight, seeing it all as a continuous frieze of interacting activity.

What the voyage across the Atlantic had really been like for Tom and his father was a test of endurance.[2] In another of his economical gestures, Mr Trollope had taken steerage passage for them. Tom made one visit to the dark, crowded, noisome steerage quarters on the *Corinthian* and knew he could not sleep in such surroundings. Mr Trollope, incapacitated by one of his headaches, stumbled half-conscious into the berth assigned him, but Tom announced that he would sleep on the open deck rather than spend a night there. The other steerage passengers snorted in derision. Let him try it and he would soon see that even these quarters were preferable to the discomforts of the deck. But Tom was not deterred.

Wrapped in his greatcoat, of the sort called 'dreadnought', he found the first night on deck an interesting novelty. The weather was still mild for September, the planks beneath him not over-hard, and the fitfulness of his sleep no real annoyance. The next night was less delightful, and soon after that the weather turned wet and cold. But Tom had pledged himself and would not yield. He descended into the steerage each day to do what he could to ease and tend his father but spent the rest of the time above deck. One night the ship

encountered a storm so severe that half the sails were blown from
the yards, and Tom rode out that night clinging to the bulwarks.
But he kept to his resolution for all the thirty-eight days of the
voyage. When the ship finally dropped anchor in New York harbour,
he felt almost as crippled as his father. However, he was consoled
in his fatigue by the fact that he had not given in.

The journey westward was rough and generally comfortless.
Hours of jolting in stagecoaches alternated with a few hours of
restless sleep in dirty inns. After days of land travel they boarded a
steamboat and were exposed to that American experience until they
arrived at Cincinnati. Finally there they were, at a roomy, bright-
looking house with green blinds, set in open but unkempt grounds.
More important, they were welcomed with almost hysterical delight
by Fanny, Henry, Cecilia, Emily, and Hervieu.

What Tom remembered of the next few months mostly had to do
with social and sightseeing activities. Fanny was eager to introduce
her husband and son to the friends she had made in Cincinnati. The
friends were all eager to be hospitable to the visitors. Dr and Mrs
Price, parents of two pretty daughters, entertained the Trollopes at
dinner parties and at frequent dances they held for the pleasure of
the young people. There were also theatricals at the Price house,
just as there had been back at Julians, and Tom enjoyed playing
Falstaff in *The Merry Wives of Windsor*.

He was also pleased to meet and become acquainted with the
talented young artist of Mr Dorfeuille's 'Hell', Hiram Powers. He
talked viniculture with Mr Longworth. And unlike his mother, he
was not offended by the manners of the Americans he met in the
course of an ordinary day—shopkeepers, jitney drivers, or washer-
women. To Thomas Adolphus, their open, forthright remarks,
which Fanny found unduly familiar, were disarming, helping to
banish his shyness. 'Doubtless there were many causes of anxiety for
my elders,' Tom recalled later, 'but to the best of my remembrance
they touched us young people very lightly.'

His elders did indeed have concerns of some moment, which they
discussed privately. This whole American experiment had to have
some purpose. Thomas Anthony had envisaged a commercial
venture and thought of Cincinnati as the location. And Fanny, who

had spent eight months in the little city observing the manners and resources of the city's inhabitants and assessing their needs, had dreamed up the special sort of project on which she and her husband should embark.

She described her vision to her husband—a bazaar that would supply as many of the town's civilized needs as possible. It would stock a variety of specialized merchandise: leather goods, silverware, china, cutlery, laces, and other items of English or European manufacture that were not available in Cincinnati. But, Fanny went on excitedly, that would only be the beginning. She went on to describe the other amenities the bazaar would provide; the ice-cream parlour and tea-room for Cincinnati ladies; the room where Cincinnati gentlemen could get the latest stock market quotations while sipping juleps; the art gallery. She said that a large hall suitable for lectures or concerts was obligatory and then spoke of further inspirations. A huge globe, located in some central spot, would be a nice touch. There might be some special attraction for children. Finally, the bazaar might also include an area where some of the crafts of Cincinnati artisans could be displayed and sold—embroidery, quilts, elegant pincushions and pen-wipers, firescreens, bookcovers, and other artifacts that Fanny knew the ladies of Cincinnati created in the many hours when their husbands were involved with business or eating at the hotel.

It had to be Fanny's vision. Thomas Anthony's mind did not run to such a mix of sociability, culture, education, entertainment, and nice things to buy. But as Fanny explained the possibilities, it began to seem not such a bad idea to him. Together they looked for a site for this bazaar and finally settled on a location a little distance from the centre of town, near the river. A purchase price of $1,635 was agreed on, and papers were signed.

They also discussed what sort of building should house this unique enterprise, and Fanny was bursting with ideas here also. She had Hervieu sketch some of her inspirations.

In the meantime, walks, parties, and excursions continued. Fanny suggested that her husband and sons might be interested in an expedition across the river to Bone Lick, in Kentucky, where a remarkable religious sect, the shaking Quakers, had a settlement.

She thought it too rigorous a trip for herself and the girls in the cold of early December, so father, sons, and Auguste Hervieu went without them and returned with a detailed report on the curious customs of these celibate people, their grotesque singing and dancing, and their amazing prosperity as farmers and craftsmen.

Real winter settled in, and the Trollopes amused themselves by skating on frozen ponds nearby. At home, they sat by the fire, reading, playing chess, or playing cards.

By mid-February, however, the winter weather was moderating and the ice in the river beginning to break up. Thomas Anthony began to think about returning to England, where Tom was to enter Oxford in the spring. Fanny went about collecting buffalo robes in which they could wrap themselves against the cold as they travelled and 'double boots', or overshoes.

Just then the Cincinnati newspapers announced the approaching visit of Andrew Jackson, the President-elect, who planned to stop briefly in the city en route from his home in Nashville, Tennessee, to the nation's capital in Washington, D.C.

The Trollopes had all been entertained the previous summer by what they had seen of an American political campaign when the incumbent President, John Quincy Adams, was vying against the backwoods hero Jackson for the chief office of the land. Cincinnati, a western city, was predictably pro-Jackson, and most political stump meetings began and ended with loud shouts of 'Jackson forever!'

Fanny thought that if the hero himself were to appear in Cincinnati, her husband and son should wait for his arrival. Perhaps they could even book passage east on the same vessel by which he was travelling.

They learned that the General had arrived in Louisville, across the river, and was due in Cincinnati in a few hours. Thomas Anthony and Tom hastily finished packing their bags and walked from the Mohawk cottage to the city, accompanied by the family. They joined a crowd at the landing place and soon saw a steamboat approaching up the river, escorted by a steamboat on either side. Cannons boomed as the boats churned past the wharves, executed a turnabout, and then swept back again to manoeuvre a graceful landing. Fanny, pleased by spectacles, thought it was beautifully done and was surprised that there was no cheering from the crowd. She could not accustom herself to the silence of most American crowds everywhere except at revival meetings.

Carriages were waiting at the water's edge to convey the General to the hotel where he was to spend his few hours in the city, but when he disembarked he indicated that he preferred to walk. The silent crowd parted, leaving a lane. Fanny was impressed by the General's appearance. A tall, gaunt man, his grey hair carelessly but not ungracefully arranged, he looked like 'a gentleman and a soldier' to Fanny. He was dressed in deep mourning, having recently lost his wife, a fact that should have been known to the avid newspaper readers of the city. Still, Fanny heard someone near her cry out, 'There goes Jackson, where is his wife?' And she was pained to hear another voice cry, 'Adams forever!' But these were the only shouts that broke the silence.

After a suitable interval. Thomas Anthony and his sons, Tom and Henry, joined the group of citizens who were gathering at the hotel to be presented to the President-elect. In due time the three Trollopes made their way up the line and shook General Jackson's hand. After which, Mr Trollope hurried from the hotel, booked passage for himself and Tom on the General's steamboat, took a hasty dinner with Fanny, Henry, and the girls, and then, at the appointed hour, got Tom, himself, and their luggage aboard.

Later, in letters from Thomas Anthony, Fanny learned that her husband had held several conversations with the General during the journey and was much pleased by his intelligence and manner but 'deeply disgusted by the brutal familiarity' to which he was exposed at every stopping place. Thomas Anthony reported one encounter in detail. He was at the General's elbow when a greasy fellow accosted him thus:

' "General Jackson, I guess?"

'The General bowed assent.

' "Why, they told me you was dead."

' "No! Providence has hitherto preserved my life."

' "And is your wife alive too?"

'The General, apparently much hurt, signified the contrary, upon which the courtier concluded his harangue by saying, "Ay, I thought it was the one or t'other of ye." '[3]

Fanny shook her head over this new example of American manners, but by the time the letter reached her, she was far too busy to ponder it for long.

The bazaar was beginning to take shape in the drawings of a young architect she had found and she was in a ferment of creativity making suggestions and changes. The sketch for a modest two-storey building that the architect had first presented to her seemed quite inadequate. She wanted something more elaborate and unique. She was a woman of taste and had travelled widely in England and to some extent in France and was familiar with both ancient and modern buildings of beauty and dignity. But now she seemed impelled to erect something different from those European structures, thinking perhaps that only something astonishing would draw the crowds as Mr Dorfeuille's 'Hell' did.

One of her first suggestions was a central rotunda covered with a small dome. Auguste Hervieu had been working for some time on a grand historical painting of La Fayette landing at Cincinnati, and it could be exhibited to greatest effect in a rotunda. Fanny also wanted great windows across the front of the building, set off by Grecian columns, and arches of some sort over the windows, pointed arches, perhaps something in the Moorish style. The pediment above must also be decorative; she left it to the architect to devise something.

Fanny was generally pleased with the sketch that finally emerged, contenting herself with the thought that further changes and elaborations could be made as the building progressed. Since the whole project of the bazaar was to provide a career for Henry, she often had him at her side as she set about hiring a contractor and workmen to start the actual construction.

Just how Thomas Anthony had raised the money to make a down payment on the land where the building was to stand, how he was providing funds for the construction, and how he was going to arrange to purchase and ship two thousand dollars worth of goods from England to Cincinnati, as he had promised his wife to do, is a mystery to later generations. It may well have been a mystery to Fanny also, who could not have been privy to any of her husband's figures. She and the children would have starved during the first months in Cincinnati but for Auguste Hervieu's generosity. Her husband had taken steerage passage for himself and Tom to cross the Atlantic. When he arrived, he told her that he had moved from Julians Hill to a much smaller house at Harrow Weald to save money. Still, he had taken it for granted that they should proceed with the bazaar as a commercial venture. And so, Fanny was proceeding.

When the contractor saw the plans for the building, he shook his head in disbelief, and as the structure began to take shape, there was a great deal of laughter among the workmen. The design seemed outlandish to them, another notion of that 'English old woman'. Fanny ignored their laughter, but it was not so easy to deal with suppliers of wood, brick, tile, and other necessities when they procrastinated in their deliveries. The chief source of their reluc tance seemed to be their bewilderment at Mrs Trollope's plans. They did not see that Cincinnati needed such a building, and who was she anyway, to come from England and impose some curious bazaar upon their city? Fanny tried to speak reasonably with them all, saying that she hoped the bazaar would be an ornament to the city and that it would offer not only attractive foreign goods for sale but provide a marketplace for local crafts. Heads still shook in doubt. A low, murmuring groundswell against 'foreign notions' had begun.

It was no help to Fanny that a book by an Englishman, Capt. Basil Hall, about his travels in America, appeared that summer of 1829. By and large Cincinnati was not a book-reading town, but word about this particular book seemed to spread by osmosis. Some arrogant Englishman had come visiting the country and then written a book extremely critical of it. It made no difference that Captain Hall had prefaced his book, *Travels in the United States*, by writing that he had come to America with every prejudice in its favour, eager to admire everything in the new republic, and that he had found much that he did admire.

All the talk centred on what he had not admired. He had written that many things in America were unfinished and showed careless- ness and haste in their manufacture and that Americans 'always stop at that point, when the business in hand has reached that condition which is most certain of procuring for it a ready market . . . suited to the average taste of consumers.'[4]

He wrote that Americans seemed unable to forget their victory in the Revolution, and though he found that understandable, he felt that it was 'utterly out of nature' for them to expect the British, who had been defeated, to wish to spend the same amount of time reflecting on the outcome of that war.

He wrote of the endless hunger of Americans for praise of their country and the way they insisted in every conversation that the United States be acknowledged the finest, greatest, most wonderful country in the world. Captain Hall suggested that this self-praise bordered on bad manners.

Even the illiterate in Cincinnati were soon aware that an Englishman had written a book criticizing American manners, patriotism, and craftsmanship. The native resentment was unanimous.

Perhaps it was only natural that some of that ill-feeling spilled over on to Fanny Trollope and the structure she was foisting on Cincinnati. Did she think her building was something better than Americans could manage for themselves? The workmen idled at their tasks and clamoured for their wages.

Unfortunately, no remittances came through from Thomas Anthony for several months. Fanny asked the men to be patient; they would get their money. They laughed at her and threw down their tools. Once again, as during the winter before, Fanny had to turn to Auguste Hervieu, who lent her what he could. The work commenced again, in a desultory way.

Looking at the building that was taking shape. Fanny felt both excited and frantic. She thought it was a lovely building, different and imaginative, and surely the people of Cincinnati would learn to like it. But why was there no letter from Thomas Anthony? How could she go on without more money? And when would the shipments of goods begin to arrive?

She felt feverish with impatience. And suddenly she was shivering, her teeth chattering. She could not believe it at first, not even when the shivering stopped and the fever swept through her again. She had never been really sick in all her life. But before long she was in bed at the Mohawk cottage, her fever raging and then subsiding as her body was racked with shudders and the bedclothes were soaked with sweat. Somewhere, somehow, she had picked up malaria, and for several weeks it seemed very likely that she would die of it.

12

Disaster

Trollope's Folly. The nickname arose spontaneously in Cincinnati and was joyfully and unanimously used in referring to Mrs Trollope's empty, not quite finished building. There it stood, a fantastic hodgepodge, good for nothing, ridiculous evidence of what some English people thought Americans would put up with.[1]

The report went around that the 'English old woman' who was responsible was lying ill in her cottage in Mohawk. A delegation of workers made its way to her, angry over their unpaid wages. Henry met them, nervous and unsure, and explained that his mother was very sick. He assured them that they would be paid as soon as she had recovered, but this did not satisfy the men. They had contracted to work for such and such a wage, and if they did not have their money, they figured they might take the matter to court. There were ways of settling these things in America, they said, where freeborn men were worthy of their hire. At some point Auguste Hervieu appeared. His reassurances in his still broken and accented English did not calm the men. They would have satisfaction or sue for their rights. Hervieu would have been happy to give them some partial payment from his own funds, but Mrs Trollope was dangerously ill. He had no idea what expenses would be entailed in restoring her to health. Neither did he have any idea when some further remittances would come from Mr Trollope in England. He could only reiterate that the men would be paid as soon as possible.

The workers moved away, still unsatisfied, and murmuring about courts of justice.

The days went by, and Fanny continued to burn and shiver. Dr Price came regularly, took her pulse, felt her forehead, and left more calomel. The illness would have to run its course.

Some months before her illness Fanny had managed to improve

the situation in regard to 'help' by locating an expatriate English-woman who was happy to take service as a cook and then, later, a tidy young Frenchwoman who was equally pleased to be hired as a governess for the girls. And so, for a while, meals continued to be served, the girls did their lessons, and there was someone to tend to Fanny's needs.

But money to pay these women had now run out. They had stayed on, week after week, not wishing to leave, but they had to consider their own futures.

And then, when the mood in the cottage was at its lowest, the promised shipment of goods from Thomas Anthony arrived. Henry tiptoed into his mother's room to whisper the news to her, hoping it might work some reviving magic. He saw her eyes open and flutter. He saw her try to smile. He smiled back and hurried out of the room.

Henry and Hervieu could hardly believe their eyes when they opened the first crate. It was filled with cheap bits of trumpery—souvenirs such as one might buy at a seaside resort. This was not the sort of merchandise Fanny had talked about for the bazaar. She had talked of fine leather goods, china and cutlery, articles of a kind unavailable in Cincinnati. What sort of mistake had their father made? They hurried to open another crate, and this time found a collection of shawls, bonnets, and mitts. Henry and Hervieu did not need to be experts in ladies' furnishings to recognize these items as tawdry. The look and feel of them made their cheapness clear. They opened the rest of the boxes and found the same sort of merchandise. Thomas Anthony Trollope had made another of his economical gestures, similar to sending his sons to Harrow as 'charity students' to save tuition, and half-killing himself by travelling steerage across the Atlantic. He had sent two thousand dollars worth of junk across the sea to stock the bazaar.

They did not tell Fanny for quite a while. She had begun to mend. Her fever was gone. But she was thin and weak beyond belief. The girls propped her up in bed and brought her nourishing broths. She smiled at them and closed her eyes in weariness. It was several days before she put her feet over the edge of the bed and tried to stand. She soon collapsed on the bed again. She had no strength in her legs at all.

'How is the bazaar?' she had been asking ever since the fever had subsided, and both Henry and Hervieu told her not to worry. Her first concern was to regain her strength. They carried her each day to a chair by the window and brought her books to read, the works of James Fenimore Cooper to start with. The various friends she had made in Cincinnati came, bringing junkets and jellies and more books, and if she asked them about the bazaar, they tried to reassure her, saying that all would be well.

For days now Fanny sat in a sort of trance, reading *The Last of the Mohicans*, *The Deerslayer*, and *The Pathfinder*, entering another America from the one she had seen for herself in Tennessee and Ohio. But after reading Cooper, she found she could not sleep without Indians creeping through her dreams to ambush her, while panthers glared and forests closed in on her. Finally she asked for an antidote—the Waverly novels, please. Her family found them and brought them to her, and reading them, she was restored to a world she knew. There was a 'wholesome vigour' to Sir Walter Scott's writing that seemed to assuage her nerves. She began to get stronger and at last was able to stand and to walk across the room, even out to the piazza.

And just in time. For Henry and Hervieu could no longer conceal the truth from her. The workmen and contractors had made good their threats and started suits against Mrs Trollope for non-payment of wages and bills for supplies. She, or an attorney, would soon have to appear in court.

'But Mr Trollope has sent more remittances, surely,' she whispered. They had to tell her no. Well, but he has shipped goods, she insisted, looking at them anxiously. Then they had to go on with the story, trying to minimize the situation. Perhaps Papa had not really been clear about what Mother had in mind, Henry suggested.

Fanny ordered a carriage to drive her to the bazaar so that she could see for herself what had been delivered. She walked out to it, leaning on Henry's arm, and they drove to the bazaar. She stared at the building a moment before alighting. It really was a cheerful structure, a pleasant conceit, the sort of thing that might have amused the Prince Regent himself back in the days when he was indulging his fantasies at Brighton. Then, supported by both Henry and Hervieu, she got out of the carriage and climbed up one side of the divided stairway that led to the great central door. Inside, breathing in the smell of new plaster and wood, hearing the echoing emptiness, she looked at the contents of the crates.

She had never been a woman to scream or cry or carry on. She did not do so now but signalled Henry and Hervieu that she wanted to go back to the carriage.

She chose to forget all that happened next. The frantic manoeuvring to sell or auction off the merchandise that Thomas Anthony had sent to various merchants around the city, the sheriff's auction of the building itself, these events she endured but managed somehow to keep at a distance. Later she wrote, 'It was no very agreeable conviction which greeted my recovery, that our Cincinnati speculation for my son would in no way answer our expectation.'[2]

It was difficult to see the dream of her beautiful bazaar come crashing down in a tumult of legal actions, hard bargaining, and haggling, but worse was to come.

She and her family were evicted from the Mohawk cottage for non-payment of rent, and what furnishings they owned were seized to be sold for her debts.

How was it possible? How could she have fallen into such total ruin? There was, to be sure, a habit of living in a certain style without regard to available funds. She had had an unrealistic and extravagant vision of the bazaar. There had been general mismanagement. Thomas Anthony's shipment of so much shoddy merchandise was simply the final straw. Fanny explained the failure to friends later by saying that she and her husband were too ignorant of commercial enterprises to undertake such a venture.

A sympathetic neighbour took them in. Fanny and the two girls slept in the one spare bed; Henry and Hervieu on the kitchen floor. They were all grateful for such accommodations while the slow process of disposing of the merchandise from England went on.

At this point, Henry fell ill with a return of the fever he had contracted at New Harmony. The people with whom they were staying tried to reassure his mother. The young man was simply suffering from the 'bilious fever' that was common in the area. After a few days his fever subsided, and he seemed recovered. Then, a few days later, he was seized by a sudden convulsion that shook his whole body while his face took on a livid hue. Again the Trollopes' hosts were not alarmed. 'It's only the ague,' they said. 'Lots of folks get it hereabouts. It comes and goes.' And so it did with Henry. He would seem quite well for a few days, and then the ague fit would overtake him.

To get Henry out of Cincinnati, out of America altogether, and back home in England was now Fanny's chief goal. The country that was to have provided him with some sort of future security seemed likely to kill him. She was almost as eager for herself and her daughters to be gone, but she thought their departure must wait. Henry must go now, before the river was frozen and the boats stopped running. Now, so he would arrive in England before spring, when it had been agreed between Fanny and her husband that Thomas Anthony would return to Cincinnati. Once again letters between Fanny and her husband seemed to be miscarrying. She was not at all sure that he had received any word about the failure of the bazaar. Henry must carry the news in person.

Once again she had to appeal to Auguste Hervieu for funds, and he came to her aid once again and lent her the money for Henry's journey. Somehow, by giving drawing lessons and taking portrait commissions, he earned enough to come to the rescue when the emergency was extreme.

Henry was hurried aboard a steamboat, given the name of a man in New York who was acquainted with both his father and the Wright sisters and to whom he was instructed to apply for help in arranging his transatlantic passage, and sent on his way.

Fanny watched the boat churn off up the river. How wonderful if she and Cecilia and Emily and Hervieu could have been aboard also. She yearned for England and home. But a welter of details still attended the final disposition of the bazaar and its merchandise. She had to stay in Cincinnati a few more weeks. And at the end of that time the river would probably be closed to steamboats for a month or so because of ice.

She might have been frantic with impatience except for the idea that had been at the back of her mind for months now, as she made notes on her American experiences. The idea now loomed as something tangible she could do. She could write a book.

Frances Wright had done very well with her *Views of Society and Manners in America*. That book, of course, had been altogether laudatory, pleasing both to Americans and English liberals sympathetic to republican principles. But Captain Basil Hall had also written a book, a great deal more critical of America, and from the stir it had created in Cincinnati Fanny imagined it must have caused talk in England as well, which meant that he must have made some money from it. Yes, she should at least try her hand at a book.

She was not worried about the actual writing. She had written for her own entertainment and that of her friends since her girlhood. But she did realize that for all her months in the United States she had seen only a small portion of the country—a glimpse of New Orleans, the journey up the Mississippi, Nashoba, and then Cincinnati and its environs. To write any sort of book about America she really should tour some parts of the East and visit some of its older, more famous cities—New York, Washington, Philadelphia. And could any book about the United States be complete without some description of its greatest natural wonder, Niagara Falls?

It occurred to her that the interest in such a book might be enhanced if it had illustrations, and there she was with an artist very nearly at her elbow. If Auguste Hervieu would consent to join her in the project and the book sold, he might actually see a little profit from his efforts, a tiny return for all she owed him. She spoke to him about the idea, and he was enthusiastic. And he was once again ready to advance money so that she, the girls, and he could not only travel to the East but make it a real excursion, taking in as many areas and cities as possible to provide material for the book.

This offer was possible because, amid all Fanny's disasters, Hervieu was having a bit of success. He had completed his great historical painting, which was to have contributed to the glories of the bazaar. The subject was the landing of La Fayette in Cincinnati, and Hervieu had decided to add local interest by painting the likenesses of more than forty of Cincinnati's most prominent citizens among the figures gathered on the shore to greet the hero. When this painting was exhibited in the upper gallery of the bazaar, it was as widely admired as the rest of the place was deplored. Visitors thronged to pay a small admission price for the privilege of viewing themselves or their neighbours immortalized in oil on canvas. Timothy Flint was so pleased by the painting that he declared in his *Western Monthly Review* that the proper place for it was in the halls of Congress.

Such praise, along with the funds the exhibit of the painting brought in, encouraged Fanny and Hervieu to think that the journey east might be mostly financed by exhibiting the canvas in cities along the way.

Fanny was now full of impatience to depart. She shed no more tears over the fate of her bazaar, the main floor of which had become an untidy market. She did make one last attempt to earn a few dollars by staging what she hoped might be a series of elegant entertainments in the great lecture hall of the building. Her theatrical acquaintances, Mr and Mrs Drake, were persuaded to offer dramatic readings. Fanny arranged for musical interludes and offered tea and coffee at intermission time. But attendance at the first presentation was sparse. Fanny, it seemed, had won all the success she was to achieve in Cincinnati with her inspirations for Dorfeuille's Western Museum.

After the second entertainment attracted an audience of twelve, Fanny gave up the project and only wanted to see a break-up of the ice in the river. By the middle of February the ice seemed to be melting. She was ready to rush with her family, Hervieu, his painting, and all the assembled luggage, to board the first steamboat heading east. Her friends urged caution. The first thaw could be dangerous. Floating chunks of ice, some very large, whirled about in the river, piled up against each other, or crashed into boats with great violence. Little rivers that were tributaries to the Ohio discharged their piled-up ice and created ice jams and whirlpools along the way.

So she restrained herself. But she had begun already to rise before dawn from the crowded bed she shared with Cecilia and Emily. Bundled up in a dressing gown, she lighted a candle, got out ink bottle, paper, and pen, and started to write the book that she hoped and prayed would (with Hervieu's illustrations) bring some return for her two years in an alien land.

13

Harrow Weald – Travels in America – Slavery

The farmhouse, Harrow Weald, to which Thomas Anthony had moved after renting Julians Hill, might have had a picturesque charm on a sunshiny day. On a grey day, the heavy trees surrounding it seemed to submerge it in funereal gloom. Nothing had been done about lawns or gardens or shrubs. Grass grew high and untended, and when the wind blew, the branches of the trees scraped the house in a fretful way.[1]

In the dark of an April midnight the house had an almost haunted appearance. On one such night in 1830 someone knocked on the front door. Tom was home, and by midnight, he was asleep in a downstairs room. The knocking finally wakened him, and he groped his way to the door.

Outside stood a thin young figure, drooping with fatigue over a huge carpet bag at his feet.

'Tom!' said the figure, straightening a little.

'Good God!' said Tom. 'Henry? Is it really you, Henry?'

His brother was home from across the sea. His ship had docked at Liverpool, and he had just enough money to pay the coach fare to London. Arriving in the city without a penny, he had seen no alternative but to walk the twelve miles to Harrow Weald, lugging his bag.

Thomas Adolphus picked up the bag and drew his younger brother into the house. He lit a candle and began asking questions. But Henry was far too exhausted to talk. All he wanted was a place to lie down and sleep. Tom led him to a sofa, said good-night, and blew out the candle, wondering very much about events in America.

Next morning, somewhat restored, Henry greeted his astonished father and his young brother, Anthony, who was home now from Winchester. Henry had no time to ask about that. His father thundered a barrage of questions at him. Why was he back in

England? Where were his mother and sisters? What was happening in Cincinnati? How was the bazaar progressing?

Obviously, the letters Fanny had written to her husband had never reached him.

As the story of the disaster in Cincinnati gradually emerged, Henry's answers to his father's questions grew more and more defiant and defensive and his father more flushed and incredulous. All had been lost? Everything? The building? The merchandise he had sent? Yes. All. And where, again, were Mrs Trollope and the girls? Again Henry repeated that his mother had decided to make a brief tour of the eastern part of the United States before returning to England. She had an idea of writing a book about it, Henry said. Finally, his rage and stupefaction reducing him to silence, Thomas Anthony retired to his room, and Henry could relax a little.

It was the beginning of a long, dreary stretch for Mr Trollope and his three sons. Tom was perhaps the least unhappy. He did not receive the election to New College that he had hoped for, and he finally enrolled at Alban Hall at Oxford. This was not so prestigious as some of the other colleges, but Tom had an easy way of accepting what befell. Eventually he left Harrow Weald for Alban Hall. Not long after that, Mr Trollope arranged for Henry to attend Caius College at Cambridge, and Henry departed, leaving Mr Trollope alone with Anthony.

Anthony was fifteen, big for his age and awkward. He had been unhappy at Winchester, but he was even more unhappy when his father suddenly brought him home from that school, possibly because he could not keep up with the bills. Now, although he was somewhat old for it, he was again going to Harrow-on-the-Hill. Twice a day he trudged up the lane from the farmhouse to the school, through dust or mud depending on the weather, and twice a day back again. Again he was a despised day boy, a charity case, an outcast, fair game to be taunted by any of the boarders. One day, goaded too far by another student, Anthony doubled his fists and fought his tormentor. Once aroused, he would not back down and fought on until one of the masters finally intervened to stop the struggle. Anthony was secretly pleased that he had mauled his opponent so badly that the boy had to leave school for a while.

As for Mr Trollope, he moved in a fog of bitterness and misery that insulated him from any of Anthony's problems. When he was feeling well enough, he went out to join the bailiff and supervise activities on the farms at Julians and Harrow Weald. But when his headaches overcame him, as they did more and more frequently these days, he shut himself up in his room and suffered through the attacks with ever larger doses of calomel. When he and Anthony took their meals together, they were slapdash affairs, served up by the serving woman in the kitchen. Now and then they exchanged a few words. There were times when Anthony, hostile though he was towards the father who kept shunting him from one school to another, felt a sympathetic kinship with the unhappy man. Both of them seemed to be misfits, abandoned by the woman who had once made home life cheerful and alive with the comings and goings of neighbours. Who knew when she would return? In the meantime, the two of them plodded through the days and nights in their private orbits at Harrow Weald.

In America Fanny was beginning to enjoy herself. The ice on the Ohio River was finally broken, and there was a journey to make, up the river on another of America's splendid steamboats, so comfortably appointed for the gentlemen, so restricted for the ladies. Never mind, she and the girls could sit outside on the canopied deck through most of the days, observing the scenery and noting how the riverbanks gradually grew more cultivated as the boat travelled further and further east. They saw richer farms, well-tended houses, sleek animals in the patterned fields. Fanny forgot about being penniless. She put the disaster in Cincinnati behind her and remembered instead only the curious and interesting aspects of life there. These memories she was now writing down in odd moments, getting her book underway. With Cincinnati behind her she could recall some absurd encounters.

The boat steamed along, and Fanny's pen scratched over the paper on the writing table in her lap, recalling various expressions of the American dislike and distrust of the English:

'Well, now, I think your government must just be fit to hang themselves for that last war they cooked up; it has been the ruin of you I expect, for it has just been the making of us.'

Or . . . 'Well, I do begin to understand your broken English better than I did; but no wonder I could not make it out very well at first, as you come from London, for everybody knows that London slang is the most dreadful in the world. How queer it is now, that all the people who live in London should put the *h* where it is not, and never will put it where it is.'[2]

Then the boat was coming in for a landing at Wheeling, still in Virginia in those days, a slave state. This soon plunged Fanny into philosophical difficulties.

They arrived at two o'clock in the morning and had to disembark at once with all their luggage since the steamboat was going directly on. However, 'We were instantly supplied with a dray, and in a few moments found ourselves comfortably seated before a good fire, at an hotel near the landing-place; our rooms, with fires in them, were immediately ready for us, and refreshments brought, with all that sedulous attention which in this country distinguishes a slave state.'[3]

It hurt her to note this and report it, for she felt slavery was wrong. But there it was. She was 'immediately comfortable, and at my ease', in a slave state and felt that the intercourse between her and those who served her was 'profitable to both parties and painful to neither'.[4]

She struggled with the problem, for she had come to the United States fired with the anti-slavery ideals about which Frances Wright had spoken so eloquently. She had looked forward to a land where every man and woman was guaranteed the right to life, liberty, and the pursuit of happiness. Instead, she had found a country where everyone talked constantly of 'freedom and equality', but behaved in ways that seemed to make such words a mockery. She remembered the young women who had come to 'help out' and then acted with arrogance and incompetence, too proud for the work they had contracted to do but unqualified for anything else. The doctrine that no person should be a servant was false, she concluded, 'for in point of fact the man possessed of dollars does command the services of the man possessed of no dollars; but these services are given grudgingly, and of necessity, with no appearance of cheerful good-will on the one side, or of kindly interest on the other'.

Later, after more time spent in the slave states, Fanny became aware of something else not so pleasant—the unhappy influence of slavery on the *owners* of slaves. Finally she would confess that she 'could not but think that the citizens of the United States had contrived, by their political alchemy, to extract all that was most noxious both in democracy and slavery and had poured the strange mixture through every vein of the moral organization of the country'.[5]

She was still enjoying the quiet service that seemed to go with slavery as she, the girls, and Hervieu lingered awhile in Wheeling before boarding a stagecoach to travel over the Allegheny Mountains to Maryland.

Fanny was now making careful notes of everything for her book, describing the coach that had no step, so that entrance had to be effected by a ladder, putting females somewhat in the predicament of sailors who 'in danger, have no door to creep out'. But soon she was noting the beautiful countryside, and as the coach, ascending and descending foothills, mounted higher and higher, she was enraptured by scenery like none she had seen before. 'It is a world of mountains rising around you in every direction, and in every form; savage, vast and wild; yet almost at every step, some lovely spot meets your eyes, green, bright, and blooming, as the most cherished nook belonging to some noble Flora in our own beautiful land. It is a ride of ninety miles [to Hagerstown, Maryland], through kalmias, rhododendrons, azaleas, vines, and roses; sheltered from every blast that blows by vast masses of various coloured rocks, on which—"Tall pines and cedars wave their dark green crests":— while in every direction you have a back-ground of blue mountain tops, that play at bo peep with you in the clouds.'[6]

Hagerstown, where they were delayed for a day by what Fanny considered a 'Yankee trick' in scheduling, was a small place, but it had the most comfortable inn the Trollopes had yet encountered. Instead of being scolded for wanting a private sitting room, as they had been in Cincinnati, they were offered two, without even asking, and they were summoned courteously to meals that were not only abundant but even elegant.

From Hagerstown their itinerary led them to Baltimore, and Fanny thought this the handsomest city she had yet seen in the

Union. The skyline offered domes and steeples. There were fine
public buildings and private dwellings lavished with white marble.
They were lodged in an excellent hotel, and they found a number of
interesting and civilized sites to visit—a cathedral, an art museum
run by one of the Peale brothers (they were all artists). They looked
in on an 'infant school' run by an amiable Englishman, and Fanny
was astonished by the well-bred behaviour of the children, so
different from the undisciplined activity of the children she had
observed in Cincinnati. She was sorry altogether to leave Baltimore.

She was now getting a very different view of the United States
than she had had west of the Alleghenies. In Washington, D.C., she
was greatly impressed by the architecture of the Capitol. She had
not expected to see so imposing a building in America and admired
its façades, both western and eastern, and the way it stood 'so finely
—high and alone'.[7] She did not join in the laughter of some
foreigners because the plan of the city was upon such an enormous
scale and so little had been executed. The plan seemed good to her,
and what had been done so far had been done well. She admired
Pennsylvania Avenue, lined with stylish shops as it extended towards
the mansion of the President, and as she toured the Capitol building,
she saw details ignored by many visitors. In the lower part of the
building, below the rotunda, she walked through a hall, the ceiling
of which was supported by pillars, and the capitals of the pillars
struck her as especially fine. 'They are composed of the ears and
leaves of the Indian corn, beautifully arranged, and forming as
graceful an' outline as the acanthus itself. This was the only instance
I saw in which America has ventured to attempt national originality;
the success is perfect. A sense of fitness always enhances the effect
of beauty.'[8]

But in Washington, as everywhere in the United States, she was
troubled by the disparity between the incessant talk of liberty and
equality and the actual behaviour of the citizens. 'It is impossible
for any mind of common honesty not to be revolted by the contradictions in their principles and practice. They inveigh against the
governments of Europe, because, as they say, they favour the powerful and oppress the weak. You may hear this declaimed upon in
Congress, roared out in taverns, discussed in every drawing-room,

satirized upon the stage, nay, even anathemized from the pulpit; listen to it, and then look at them at home; you will see them with one hand hoisting the cap of liberty, and with the other flogging their slaves.'⁹

As it happened, her visit in Washington, D.C., coincided with the efforts of Congress and President Andrew Jackson to evacuate the Cherokee Indians from the grounds that had been ceded to them by treaty in Tennessee and Georgia. 'If the American character may be judged in their conduct in this matter, they are most lamentably deficient in every feeling of honour and integrity,'¹⁰ Fanny wrote.

She was pleased to be allowed to attend some sessions of Congress. In England, ladies were not admitted to the House of Commons. The eloquence of a 'thorough horse and alligator' orator from Kentucky amused her, especially when he begged his colleagues to 'go the whole hog' on some issue. Mainly she was impressed by the fact that most debates seemed to turn on one theme—the entire independence of each individual state. And she was distressed, as she was in every public place, by the constant tobacco chewing and spitting of the men.

Through all of this sightseeing, she and Hervieu had been suffering some personal disappointment. The plan to exhibit his huge painting in the cities through which they passed was not working out as profitably as they had hoped. And despite Timothy Flint's encouragement, no one they approached in Washington seemed interested in buying the painting to grace the halls of Congress. Fanny tried to cheer Hervieu with the thought that the painting would have better success in Philadelphia and New York.

They did not leave for those cities immediately, however. Soon after arriving in Washington, D.C., Fanny had managed to locate an old friend, the oldest Garnett daughter, Anna Maria, who had married an American, Charles Stone, in 1804. Now a widow, Mrs Stone was living about ten miles from the capital in a town called Stonington, near the great falls of the Potomac. Once Fanny had found her and the two women had embraced, overjoyed to see each other again after so many years, it was arranged that the Trollopes and Hervieu should spend the coming summer months with Mrs Stone.

The summer was a return to the sort of life that Fanny had known of old. Every fine day the little group would take a walk to some scenic spot in the vicinity, of which there were many. Then they would return, nicely fatigued, to sit on the veranda and sip iced tea or sangria while some one of the group played Mozart on the pianoforte in the parlour. In the early morning hours, before the others rose, Fanny worked on her book, catching up on the notes she had made of the sightseeing since leaving Cincinnati.

But by August of 1830 it seemed time to move on. There was still much more she had to see in the East before she would have a manuscript of enough consequence to offer a publisher. She must visit Philadelphia, New York City, and above all, and at whatever cost, she must travel to that wonder of American wonders, Niagara Falls.

14

Return to England –
'Domestic Manners of the Americans'

King George IV, once England's Prince Charming but of late years grown fat, dropsical, ill-tempered, and despised, was dead. William, Duke of Clarence, who had only recently seen the likelihood of ascending the throne, was king. The former Princess Adelaide of Saxe-Meiningen, whom William had finally been persuaded to marry, was queen. But these changes made little difference to most English people. The subject that had them so agitated was the matter of reform—reform in districting for the election of members of Parliament, reform in voting rights so that a greater percentage of the population would have some say in their government. Tories and Whigs stood sharply divided, the Tories appalled at any change in the established order of things, the Whigs pressing eagerly for a wider franchise, a more representative democracy. Tories and Whigs alike considered William's ascension from the point of view of what he might do to tip the balance either way. They wondered if the Tory Duke of Wellington would be allowed to remain as Prime Minister and if not, who would be taking his place.

Most of all this was just a distant racket to the occupants of Harrow Weald, though Thomas Anthony, affirming liberal principles, hoped for a new ministry that would begin to take some steps towards reform. None of it meant anything to young Anthony. For him, there was a brief respite from constant misery when his brother, Thomas Adolphus, came home in late summer on holiday. Tom encouraged activity. He and Anthony went for long walks, testing each other for endurance. One day Tom acquired some 'single-sticks with strong basket handles', and he and Anthony had a bout with them. Both ended up with a great many bruises and welts, but Tom, gracious to his younger brother, conceded that Tony was his superior in quickness and adroitness, and also in bearing pain. On another occasion, hearing of a grand exhibition at Vauxhall, the brothers set out to walk to it. They each had the necessary shilling for admittance but no other money with which to buy refreshments or other entertainment. They managed to enjoy themselves even so. Tom was pleased by the fireworks, and Anthony joined in the country dances, his awkwardness and shyness put aside for a few hours as he pranced and swung partners in safe anonymity. Long after midnight they started the long walk home to Harrow Weald, arriving at dawn physically exhausted but refreshed in spirit.[1]

But nothing, it seemed, could go easily or happily for long at Harrow Weald. As Tom's holiday came to an end, his father contrived to cause new difficulties for his son. The master of Tom's college, Alban Hall, had recently issued stringent rules in regard to a prompt return from holiday. For some reason that Tom could never remember later, Mr Trollope insisted that Tom remain at home a day past the date that he was due to return to Oxford. When he did return, Tom was told he must either pay a fine or be expelled. He wrote to his father explaining the ultimatum. His father replied that he would not pay a fine under any circumstances.

The matter was finally compromised by Tom being transferred to Magdalen Hall, an even less prestigious college at that time than Alban Hall, generally attended by misfits. There was little studying and a great deal of drinking, but Tom isolated himself from the surrounding anarchy, drank very little because he did not care for wine, and read a great deal, totally at random.

Soon after this, Henry came home to Harrow Weald from Caius College. Lack of funds to keep him there and his own lack of application both contributed to his return. Thomas Anthony greeted his second son without enthusiasm and retired to his room. If young Anthony had hoped for a companion he was mistaken. Henry showed none of the sympathy that Tom had sometimes offered. At loose ends at Harrow Weald, Henry recalled the one scientific subject to which he had been introduced at New Harmony in Indiana—geology. He roamed about the fields and hills of Harrow looking for rock formations and brought specimens home to study. He had little to say to his younger brother. Anthony was almost relieved when his father decreed that Henry should go to London each day and begin reading for the Law.

Letters came from America more frequently as Fanny reached the eastern coast, where transatlantic mail service was more reliable. Husband and sons heard from her in New York, in Philadelphia, and in Buffalo. By the spring of 1831 they were reading that she was beginning to plan her return to England. After that, what conversation there was in the farmhouse consisted of speculation as to when she might arrive.

The days passed, and the weeks passed. Father and sons gave up any momentary expectation and drudged on in their melancholy ways. Then, one day, suddenly there she was, along with Cecilia, Emily, and Auguste Hervieu.

Fanny created her own flurry of delight as she greeted her husband and son. 'Tony!' she cried, 'How you have grown! I would hardly have known you. Come and kiss your mother.'

But she had been gone too long. She had written him too infrequently, remembering him chiefly in messages to Tom that were to be relayed to him. He was the only one of the family who had never been in America with her. He stood stiff and withdrawn as she tried to caress him. Still he could not keep his eyes off her as she darted about, laughing, exclaiming, deploring. 'Oh, no, you can't have been living like this all the time I've been gone.' Chairs were pushed into new positions, blinds drawn up, abandoned dirty dishes gathered and put into the sink, even as she poured forth her greetings, news of the voyage, her joy in being home.

It would be years before Anthony could come to terms with his feelings about the mother who seemed always to abandon him, ignoring him for the cheerful, biddable Tom, clever, high-strung Henry, and the girls who trailed about after her like ducklings. At this time he felt only a stubborn rejection. But he could not help watching her, and in the long, rambling fantasies with which he beguiled his walks to and from school, there was always some bright, witty young woman as part of the action. Not a mother—never a motherly figure, but always a surprisingly independent young woman with a glint of mockery in her talk. Such women inhabited his imagination. But as for mothers—he had to invent them. He felt he had never had one himself.

Tom came home from Magdalen one day and was astonished to

find his mother and sisters and Hervieu returned. He was surprised also to see that in the short time his mother had been home the house seemed subtly changed and not so comfortless. Tom had no idea what his mother had done. Whatever it was, Harrow neighbours, who seemed to have disappeared during her absence, were dropping in, lingering for tea, eager to hear everything Mrs Trollope had to tell about her adventures in America. The Drurys were seen again. Lady Milman drove by. Her sons, Sir William and the Reverend Henry (already winning recognition as a poet and dramatist), came with their families, and the Trollopes were invited, in return, to Pinner.[2] Although the Grants were no longer next-door neighbours, as they had been at Julians Hill, they made their way to Harrow Weald even so. Laughter was heard in the dilapidated farmhouse.

There is no record of how Fanny and Thomas Anthony talked privately after their long separation. Did he berate her for the loss of the bazaar at Cincinnati? Did she, feeling unjustly accused, charge him with sending shoddy merchandise when the whole idea had been to offer elegant commodities not otherwise obtainable to the residents of Cincinnati? Whatever the accusations, explanations, and justifications were that they exchanged, they kept them between themselves. Henry had already told his father of his mother's project of a travel book about her American experiences. Fanny, always eager to put thoughts of grief or disaster behind her, surely preferred to talk about that and the possibilities of finding a publisher for the project rather than dwell at any length on the catastrophe in Cincinnati.

Thomas Anthony read through Fanny's manuscript. The lively descriptions of Cincinnati characters and customs almost carried the sound of his wife's voice—light and mocking and making the most of everything that was hypocritical or ridiculous. He nodded when he came to the descriptions of some of the eastern scenes he had visited also. She had done very well with Niagara Falls, a sight he had been almost too blind with headache to encompass. 'It is not for me to attempt a description of Niagara', she had written, 'I feel I have no power for it'. But she had gone on to tell of the 'wonder, terror and delight' that completely overwhelmed her, and then of the days she and her group had spent picking their way down slippery paths to be immersed in spray and rainbows and glory. He must also have approved her joy in the passage down the Hudson River and her pleasure in the elegant hospitality she had known in New York City.

But finally he would have to come to her summation of impressions of America, a summation based far more on the months she had spent in Cincinnati than on any of the travels afterwards.

'I suspect that what I have written will make it evident I do not like America.

'Now, as it happens that I met with individuals there whom I love and admire, far beyond the love and admiration of ordinary acquaintance; and as I declare the country to be fair to the eye, and most richly teeming with the gifts of plenty, I am led to ask myself why it is that I do not like it. I would willingly know myself.'

She tried to explain it. She was not speaking of her friends there or her friends' friends. 'The small patrician band is a race apart; they live with each other, and for each other, mix wondrously little with the high matters of state, which they seem to leave rather supinely to their tailors and tinkers, and are no more to be taken as a sample of the American people, than the head of Lord Byron as a sample of the heads of the British peerage. I speak not of these, but of the population generally, as seen in town and country, among the rich and the poor, in the slave states, and the free states. I do not like them. I do not like their principles. I do not like their manners. I do not like their opinions.'[3]

Fanny wrote that as a woman and a stranger it would be unseemly for her to say that she did not like the American Government, and so she would not say so. The Government suited the American people, and that was that. She condensed to one paragraph the settling of America by people who had banished themselves (or been banished) from the mother country, the manner in which the mother country had 'sent them gay and gallant officers to guard their frontiers', and then taxed their tea in consequence. In equally glib phrases, she took care of the Revolution, 'so they could have their own way in everything'. 'Let us make a government that shall suit us all, let it be rude, and rough, and noisy, let it not affect either dignity, glory or splendour . . . let every man have a hand in making the laws, and no man be troubled about keeping them.'

This was, perhaps, the chief burden of Fanny's complaint. It seemed to her that the doctrine of freedom for all meant that in practice the naturally orderly obeyed the laws while the disorderly flouted them at will.

There was a final irritation. 'A single word indicative of doubt, that anything, or everything, in that country is not the very best in the world, produces an effect which must be seen and felt to be understood. If the citizens of the United States were indeed the devoted patriots they call themselves, they would surely not thus encrust themselves in the hard, dry, stubborn persuasion, that they are the first and best of the human race, that nothing is to be learnt, but what they are able to teach, and nothing is worth having, which they do not possess.'[4] This arrogance of 'free-born Americans' had really offended her. And it seemed to her that their insistence on an equality of nature, a very different thing from equality of opportunity, was a pernicious doctrine. She had her own farewell to Americans:

'If refinement once creeps in among them, if they once learn to cling to the graces, the honours, the chivalry of life, then we shall say farewell to American equality, and welcome to European fellowship one of the finest countries on earth.'[5]

Thomas Anthony, a Whig and a liberal all his life, might have been excused if he had asked his wife to modify some of these statements. Presumably he did not.

Louder, more enthusiastic approval came from the Milmans. Fanny asked Henry Milman, experienced in literary matters, to read the manuscript and give her his suggestions and criticisms. As he finished each chapter, he passed it on to another member of the family. Soon one or another of the Milman clan was climbing the stairs at Harrow Weald to the little room where Fanny worked, crying, 'More book! More book!' Fanny was 'vastly delighted' by this response. It might signify nothing in the larger world, but it encouraged her to do the final polishing.

She turned to another literary friend, Mary Russell Mitford, for advice about where to submit the manuscript, and Miss Mitford suggested her own publishers, Whittaker and Treacher, and said she would write to them recommending the work to their special attention. The moment had come. Auguste Hervieu tidied up the sketches he had made to illustrate some of the more provocative passages in the manuscript: a theatre scene, a picture of some American gentlemen lounging about chewing tobacco, a backwoods scene, a sketch of a young lady at her toilette. There was nothing more to do but bundle up manuscript and drawings and dispatch the parcel to Whittaker and Treacher in London.

Fanny tried to prepare herself for rejection and even considered the sort of gainful employment she could find if she won no acceptance as a writer. She recalled that women of her age and class were sometimes hired as supervisors of tutors and courses of studies in grand private homes or small schools. Perhaps she could find such a post if the dream of writing failed. She would have to do something, since they had obviously reached another financial nadir. It seemed improbable after the years of comfort at Julians, but there were not even pillows for the beds at Harrow Weald nor beds enough for all the family. The clothing situation was equally desperate. After three years of travel, Fanny's wardrobe was almost in tatters as was the girls', and they had outgrown their clothes as well. It was clear now that Thomas Anthony's attempts at farming the land at Julians, Julians Hill, and Harrow Weald were simply driving the Trollopes further into debt.

Fanny had one comfort in this time of suspense. Her husband had found a new project to engage him, and his spirits were accordingly quieter. It hardly mattered that the project seemed grotesque to her. What Thomas Anthony had embarked upon was a comprehensive *Encyclopaedia Ecclesiastica*, to embrace the whole history of the Christian Church, its rites and ceremonies, orders, denominations, and so forth, all presented in alphabetical order. Fanny must have shuddered when he first outlined his plan to her—a scheme even more grandiose than any plan for becoming a gentleman farmer or establishing a commercial enterprise in America. But she suppressed her incredulity quickly when she realized what this new interest could mean.

'I cannot express my delight at his having found an occupation,' she wrote to Tom at Oxford. 'He really seems quite another being; —and so am I too, in consequence.'

Thomas Anthony, absorbed in research in the old books in his study, was a far easier person to live with than a tormented man roaming about spreading gloom, and pouncing on anyone not engaged in some useful task.

Small bits of encouraging news trickled in from London. An editor at Whittaker and Treacher had the inspiration of sending Mrs Trollope's manuscript to Captain Basil Hall for assessment. Fanny had devoted several appreciative pages to the captain's book about America. He read her manuscript and was delighted with it, in part because her observations tallied so frequently with his own and in part because he felt the book was written with great verve and humour. He not only sent an enthusiastic report to Whittaker and Treacher but got in touch with Fanny personally to congratulate her. As Tom recalled it, Captain Hall suggested the book's title, *Domestic Manners of the Americans*. When it was definite that Whittaker and Treacher were accepting the book for publication, Captain Hall met Fanny in London and advised her as the contract was proposed, drawn up, and signed.

The book was accepted! With such good news Fanny felt free to purchase some tea, butter, and other needed supplies for her deprived family. She ceased brooding about the possibility of looking for work as a supervisor of studies. From the moment she had started her book on America, she had thought that if she could sell it, she would try her hand at a novel. During the weeks of waiting to hear from the publishers she had already begun to concoct a plot —an English aristocrat forced by some tragic turn of circumstances to seek exile in America. Each morning now she rose early and shut herself up in the little room at the head of the stairs that the girls had begun to call The Sacred Den and worked away at the novel.

More encouraging news came from London. Henry Milman, who was up in the city, wrote to his sisters, and they hurried to Harrow Weald to report to Fanny. A copy of the manuscript had been shown to John Gibson Lockhart, Sir Walter Scott's son-in-law, but more importantly, editor of the popular Tory publication, *Quarterly Review*. Lockhart had read the book and declared it was 'the cleverest woman's book he had read in a long time.'[6] Lockhart was setting aside forty pages of his spring issue of the *Quarterly* for a laudatory review of her book along with copious excerpts from it.

Fanny began to feel nervous and edgy. She went to visit old Lady Milman at Pinner for a day or so to calm her nerves and heard further reports from Henry in London of others who had read the book before its publication and found it extremely entertaining. Fanny now feared that the book was being 'over-puffed beforehand, and that it will fall sadly flat afterwards.'[7] She clutched at Lady Milman's placid hope that she would be ready with 'something else' when the book came out, and she hurried home to spend some more time working on her novel.

Thomas Anthony had prepared a prospectus for his vast work by this time and sent it off to the eminent publisher, John Murray, famed for bringing Lord Byron's work into print. One of Murray's readers had been impressed by Mr Trollope's proposal, and Mr Trollope was summoned to London to talk over the possible publication of his encyclopaedia in a serial form.

Fanny was pleased to submerge her own anxieties in her husband's interests and drove into London with him when he went to confer with Murray. Later Thomas Anthony reported some of his conversation with Murray to her with a certain dour satisfaction.

'By the bye!' Murray had said, '*Trollope*—who the devil *is* Mrs Trollope? Her book is the cleverest thing I ever read. I have read it through. So spirited!'

Mr Trollope had replied gravely, 'The lady is my wife.'

'Why did she not bring it to me?' Murray said. 'It will sell like wildfire! She ought to have brought it to me. But I will help it all I can. You must introduce me to her.'[8]

Fanny wrote excitedly about that interchange to Tom. 'There, my son, what do you think of that? May I not say like Lord Byron, "I awoke one morning and found myself famous"?' At the same time she feared that this promise of success might be another mirage. She had been tricked by several false visions now—the American dream, the Nashoba utopia, the New Harmony school, the Cincinnati bazaar.

At about this time, Thomas Anthony became interested in resuming his legal career through an appointment to a London magistracy that had recently fallen vacant. By a freak of chance Uncle Adolphus Meetkerke, that stout old Tory, had some friendly connexions with the new Whig ministry. Now the father of a brood of children and feeling a twinge of sympathy for the lost expectations of his nephew, Uncle Adolphus had called on the new Home Secretary, Lord Melbourne, and spoken on behalf of Thomas Anthony Trollope. Lord Melbourne had been quite civil and suggested that Mr Trollope write to him applying for the magistrate's post, which Thomas Anthony promptly did. Lord Melbourne acknowledged the letter in a gracious fashion, and Thomas Anthony had believed that the post was as good as his. For several weeks he moved about Harrow Weald in what was, for him, an aura of positive good temper. The girls brightened. Henry, home from another unfruitful day of reading law in London, no longer provoked angry outbursts from his father. Fanny could not bring herself to suggest that Lord Melbourne's letter might have been merely a polite acknowledgment of her husband's application and nothing more.

Then what Fanny had feared all along came to pass. Another barrister was appointed to the vacant post. Thomas Anthony took the blow standing, as once before he had taken the blow of losing the Meetkerke inheritance. He locked his face, said nothing, and retreated to his room and his *Encyclopaedia Ecclesiastica*.

'The bubble has burst, my dearest Tom,' Fanny wrote. 'The magistracy can be dreamt of no more by any of us.'[9]

Grieving for her husband, who was soon felled by another of his headaches, Fanny refused to let any of the advance approval of her book seduce her into fantastic dreams. All she hoped for, all she wanted ,was a modest financial return on her travel book and enough recognition so that she would be able to sell the novel on which she was working for another modest sum, and then perhaps begin on another novel.

She was holding to this level of expectation when *Domestic Manners of the Americans* was published on 19th March, 1832, nine days after her fifty-second birthday. After which, confounding her doubts, she did awake one morning like Lord Byron and find herself famous.

PART THREE

Pen in Hand
1831–1836

15

Fame – Criticism – Julians Hill –
'The Refugee in America'

She sat at the long table in John Murray's red-panelled dining room, candlelight winking off the silver to make pools of rosy light in the wine glasses. On either side of her and across the table were some of the literary figures of the day—John Lockhart, editor of the *Quarterly*, and his wife; her new friend, Capt. Basil Hall and his wife; the writer, Walter Savage Landor; and, at the head of the table, John Murray himself. The group was gathered to honour her, the author of 'the book of the season'. She parried the compliments heaped upon her with a breathless good humour and incredulity.

Another evening she was at the Misses Berry's splendid home on Curzon Street. She had accepted this invitation reluctantly, for she knew the Misses Berry only by their reputation for elegant entertainment of the titled and wealthy. But here again she was the star of the evening. Writing about it to Tom, she took refuge in her old 'quizzing' style.

'The Countess of Morley told me that she was certain that if I drove through London proclaiming who I was, I should have the horse taken off and be drawn in triumph from one end of the town to the other! The Honourable Mr. Somebody declared that my thunderstorm was the finest thing in prose or verse. Lady Charlotte Lindsay *implored* me to go on writing—never was anything so delightful. Lady Louisa Stewart told me that I had quite put English out of fashion and that everyone was talking Yankee talk.'[1]

It was, of course, very pleasant suddenly to become a celebrity at the age of fifty-two. Pleasant, after the years of poverty, anxiety, and disaster, to be so showered with invitations that she drove in to London, with Cecilia to keep her company, to stay for several weeks, greeting old friends and making new ones.

Reading the reviews her book was receiving was a more mixed

experience. In the *Quarterly* she saw herself described as 'an English *lady* of sense and acuteness, who possesses very considerable powers of expression'. Her book was not only 'clever and amusing' but dealt intelligently with almost every aspect of American life. Her chapters on religion in America were especially recommended to those 'in any way distrustful of the benefits of the established church'.[2]

On the other hand, she found herself denounced in the *Edinburgh Review* for writing a 'spiteful, ill-considered and mischief making book'. That reviewer surmised that the book's hostile tone was caused by the author's disappointment in a commercial venture in the United States and further charged that she had indicted a whole nation from very limited observations. Finally, 'Returned to Harrow, her preface of March 1832 is an express advertisement against the Reform Bill. Four-and-thirty chapters of American scandal are dished up with the immediate purpose of contrasting the graceful virtue of a boroughmonger with the profligate vulgarity of a ten pound franchise'.

But there it was, really—the chief reason why the book was being 'talked of everywhere, and read by all sorts and conditions of men and women'. The timing of its appearance could not have been more fateful. The issue of the Reform Bill (which threatened the 'graceful virtues' of boroughmongers) was agitating people all over England. The working people of Bristol had rioted during the winter when it seemed the bill was doomed. During the spring of 1832 Londoners were fearing the same sort of disturbances. Tories of the middle and upper classes, who wanted no part of reform and dreaded its supporters almost equally with the current epidemic of cholera morbus, seized on Mrs Trollope's book about America as proof positive of what would happen if egalitarian principles were adopted in England. Manners would disappear. Refinement would vanish. Every oaf would set himself up as good as a lord. And they cited Mrs Trollope, chapter and verse, to prove it.

The Whigs, meanwhile, convinced that changes must be made if England was to survive in the new industrial age, were bound to find the book prejudiced and reactionary, if not downright false, in its portrayal of a democratic society.

Fanny was distressed by charges of exaggeration and invention in the Whig reviews. Over and over, she insisted to friends and acquaintances that she had not described any scenes or behaviour that she had not personally witnessed. And this was true enough. But it was also true that in her book she had spent few words describing those individuals in the New World whom she had grown to love and admire, 'that small patrician band' that was 'a race apart'. Instead she had focused her attention on those elements of a new society that were bizarre, aspects that were easy targets for her mocking style. Indeed, in the shock of her immersion into an alien society, she did see some American traits and tendencies very clearly. A decade later, Charles Dickens would visit the United States and react almost identically in his *American Notes*. Later his novel *Martin Chuzzlewit* would further amplify the same observations into a wildly comic chronicle of American arrogance and 'cuteness'.[3] A hundred and forty years later it is still possible to see various American obsessions neatly pinned down by Frances Trollope in the pages of *Domestic Manners*.

Though she was troubled by the criticism her book was receiving in England, Fanny was not bothered at all by the American response. After her flat admission that she did not like Americans she could hardly have expected a favourable verdict when a pirated edition was published in the United States. Unfortunately, she gained nothing from the sales that outrage against her book had encouraged. She might well have been amused if she had read the foreword to one American edition, written by James Kirke Paulding. Paulding had been a youthful friend of Washington Irving, and both of them, in their early days, had been eager to mock the pretensions of their countrymen. The two of them, along with a few friends, had enjoyed themselves some twenty-five years earlier by publishing a magazine called *Salmagundi*, in which they laughed immoderately at the boasting of the young American republic. Paulding's preface to the American edition of *Domestic Manners* was another elaborate exercise in mockery. He affected at first to be astonished at such a moderate and good-humoured report on the country. So many American foibles had been overlooked or ignored, such as the fact that in the United States it was the universal practice for 'gentlemen, as soon as they have finished their dinner, to call for a pitchfork or a chestnut-rail, wherewith to pick their teeth. Some prefer one, some the other; but on the whole the pitchfork is the favourite. . . .' But soon Paulding was launched on his main theme, his suspicion 'that the author is not what she pretends to be, an English lady.'[4] Many clues had led him to this surmise: the unlikelihood of such a woman writing so fully about bugs and spitting or repaying American hospitality with unfriendly reports on domestic matters. After a good deal of mock-solemn evaluation of such evidence, he proposed that the book had actually been written by Captain Basil Hall (or All, as Paulding believed the English pronounced his name), masquerading under the curious name of Trollope.[5]

Back at Harrow Weald after the London interlude, waiting for the first financial returns on *Domestic Manners*, Fanny worked feverishly on her novel, *The Refugee in America*. Now was the time to have it published, while her name was fresh and controversial in the public mind. If the book came out soon, she might realize a really helpful sum to augment the money she was now expecting from *Domestic Manners*. She had dreamed up a melodramatic plot: a young English lord, provoked into a scuffle with an unsavoury character, whom he presumably kills, the young lord's escape under the aegis of a well-to-do friend of his family and his subsequent journey to America with the friend and the friend's beautiful daughter. Once Fanny had her characters in the United States, she had plenty of backgrounds for her story, plenty of curious characters to give local colour, not to mention an assortment of villains from England on the trail of her hero to give the plot endless twists and turns.

And then another shower of invitations that she could not resist drew her to London again. 'I hope the whirl of engagements in which I live will be of advantage to me—to us, rather,' she wrote to Tom. 'But I almost doubt if I shall not lose more than I can ever gain. It is true that everybody ʾlls me they are longing for the novel, but the novel has yet half a volume to be finished, and I can scarcely find an hour in each day to give to it.'

She was enjoying herself all the same. At last she had some money in hand from the sales of *Domestic Manners*, which was going into a second edition. She could buy new clothes for Cecilia, Emily, and herself, and a few comforts for Harrow Weald. She went with Cecilia and Henry to the theatre. She saw to it that Henry, through the courtesy of Captain Basil Hall, was introduced into the London Geological Society, an organization that interested Henry far more than law books. And the 'evenings' and 'mornings' were 'incessant'. 'God bless you', she concluded a letter to Tom, 'and preserve the brain of your venerable mother through this whirl'.[6]

By the end of the summer she had received one thousand pounds in royalties for *Domestic Manners* and felt rich enough for almost anything. Certainly rich enough to move her family from the dim discomfort of Harrow Weald back to the sunshiny space of Julians Hill. Fortunately, that pleasant residence was available, so Fanny quickly paid half a year's rent and taxes and arranged for some new fixtures, a new bed, sofa, pillows, and other such items. The Milmans and the Grants cautioned her to be prudent. She must not expect her book to continue earning such large sums, and she had no guarantee at all as to what her novel might bring. But the moment was what counted with Fanny. She wanted her family out of the melancholy Harrow Weald, and at the moment she had funds to arrange it, and no cautionary words could stop her. With relief and triumph she saw her family resettled in the comfortable quarters Thomas Anthony had abandoned two years before.

Somehow, in spite of the turmoil of moving, she managed to finish her novel, *The Refugee in America*, deliver it to Whittaker and Treacher and receive an advance of four hundred pounds. After which, she began at once on a new novel.

At fifty-two she had become more than a celebrity, she had become a professional. On some basic level she had recognized that her husband's dreams—of farming, of business in America, of the law—were all bubbles due to burst. If the family was to have any sort of income, she was the one who could and therefore must provide it.

Accordingly, she continued in the pattern she had begun in Cincinnati, rising at four or five o'clock in the morning, before the rest of the family was awake, writing for three or four hours until the household began to stir, then joining her husband and children for breakfast and making plans for the day.

For Fanny, it was almost reward enough that life at Julians Hill now followed a gracious and civilized course. Visitors were welcomed at luncheon, tea, or dinner, and visits were made in return, to the Grants, the Milmans, the Drurys, to brother Henry at Fulham, and to others even further afield. Picnics; walks; excursions; evening entertainments; musicales; card parties; theatricals; charades; visits to art galleries, to the theatre, to concerts; easy discussion of books, poetry, music, scenic beauties—all these made up the good life to Frances Trollope. They made up the 'refinement' she had missed in America, where so few clung to 'the graces, the honours, the chivalry of life'. If she had to work very hard to achieve those graces for her family, she hid every sign of her effort. Her children should have grace with seeming ease.

She was amused when Cecilia, Emily, Henry and Hervieu, with some sporadic help from Anthony, began a family newspaper in the autumn of 1832. They called their production *The Magpie*, pasted the contributions in a scrapbook, and had a very select group gather once a week to hear the offerings read aloud. Sometimes Fanny favoured them with a small item, which she signed 'Grub Street'. The whole enterprise was just the sort of cheerful family activity that Fanny liked to see her brood enjoying.

The Refugee in America was published in January 1833, and Fanny was shocked when the *Quarterly Review*, which had been so generous in praise of *Domestic Manners*, criticized it harshly. The hurt was even greater when she heard a rumour that Captain Hall had written the review. Forthright as always, she wrote to ask him if this were so. Captain Hall replied at once, denying the charge but also warning her against being too wounded by hostile notices. 'You must be aware that, having written such a book as your travels, you necessarily raised an immense host of vindictive vulgar active enemies. . . . You have had the boldness to publish your opinions on America and having thereby incurred the risk of censure and ridicule you must not shrink from the endurance.'

Relieved that her friend had not written the unkind review, Fanny hardly needed his good advice. If she was going to write for a living, she knew she must ignore criticism. Sales were what counted. With *The Refugee* selling respectably, she pushed thoughts of it aside to concentrate on her new novel. This was a tale wholly removed from her American experiences, a pure flight of fancy about intrigue in an Italian cloister in the sixteenth century that she was calling *The Abbess*.

From time to time when her inspiration or imagination flagged, she amused herself by concocting a humorous narrative verse about a mother's problems in seeing to it that her daughters were suitably married. Such problems were still academic to Fanny. Cecilia was only seventeen and Emily fifteen, but the subject of marrying off daughters was a staple of the current fiction.

Fanny made a farce of it in romping rhymes that had no pretence to poetry.

> Few have yet learned how far, by care and skill,
> A well-taught girl may marry whom she will.
> The Mother's Manual, it is hoped, will prove,
> A useful treatise in the school of love.[7]

The heroine of Fanny's comic verse was Lady Hook, 'a widow, the wisest and best/That ever six fatherless daughters caressed'. And 'In less than six years from her husband's demise/She had married six girls and each match was a prize'. Her sister, a Mrs Philtre, had also been bereft and left with three young daughters, but fortunately she had her sister to give her lessons:

> Let your girls learn Italian—I have known it lend grace
> More than once, to a very indifferent face.

The clever mother also advised her sister to teach the girls to waltz, and

> There's another thing still, which I've known to succeed,
> And produce great effect with most wonderful speed. . . .
> This is rhyming offhand. It seems always so clever.

Certainly Fanny had the knack of rhyming offhand with wonderful speed, and there was still another personal note in her final advice:

> Let all expenditure that meets the eye
> Be pushed to what your utmost means supply;
> And what is wanted to augment the sum,
> Be scraped in quiet privacy at home.

Her own family was sent into gales of laughter as she read the verses aloud around the tea table. Auguste Hervieu, artist-in-residence, hurried to make a series of sketches to illustrate this 'essay in verse'. For Fanny it was a pleasant change from working on *The Abbess* to take the completed package in to London and sell it to a new publisher, Treuttel and Wurtz and Richter, who thought it would do well as a gift book.

Once again she was widely entertained, for she was still a celebrity. A portrait of her that Hervieu had painted hung in Somerset House, a public building of some renown near Piccadilly, which frequently featured pictures of notables. Cecilia went to look at it but was chiefly caught by a critic's comment: 'The painter has not flattered her good looks. He has had vinegar in his brush too'. Cecilia wrote Tom, 'Mama now goes by the name, at home, of Old Madame Vinegar'. Actually, it was rather a charming picture, showing a small piquant face (under a lacy cap, in the fashion of the day), with wide-set eyes and wide cheekbones. The eyes held a look of sadness, oddly at variance with the smile that seemed to lurk at the corners of her generous mouth.

A plan for still another writing project came to her that winter of 1833. She recalled that John Murray had regretted not publishing her American travel book, and she now asked him if he would be interested in a travel book about some other locale, Belgium, for instance and western Germany (she had been cherishing a desire to visit her friend Julia Garnett Pertz, now living in Hanover, for some time). Murray was agreeable to the idea, so she returned to Julians Hill in good spirits. She thought she would take Henry with her. He was getting nowhere with his law studies. Maybe on a holiday with him she could get some clue to a more profitable direction for him. And of course Hervieu would go with her to do the illustrations.

Somehow she never thought of taking Anthony. He was still attending Harrow-on-the-Hill, two miles closer now that the family had moved from Harrow Weald to Julians Hill, but Anthony found the journey between home and school miserable all the same.

He studied for and took the examination for a scholarship to Trinity and, not very surprisingly, failed it. No one seemed unduly disturbed, although it signalled the end of Thomas Anthony's hopes that all his sons would follow in his footsteps from Winchester to Oxford. How was it possible that Fanny, who found her greatest enjoyment in the happiness of others, could have been so unaware of Anthony's needs? The mystery of young Anthony's unhappiness and his sense of exclusion runs like a dark thread through the years of his mother's American adventure, the family's misfortunes, and his mother's triumphant rescue of them all.

16

Travels in Belgium – 'The Mother's Manual' – 'The Abbess' – Eviction

In the spring of 1833 almost everyone at Julians Hill was laid low by influenza. The local doctor and apothecary was summoned, but his treatment seemed almost worse than the illness. He applied leeches to them all, with the result that Cecilia had hysterics, sturdy young Anthony fainted, and Henry, already anaemic after his bouts of malaria in America, was nearly drained of blood. Hervieu resisted the leeches, treated himself with various drugs and became delirious, staggering forth from the house to wander in the fields till he was discovered and brought back to his bed.

Everyone recovered in due time except Henry, who continued to show a hectic flush, and Emily, who had always been frail and who continued languid. Their mother, who had missed a few mornings at her writing desk but was never so ill as she had been in Cincinnati, worried about those two.

But now it was time to make arrangements for the Belgian tour. Anthony was going to stay with his father at Julians Hill, but Cecilia's and Emily's time was parcelled out in visits to relatives and friends—Cousin Fanny Bent in Exeter, brother Henry at Fulham, the Milmans at nearby Pinner.

Finally everyone was packed up and on their way. Fanny, Henry, and Hervieu drove to London to board the boat for the Channel crossing at the foot of the Tower Stairs.

The tour Fanny had mapped out led them from Bruges to Ghent, Antwerp and thence to the battlefield of Waterloo. There Fanny walked about the plains until nightfall, enjoying the atmosphere, which was heightened by an impending thunderstorm. They travelled on to Aachen, where Fanny was awed by Charlemagne's great cathedral and by sitting in the chair where so many emperors had been crowned.

Every day she made copious notes, Auguste Hervieu sketched picturesque scenes, and Henry looked for rock formations and out-croppings at which he chipped for samples for his collection. The tour then took them to the Rhine country, to Baden-Baden and its gaming tables, to the Harz Mountains and the Brocken. Indefatigable, Fanny mounted a mule to ascend the Brocken along with Henry and Hervieu.

They arrived at the guesthouse at the summit just as a storm broke over the mountain. The howling of the wind was terrifying. All night long shutters and doors banged about so that no one slept. Fanny found it all rather exciting, although she did write:

'Full of interest and enjoyment as this expedition proved to us, I doubt whether I can fairly recommend the ascent of the Brocken to the generality of female travellers.'[1]

All in all, the tour provided enough wonderful scenery, varied sites of historical importance, and small adventures for Fanny to work up a respectable travel book when she returned to England. It was readable, as was everything she wrote, but in Belgium and Germany she was travelling through territory the history of which was familiar to all cultured English people. It had nothing like the electricity of her book on America.

That country, so raw and new, had provoked her to a response that went far beyond the genteel reporting of sightseeing. America, by its very differences from what she had always known, had launched her as a writer in a way that her bland report on Belgium and Germany could never have done. Now, because her name was on a book, people were ready to read whatever she had to write about anywhere at all, even though the new writing lacked the spice of malice and disapproval that had made the first book so entertaining.

It was just as well that she had the notes for the book on Belgium and western Germany well in hand when she returned to Julians Hill, for she came back to impending disaster.

Thomas Anthony had suffered an apoplectic seizure during her absence. Cecilia had written to her about it, but the letter had never arrived, so Fanny had known no reason to cut short her visit with Julia Garnett Pertz in Hanover. By the time she, Henry, and Hervieu arrived in Hamburg on their way home, Thomas Anthony had recovered enough to travel there to greet them and accompany them the rest of the way.

Once again, they were in financial difficulties. Fanny was puzzled, for she had assumed that the success of *Domestic Manners* had rescued them from their straits. But she had spent the income from that book freely, and the novel that followed had not earned anything near the same amount.

Now Thomas Anthony had exhausted his resources. Lord Northwick, their landlord, had grown weary of not receiving the rent for the Julians property, contracted for so long ago. He was sending threatening letters that frightened Thomas Anthony into ever more severe headaches. The Trollope young people called him the Monster of Harrow, and though Fanny laughed, she realized the man was not unjustified in demanding the rent for his Harrow properties.

Unable to get any clear view of their situation from Thomas Anthony, she consulted her brother, Henry Milton, and he went to his solicitor for advice. It was all very muddling considering that Thomas Anthony Trollope was himself a barrister of much learning. The solicitor consulted by Henry Milton discovered that Mr Trollope had given up deeds to various pieces of property as collateral on loans without securing receipts. He had also made use of much of Fanny's marriage settlements without any proper registration of those transactions. (Loans in those days seem to have been transacted in an offhand way by signature to notes that were then transferred from hand to hand in a fashion baffling to later generations. Young Anthony, only half-listening to the family agitation, would make great use later of such lightly undertaken obligations in plotting his novels.)

To Fanny, correcting proofs of *The Abbess* and turning her notes on Belgium and western Germany into a travel book, a chief concern was that whatever was left of her dowry and her inheritance after her father's death be converted into an annuity in her name and her daughters' so that Lord Northwick could not seize them in payment of his claims. This was accomplished, with her brother's assistance, and after that she tried to think calmly of what they *could* do if Lord Northwick made good on his threats.

In the autumn of 1833 *The Abbess* and *The Mother's Manual* were published, and Fanny hoped for some royalties from them. She had an advance from John Murray on her travel book, and as she wrote the last chapters about Belgium, she was already thinking of another novel.

Through the winter of 1834 she contrived visits and other occupations for Cecilia and Emily and began the novel that she was calling *Tremordyn Cliff*. And then, late in March, she had a warning that Lord Northwick's patience had expired. He was about to institute eviction proceedings against the Trollopes at Julians Hill.

17

Exile – Illness – Henry's Death

For once Anthony was the one Fanny summoned. 'Dear Tony', she said, 'I need you to drive your father in to London this morning. Will you bring the gig and horse around at once?'

Thomas Anthony had been ill. He looked drawn and yellow as he came slowly out of the front door to climb into the gig beside Anthony. Anthony knew it was only because his father was sick that he was allowing anyone to drive him. And only after they had travelled a mile or two through the chill early morning did Mr Trollope tell his son why he was going to London. Anthony was to see him aboard the Ostend boat at the Tower Stairs. But that was all he said. Anthony had heard some talk about a possible move abroad, but he had no idea that his father was going first, and so abruptly, in order to avoid possible arrest for debt.

He saw his father aboard the boat and headed for home. Shortly before he arrived at Julians Hill, a man who had worked for the Trollopes as a gardener in their more prosperous days stepped out from a lane and flagged him to a stop. In urgent whispers he told Anthony that the sheriff's men had already arrived at Julians Hill to seize all the Trollopes' possessions. If Anthony continued on his way, they would surely take possession of the horse, gig, and harness as well.

For years Anthony had filled his lonely hours with secret dreams of heroics. Now he had an opportunity to act. Flicking the reins on the horse's back, he started up, turned down the next lane, and drove to the village, where he offered to sell the entire equipage to the local ironmonger. After some bargaining, Anthony settled on seventeen pounds. And then the ironmonger informed him that seventeen pounds was, as it happened, the exact sum due to him by the Trollope family.

Anthony returned on foot to Julians Hill, where the sheriff's men had indeed taken over. They seemed to be everywhere, itemizing possessions, pushing furniture here and there, and consulting each other about the exact nomenclature of various articles.

His mother should have been a figure of stoic sorrow, standing by as her home was dismantled in shame and disgrace before her eyes. And Frances Trollope was very quiet, nodding soberly as the sheriff's men apologized from time to time for the inconvenience they were causing her. However, a strange undercurrent of merriment seemed to hum under the proceedings. Anthony saw his sisters and the two Grant girls appear surreptitiously from time to time and then, giggling softly, disappear again. Soon he discovered what they were up to. Piece by piece, they were picking up various bits of bric-à-brac, hiding them in their arms or aprons, and then hurrying them across to the Grant property. The sheriff's men, not unaware of what was going on, frowned appropriately from time to time and then disregarded the whole charade.[1]

Fanny had already made an appointment with Lord Northwick to arrange for buying back some of her more cherished items of furniture. After the family had spent the night with the hospitable Grants next door, she met with his lordship and completed those arrangements. Trunks packed with clothes, books, papers, and other necessities were sent on their way to London and the Ostend boat, and Fanny and the family were getting ready to follow when the local doctor arrived and asked to speak to Fanny alone. Like everyone else in Harrow he knew of the dispossession and Mrs Trollope's plan to settle the family in Belgium. The doctor thought it his duty to warn her that young Henry's lungs were badly affected and that the low Belgian coast was likely to aggravate his condition.

Fanny had held herself steady through the turmoil so far, quietly seeing her husband off, quietly watching the disintegration of her home. Now she anxiously made distracted, spur-of-the-moment decisions. She sent Anthony and Hervieu to London to get the trunks and other luggage off the Ostend boat. She asked Mrs Grant to be kind enough to let Anthony, Hervieu, and the two girls stay on for a while with her family. Then she set off with Henry to board the coach for Exeter and Cousin Fanny Bent, the unfailing family backstop in case of need. She had no clear notion just how Exeter and Cousin Fanny might be helpful to Henry. She simply had to settle him somewhere.

She stayed with Cousin Fanny for several days, discussing Henry's health with her privately, urging her to make sure he ate nourishing meals and got a great deal of rest. Then she returned to Harrow and sent Cecilia and Anthony on to Ostend to join their father. The manuscript for *Belgium and West Germany* had been completed and sent to Murray, but she wanted to commission her brother, Henry, to take charge of the proof sheets and correct them when they were ready. By now it was also absolutely necessary to borrow some money from him and from her old friend Lady Dyer as well. These depressing duties completed, she gathered up her bags, boxes, and papers, and with Emily in tow, herself left England for Belgium.

The British consul and his wife, Mr and Mrs Fanche, were long-time friends. They had a large house in Ostend and were happy to have the Trollopes stay with them as long as they wished, but Fanny could not rest until she had her family under her own roof. She finally found a house she thought would do, just outside the city walls of nearby Bruges, a big, roomy place known as the Château d'Hondt. She leased it and somehow, during the next weeks, managed to furnish it with borrowed items, used furniture bought cheaply and, after a while, the pieces from Julians Hill that she had arranged to buy back from Lord Northwick.

By the end of May, Tom, graduated at last from Magdalen Hall, arrived in Bruges to find his family established in the Château d'Hondt. To Tom it seemed that his mother had worked her usual magic, once again creating a home that was pleasant and comfortable and a magnet both to friends who lived in Belgium and to those who were visiting from England. His father was once again ensconced in a study, surrounded by his books, papers, and endless notes. His mother had fitted up another Sacred Den for herself, where she wrote away on *Tremordyn Cliff* each morning before the rest of the family was awake. Even Anthony appeared less sullen here in Bruges, free at last of the misery he had known at all his schools. But soon Tom was on his way again to London where he hoped to earn his living as a tutor in the classics while he looked for a post as master at some school.

In July, Henry wrote to his mother from Exeter that he was much better and was eager to join his family. Fanny wrote to him to come and also sent a note to Tom asking him to accompany Henry across the Channel.

Tom had acquired some pupils to tutor by this time and did not think he should leave them quite so soon. However, he met Henry when he arrived in London from Exeter to see him to the Ostend boat. Tom's first sight of Henry shocked him. Henry was not better; he was very ill, and their mother was deluding herself if she thought otherwise.

Fanny was determined to believe her son's health was improved. Meeting Henry when he arrived in Bruges, she smiled in relief, telling herself he did look better. Besides, he was so lively, bubbling with plans. Henry told her it had occurred to him that he could be completely cured if he could just take a sea voyage to somewhere warm and sunny, like the West Indies. Fanny wondered a little at this dream. Surely Henry knew how little money they had, that she already owed money, and that their daily maintenance depended on her finishing the current novel. Still she smiled at him, patted his hand, and said she would see what could be arranged.

She settled him in one of the sunnier upstairs rooms of the Château d'Hondt, tried to tell herself that all would be well, and set herself the task of finding some occupation for Anthony. Someone suggested he might obtain a commission in an Austrian cavalry regiment, but he would need a knowledge of German and French. The idea of her youngest becoming a cavalryman may have seemed a little preposterous to Fanny, but she thought it would not hurt for him to study the languages. Remembering that one of the Drury clan of Harrow had established a school in Brussels, she arranged with this old acquaintance, William Drury, that nineteen-year-old Anthony should be engaged at his school as a 'classical usher', in return for some tutoring in French and German and his room and board.

Once again Anthony was packed up and sent off and, to his way of thinking, simply got out of the way. To a degree he was right. His mother had all she could handle with his ailing father; with Henry, now consumed with a sort of feverish activity; and with new fears she was beginning to feel for Emily, who was increasingly frail. In his self-absorption Anthony ignored all this, felt sorry for himself in Brussels, and was totally abstracted as he took the Drury students on walks after their lessons.

At the Château d'Hondt Fanny roused herself at dawn with cup after cup of green tea so as to write the necessary pages of *Tremordyn Cliff*. Her writing stint completed, the real burden of her day began —arranging occupation and amusement for Cecilia and Emily, soothing and humouring Henry, attending to Thomas Anthony's complaints. Exhausted by bedtime, she could not sleep, and dosed herself with laudanum. Small wonder if her novel became more and more Gothic, spiked with unlikely encounters, tragic deaths, and some passages written in a poetic cadence that made no sense at all.

By September she knew she needed medical advice about Henry, and she wanted Emily examined also. Telling the young people only that she wanted to see her publishers in London, she said she would take Henry and Emily with her to visit Tom and otherwise enjoy themselves.

Tom had found some dreary lodgings for himself in Marlborough Street. After hearing from his mother, he arranged for some rooms for her and his brother and sister in Northumberland Street. The little group arrived. Fanny visited her publishers, eager to find out if any money was owing to her. *Belgium and West Germany* had been published and received some good reviews. Fanny had even heard that King Leopold of Belgium had enjoyed the book. Perhaps such approval might help sales?

But medical opinion was urgent. One of her friends arranged for a well-known specialist to visit the Trollopes at their lodgings and examine Henry and Emily.

The specialist came and made his examinations. Fanny went with him to the door and heard his diagnosis of both young people. A little while later she came back up the stairs and said cheerfully that she wanted to take a walk in the park with Tom. Henry and Emily must amuse themselves for a bit.

Fanny and her son walked in the thin September sunlight, and Fanny told Tom what the doctor had said. Henry had tuberculosis and was going to die. There was no way to save him. Emily also had the disease, but it was possible that she might live. Fanny held herself very straight and looked directly ahead, determined that no passerby should see an old woman crying.

The next day she shared her awful knowledge with her brother, Henry Milton. Helpless with sympathy, Henry did have one useful suggestion. Cecilia should be sent to England to stay with him and his family in Fulham for a few months. This would provide her with a healthier background and also relieve Fanny of worry about her. Fanny accepted the invitation gratefully.

Sometime during this short stay in London Fanny also saw an old friend, a Mrs Freeling, whose father-in-law, Sir Francis Freeling, was in charge of the Post Office. She spoke to this friend not only of her anguish about Henry and Emily but of her concern about Anthony's future. Hesitatingly, she wondered if there might be some position in the Post Office that Anthony would be qualified to fill. It was only a random shot, but despite Anthony's conviction to the contrary, his mother did think about him now and then, and worry about his future.

Then she took her two sick children back across the Channel to the fog and damp of the Château d'Hondt. Henry was now talking excitedly of a voyage to the Mediterranean. A family friend had actually offered to arrange passage, and Fanny soothed him and made half promises. When she finally received some decent royalites on the Belgian travel book, her first thought was to repay her loan from Lady Dyer. Lady Dyer, aware of Fanny's situation, refused repayment, and learning of this, Henry begged that the money be used for the Mediterranean junket. Again, Fanny had to try to distract him.

A ray of cheer lightened the gloom when Fanny heard from her friend, Mrs Freeling, that Sir Francis had been approached and a Post Office position might be available for Anthony. Summoned back from Brussels, Anthony seemed to waken at last to the desperate situation in the Château d'Hondt. He also felt the best thing he could do for his family now was to go to London and make sure of the Post Office berth.

By mid-November Fanny heard that Anthony had been duly appointed as a clerk at a salary of ninety pounds a year. This seemed like riches to a young man who had never had any spending money, and it did not occur to either his mother or father to give him any advice about budgeting the sum. Neither of them was very expert in that matter anyway. At least it was the start of a new life for Anthony Trollope—a rather grim, lonely, unrewarding life for quite a while, until Anthony himself turned it into something else.[2]

At the Château d'Hondt, Fanny spent most of her days in Henry's room, reading to him, talking to him, soothing him however she could, interrupted now and then by calls from her husband, who also wanted attention.

The days crept on, shorter, darker, damper, and with each day Henry grew weaker. He usually woke each morning about nine, and Fanny tried to leave her writing table to be in his room then. On 23rd December 1834, she went to his room as usual, but this morning he failed to wake.

She stood a moment, realizing the fact. Then she locked the door and sat down by the bed where her son lay dead.

Later, Thomas Anthony came knocking at the door and calling to her. She answered him dully, not sure of what she said. In the late afternoon she finally opened the door and came out, told her husband that Henry was dead, and then went about doing what had to be done.

18

Paris – Madame Récamier – Chateaubriand – Thomas Anthony's Death

Rococo was the word of scorn, the adjective with which the boisterous young writers of France were dismissing everything they considered mannered, old-fashioned, and over-ornamented. Fanny heard it again and again in Paris. Among those who rejected the 'rococo' was an aspiring young novelist, Honoré de Balzac. Another who used it was a precocious poet, dramatist, and novelist, Victor Hugo. Fanny was not impressed by their efforts. She was sure that Balzac would soon be forgotten and that Hugo's dramas would never 'heave the ground beneath the feet of Racine and Corneille'.[1] Sir Walter Scott was her ideal as a novelist, and she saw no connexion between his romanticism and theirs, but if they were scoffing at Scott as rococo, and if Mozart as a composer was also old-fashioned and rococo, then she was too.

'I am, I am rococo!'[2] she wrote defiantly. And it was not all bad to be rococo in Paris in the spring of 1835. A new generation might be clamouring for public attention, but some older stars still shone brightly. Madame Récamier, for instance, was no longer young (older, in fact, than Fanny, who was fifty-five that year), but she presided over a salon noted for the grace and brilliance of its guests. Fanny had been welcomed to that salon soon after her arrival in Paris in April. Her books might not earn her quite enough for her family's needs, but they had brought her a reputation. She was that English writer with a gift for wit and satire, beloved of the Tories, disliked by the Whigs, who could be relied on to have some amusing new work published every year or oftener. So it was not surprising that along with meeting old friends like the Garnetts, Fanny was soon being introduced to such celebrated residents of the city as the Princess Belgiojoso, the Duchesse de La Rochefoucauld, and Madame Récamier.[3]

She had not come to Paris in search of such acquaintances. After Henry's death and his burial in the Protestant section of Bruges cemetery, she had little interest in social activity. Tom had come to Bruges from England with Cecilia, Cousin Fanny Bent had made the Channel crossing to offer what comfort she could. Then Tom, the indefatigable walker, had taken Cousin Fanny on a sightseeing tour while Fanny finished her novel, *Tremordyn Cliff*. Fanny was happy to have Cecilia with her again, glad to see Emily cheered by her sister's presence, but secretly fearful for the two girls to be too much together lest Cecilia be infected by the disease that had killed Henry and that was keeping Emily so frail.

Her novel was finished by February 1835, and she decided to take it to London herself and find a publisher for it. She hoped to do better with someone other than John Murray or Whittaker and Treacher, and she also wanted to make arrangements for another travel book. Paris was her desired destination because she wanted to have Thomas Anthony and Emily treated by a physician there who had been recommended to her.

The business aspects of her London trip went smoothly. A meeting with the publisher Richard Bentley had been very satisfying. He was happy to accept *Tremordyn Cliff* and also to commission a travel book on Paris for which he would advance a sum sufficient to allow her to take her husband and daughter with her.

She had hoped to be reassured in London about Anthony's progress since he was now working at the Post Office, but in this she was disappointed. She found him alone in the rooms in Marlborough Street that he generally shared with Tom, who was still in Bruges. It was distressing to discover that Tony had begun to smoke cigars and disappointing to realize that he was not making any productive use of his free time. He was neither improving himself by reading nor enjoying himself in cultivated and intelligent company.

Later, Anthony wrote of those early years at the Post Office that 'there was no house in which I could habitually see a lady's face and hear a lady's voice. No allurement to decent respectability came my way.'⁴ Anthony seemed determined to follow his own, lonely road. His mother had dozens of friends in London and its environs at whose homes Anthony might have been welcome. Anthony ignored such opportunities, preferring to spend his free time with a few co-workers from the Post Office drinking beer in pubs, roistering a little along the streets in the more sordid areas of the city, perhaps now and then becoming involved with a prostitute.

Anthony kept most of such activity secret from his mother, but she knew that all was not well. Kissing him good-bye before she returned to Belgium, she begged him to spend more time reading, studying French or Italian, or visiting family friends.

Soon after Fanny's return to Château d'Hondt Tom received a letter from a former schoolfellow offering him the possibility of a post as master at King Edward's Grammar School in Birmingham. The prospect of a real position at last sent Tom on his way to England within a day. Not long after that, Fanny was supervising the packing for herself, Thomas Anthony, Cecilia, and Emily in preparation for their visit to Paris. A tiring job at best, the packing was complicated by the great number of books and piles of notes, which Thomas Anthony needed to take with him to continue his work on the *Encyclopaedia Ecclesiastica*. But finally the four of them: Fanny, her husband, Cecilia, and Emily, were on their way.

Their apartment in Paris was in rue de Provence, not far from the newly refurbished Madeleine. Sometimes in the morning when her writing chore was finished and the rest of the family was still asleep, Fanny would walk to the cathedral, slip inside, and sit awhile in the cool dimness. She never paraded her grief for Henry, and Roman Catholicism was strange to her, but she found a certain comfort in the great dark church.

Later in the day the sightseeing and social activities would begin. In Paris the ladies who presided over salons tended to specialize, one offering musical evenings, another gathering artists around her, and still another focusing on literary people. There was even one hostess who prided herself on *salons antithétiques*, to which she invited people known to be hostile to each other. Fanny had just one criticism of all these evenings. French hostesses offered very meagre collations. Imagining herself presiding over an elegant salon, Fanny knew she would crown the evening with a hearty English supper.

Madame Récamier's interests were both literary and political. Of course, since the deposition of Charles X in 1830 and the crowning of the 'Citizen King', Louis Philippe, politics saturated Parisian life. The very dress of men on the street reflected their political allegiance. Walking out for an errand, one could recognize a Republican by his slouch hat and coat with exaggerated lapels, and Monarchist that Fanny had become, she felt a small thrill of distrust when she passed such an affirmed revolutionary. Monarchists were also divided. There were the *parceque* Bourbons (the Royalists who would support any king of the Bourbon line, which Louis Philippe was, though not in direct succession) and the *quoique* Bourbons (who were ready to support a king even if he was a Bourbon, because any monarch seemed preferable than a return to the violence of Republican rule). Many *quoique* Bourbons were members of the National Guard, and they either wore distinctive clothing or showed their quasi-official standing by carrying swords in their belts.

Madame Récamier, who had been exiled by Napoleon and who was only able to return to Paris with the Bourbon restoration, was obviously a *parceque* Monarchist. But Fanny was more interested in her literary friends. One evening, visiting Madame Récamier in her apartments at the Abbaye-aux-Bois, Fanny voiced her regret that she had not met Chateaubriand, whose book, *The Genius of Christianity*, had exerted such a profound effect on religious and philosophical thought in Europe. Chateaubriand was working on an autobiography, not to be published until after his death, but he had often given readings from the unfinished work, *Mémoires d'Outre-tombe*, before he found them too tiring and discontinued them. Fanny was disappointed to have missed the experience of hearing this famous man.

Then, one day in May, Fanny received a note from Madame Récamier. M. de Chateaubriand had been persuaded to give one more reading. A few other guests had been invited, but the occasion was especially for the benefit of Mrs Trollope and her daughters.

Tom, who had obtained his post in Birmingham but was not to commence his duties for some months, joined his family in Paris and heard a good deal about the salon from his mother. A M. Ampère had done the actual reading, but M. de Chateaubriand had been present, and Fanny had been charmed by his grace, wit, and manners. As for the passages from the *Mémoires* that had been read, Fanny had found them so affecting that she was weeping one moment and smiling through her tears the next.

Later Tom met Chateaubriand and was not so impressed as his mother. Still, he granted that 'his every word and movement were characterized by the exquisite courtesy which was the inalienable, and it would seem incommunicable, specialty of the *seigneurs* of the ancien régime'.[5] Tom surmised that this courtesy had much to do with his mother's uncritical approval.

She was also intrigued by the brilliant, restless young woman, Mme Aurore Dudevant, better known by her literary pseudonym, George Sand. Oddly enough, conservative Fanny was impressed by this bohemian who wore men's clothing and flaunted her sexual freedom. Only recently returned to Paris after a tempestuous interlude in Italy with the poet Alfred de Musset, George Sand amused herself by writing teasing words designed to offend Louis Philippe and his government. Somehow Fanny accepted all this. She proclaimed that George Sand's was 'one female pen' the productions of which 'appeared likely to survive its author'.[6]

The young musical genius Franz Liszt was also in Paris that spring of 1835, and on one memorable evening Fanny, Tom, and the girls were invited to the Princess Belgiojoso's salon to hear the Princess and Liszt perform the whole score of Mozart's *Don Giovanni* on two pianos. The Princess managed to hold her own through this demanding performance. After the last notes were struck and while their tones were still echoing through the drawing room, Liszt slid from the seat at his piano in a faint. The audience rushed to his side to lift his head, call for restoratives, and otherwise contribute to the confusion. Joining them, the Princess was as fresh as ever, seemingly unaffected by the strain of the performance.

Fanny contributed to social life that spring with a picnic for a varied group of young people in the woods of Montmorency. After the feast of chicken, ham, cheese, and other outdoor fare on the grass under the trees, most of the group wandered over to mount the donkeys that were kept for hire to explore the wood. Fanny got up on one of the small creatures and ambled about slowly, but several of the young men, Tom and Hervieu included, began to urge their mounts to impossible equestrian feats, prodding them into gallops and leaps over fences. Fanny heard their shouting and laughing at a distance. Suddenly, a white-faced young man rode up to her, and she realized that the laughter had stopped. The youth stammered out the tidings. One of the young men of the party had been thrown and had landed headlong on a pile of newly broken rocks. He was unconscious, perhaps dead.

Fanny hurried to the scene and supervised as the injured youth was moved to a nearby château and a doctor summoned. The relief was great when it became clear that the injuries were only minor. Much later, after the young man had achieved literary fame and both Tom and Anthony had become friends of his, they sometimes recalled that sunny afternoon outside Paris when it had seemed for a while that the world would never know the name of William Makepeace Thackeray.

A crowded social life and daily excursions on behalf of the travel book did not deflect Fanny from her chief goal in visiting Paris— getting expert medical opinions on both her husband and Emily. The recommended doctors came. They examined Mr Trollope and frowned. They agreed that he was in poor health, and one of the doctors estimated his age as twenty years more than it was. However, they found no specific ailment to treat, shook their heads at the report of his recurrent headaches, but seemed not to question his heavy self-medication of calomel. They examined Emily, and once again Fanny heard the word *délicate* pronounced. But again the eminent doctors had no specific treatment to suggest but spoke only of plenty of rest, fresh air, and nourishing food.

Somewhat reassured, Fanny visited a few more schools, churches, and asylums for research on her book. Auguste Hervieu polished the sketches he was making to illustrate it. By mid-June she decided it was time for the family to return to Bruges and Château d'Hondt.

Tom, who still had received no word about the Birmingham post, returned with them, and Fanny wrote steadily every morning, turning her notes on Paris into a book.

When Tom still had no word about his appointment by the first of October, he decided to go to Birmingham himself and learn how matters stood. He had not been gone more than a day or two when Thomas Anthony suffered another seizure. He was put to bed, and there was no more thought of even sporadic effort on his great encyclopaedia, advanced by this time only as far as the letter *D*.

Now, just as when Henry was so ill, Fanny's presence was demanded throughout the day at the bedside of a rapidly failing patient. It was terrible to Fanny that no doctor seemed to know what disease was destroying her husband or was able to suggest any treatment. Whatever nervous disorder had caused his violent headaches, how this disorder had been exacerbated by his excessive use of calomel, no one knew. Nor would anyone ever know what Fanny and Thomas Anthony talked about through those hours that she sat by his bed, or if they talked at all. They had loved each other once with the fervour of youth. '*Aime-moi bien. Aime-moi toujours.*' They had had seven children and worked and worried over their upbringing and sorrowed over the deaths of three. They had shared many journeys and faced a variety of disasters for which neither had reproached or blamed the other. Whatever their lives together had finally become—Fanny evolving as the financial as well as the emotional mainstay while Thomas Anthony retreated further into his glooms and desperate dreams—they had shared those lives for twenty-six years.

Thomas Adolphus returned from England on 15th October and was astonished to find his father dying. Seven days later he was dead, at the age of sixty-one.

Fanny was glad for Tom's return. She could let him take charge of the arrangements and lean on him as he escorted her and his sisters to the same cemetery where Henry had been buried the year before.

'He was, and had been, I take it, for many years a very unhappy man,' Tom wrote in his memoirs. 'All had gone wrong with him; misfortunes fell on him, one on the back of the other. Yet I do not think that these misfortunes were the real and efficient causes of his unhappiness. I do not see what concatenation of circumstances could have made him happy. . . . The terrible irritability of his temper, which sometimes in his latter years reached a pitch that made one fear his reason was, or would become unhinged, was undoubtedly due to the shattering of his nervous system, caused by the habitual use of calomel. . . . I do not think that it would be an exaggeration to say that for many years no person came into my father's presence who did not forthwith desire to escape from it. . . . Happiness, mirth, contentment, pleasant conversation, seemed to fly before him as if a malevolent spirit emanated from him.'[7]

Tom chose the epitaph for his father's tombstone, a starkly simple phrase, written in Latin: 'He has departed.'

19

England Again – 'Jonathan Jefferson Whitlaw' –
Emily's Death – Vienna

Almost immediately after her husband's death, Frances Trollope moved what was left of her family back to England and began a new novel. Thomas Anthony Trollope was dead, beyond the reach of any creditors who might gain some satisfaction by seeing him imprisoned for debt. There was no longer any need to stay in exile in Belgium. Besides, she thought the English climate would be better for Emily.

She left Tom in Bruges to take care of packing up what possessions she wanted to save from Château d'Hondt, dispose of the rest, and give up the lease on that sad house where both son and husband had died. Arrived in London, she and Cecilia and Emily moved into some lodgings that Anthony had found for them, and she looked about for a house to rent outside the city. She had no desire to return to Harrow, a now too familiar locale.

Finally she located a pleasant house surrounded by gardens in nearby Hadley, only twelve miles from London so that she could visit her publishers easily and Anthony could come to spend the weekends.

They moved in January. The garden was brown and stiff in the chill of winter, but Fanny promised Emily apple blossoms and roses in the spring and saw to it in the meantime that her sofa was in a sheltered nook warmed by the fire kept glowing in the fireplace.

The gentle, uncomplaining decline of her younger daughter was almost more difficult for Fanny to watch than Henry's feverish last days had been. Because Emily seemed to have no pain and sometimes was almost lively, hope kept reviving in Fanny that given the proper care, Emily might yet recover. But, constantly fearful that Cecilia might contract the disease that had attacked both Henry and Emily, Fanny arranged for her to spend some weeks with Lady Milman in Pinner.

After that, Fanny and Emily were alone at the Hadley house with the new maid, Cox, who was devoted to the invalid. At weekends, Anthony came, now the man of the family, the one his mother turned to when she needed male support. Anthony was the one who moved the furniture into more desirable locations, the one who stoked the fires and did the various errands. During her last months in Belgium Fanny had asked Anthony to relay messages to her publishers in London. Now he was her regular courier, bringing galley proofs of *Paris and the Parisians* back to Hadley from London, taking corrected proofs into town, making enquiries of Richard Bentley as to the sales of *Tremordyn Cliff* and the possibility of some royalties.

In the dawn hours, before Emily awoke, Fanny worked on her new novel. Once again, as with her first, *The Refugee*, she was setting her scene in America. But this time, instead of concocting a melodramatic plot that catapulted some English characters into that alien land, the whole story was indigenous to the United States.

What she planned was an anti-slavery novel, in which she hoped to show not only the evils of the institution as it affected blacks but its poisonous effects on every member of a society in which it was tolerated. She could remember very well that she had been more comfortable and better served in the slave states of America than in those that did not allow slavery. But she saw this as a result of American insistence on 'freedom and equality'—for every member of the white race. Because of this doctrine there was no white person who did not see 'service' as demeaning, making those who performed it less than 'equal'. This had led to the subjugation of black people to perform most of the labours necessary if life was to be lived in any tolerably civilized fashion. Fanny saw it leading also to a scramble wherein the cleverest, most unscrupulous, and most 'cute (the American corruption of 'acute') went after what they wanted, and devil take the hindmost.

Long years before the anti-hero had become a literary convention, Fanny Trollope was building her novel on the adventures of such a character, a handsome, plausible, and totally conscienceless rascal whom she called Jonathan Jefferson Whitlaw. In his very name she was taking a whack at various shibboleths. Brother Jonathan was the popular nickname for the American persona, and Jefferson, of course, was the promulgator of Republican principles.

She had Jonathan Jefferson Whitlaw born and raised in one of those desolate woodcutters' huts in the swampy banks of the Mississippi that she had observed with such dismay on her journey up that river. Grown to manhood, Jonathan Jefferson Whitlaw wormed his way into the confidence of a well-meaning but gullible slave owner and became the manager of his plantation, treating the slaves with carefully masked cruelty. His conviction that Negroes were something less than human did not prevent him from lusting after a beautiful young black woman, Phoebe, who loved and was loved by an intelligent young black man, Caesar.

Fanny had no difficulty in creating a large and varied cast of characters whose lives crossed or were influenced by those of her unsavoury hero. As in her previous novel about the United States, she introduced some attractive and intelligent Americans. This time an orphaned brother and sister who were trying to bring forbidden religious instruction to the slaves triggered involved complications with Jonathan Jefferson Whitlaw. A mysterious black seeress came into the story, and her strangely prophetic utterances saved Phoebe from being raped by Whitlaw. Included in the cast of characters was a family of intellectual German émigrés on a nearby plantation, which the father refused to have worked by slave labour, thereby incurring the hostility of his neighbours. Before Fanny was through, she had also brought on her stage the delicately nurtured daughter of a New Orleans widower, a girl who was discovered, at a fateful moment, to have Negro blood in her ancestry. In that time and place this was a revelation so terrible that Fanny could plot no other fate for her quadroon than prostration and death.

Darkly melodramatic, it was still a novel of more density, power, and emotional conviction than anything she had written previously. And she was writing this each morning before she went to sit by young Emily—to read to her, joke with her, sing to her, and watch her die.

The end came very swiftly, just four months after Fanny had brought her back to England. And very quietly. Like one of the soap bubbles she was blowing in the drawing that Auguste Hervieu had made of her, Emily was there one moment, and then she was gone.

This time it was twenty-one-year-old Anthony who helped his mother through the details of the funeral and tried in his own awkward way to say some words of comfort. Cecilia came home from Pinner, but her mother did not let her stay long. An invitation from the Garnetts in Paris was opportune. Once again Cecilia's little trunk was packed, and she was sent off to a happier environment to study art and perfect her French.

Alone in the bleak winter chill of Hadley, perhaps Frances Trollope allowed herself tears at last. There had been so many deaths in such a short space of time.

But once the tears were shed, the resilient force within her pushed her back, willy-nilly, into the world of the living and activity.

She finished the novel, which she called *The Life and Adventures of Jonathan Jefferson Whitlaw: or Scenes on the Mississippi.* Auguste Hervieu, still practically a member of the family though no longer living under the same roof, illustrated some of the more dramatic scenes. Manuscript and drawings were delivered to Richard Bentley.

The book was published in the late spring of 1836 and received the mixed reviews that all Frances Trollope's books so far had received. Tories in general admired the anti-American stance. Whigs were offended by her mocking aside: 'Not an ill-tempered man, only a free-born tyrant'.[1] Antislavery readers had to approve her theme and especially her satirical allusions to the anomaly of a country that boasted of its democracy while keeping a race in bondage. 'What's freedom for if we can't do what we like with our own born slaves?'[2] one character asked. And to show the poverty of one white man's dwelling in the South Fanny had written that it lacked 'the dignity of sundry half-naked negro children round the door'.[3] But critics and admirers alike had to grant Mrs Trollope's rare skill at sarcasm.

Actually, Frances Trollope's alien eye had seen the schizophrenia that was dividing the United States quite clearly, and she wrote about it with an objective acid that was impossible to partisans of either side. Years after the publication of *Jonathan Jefferson Whitlaw* there would be critics to compare Frances Trollope's book with Harriet Beecher Stowe's *Uncle Tom's Cabin* and find Mrs Trollope's the better novel.[4]

For Fanny, as always, the reviews her book received were less important than its sales and the resultant royalties. Besides, once a manuscript was out of the house, she would start on another novel. She never seemed to have any difficulty finding a new theme. When one story was completed, the idea for another presented itself, and the greater her own personal anguish or grief at the moment, the more likely she was to choose a subject that allowed her to be mocking, satirical, even spiteful. Having relieved herself on the subject of 'free-born Americans' doing what they liked with 'their own born slaves', she now remembered another type of personality that had long distressed her, the hypocritical evangelist.

Perhaps burying her youngest daughter and hearing the platitudes that had inevitably been part of the rites had recalled to her memory the way some unctuous ministers exploited the volatile sensibilities of very young women. She had memories of camp meetings and revivals in Ohio where young girls prostrated themselves before a ranting preacher who had terrified them with visions of hell. She also remembered the Reverend J. W. 'Velvet' Cunningham, the vicar of Harrow, questioning, oh so gently, the propriety of letting young girls perform in charades or theatricals while he himself made lavish use of emotional appeals to their religious feelings, usually concluding the instruction with a 'kiss of peace'.

Whatever the springs of inspiration that motivated her, Fanny's next novel again featured a villain, this time a handsome evangelical minister whose self-seeking machinations almost destroyed the quiet and traditional patterns of a small village where he had been awarded the living. She set the scene in England and called the village Wrexhill. Later, after the book was published and successful, there would be critics to write that *The Vicar of Wrexhill* was a malicious caricature of Velvet Cunningham. More likely, with the vicar as with Whitlaw, Fanny was finding an outlet for her anger at life's unfairness by attacking characters who pretended, to their own advantage, to have answers.

Tom came to Hadley in the early spring after winding up affairs in Bruges, a business he had prolonged and made more enjoyable by taking a number of walking tours in Normandy and elsewhere. By the time he arrived, Fanny had recovered enough from her grief and proceeded far enough with her new novel, *The Vicar of Wrexhill*, to be giving some thought to plans for the future.

Why not another travel book? A travel book necessarily meant an interesting journey to some foreign scene, and her first choice of destinations this time was the land that had lured her since her girlhood studies of its language and its poets. She went to London to propose a book on Italy to Richard Bentley, but he reminded her that there was, as there was so often, trouble brewing in the Italian kingdoms. He had an alternative suggestion—Austria, and Vienna in particular, might be better goals. Austria had been in favour with the English ever since Napoleon's defeat and Prince Metternich's clever parcelling out of the spoils among the victors at the Congress of Vienna. There was much of romantic, poetic, and architectural interest in Austria and its capital for a visitor to describe. Fanny nodded and accepted the new destination.

Tom still had not been summoned to the promised post at the grammar school in Birmingham, so his mother took it for granted that he would accompany her to attend to the details of travel. They would pick up Cecilia in Paris, and Auguste Hervieu would go with them too. Tom asked if a friend from his Oxford days might accompany them, and Fanny agreed, and decided also to take the maid who had been so faithful during Emily's last days. Any notion of Anthony becoming one of the party seems not to have occurred to anyone. Anthony was still employed at the Post Office. It was a post he hated and at which he did less than well, but he was gainfully employed, and Tom was not. And so, during his weekends at Hadley, Anthony could watch as his mother, Tom, and Auguste Hervieu pored over maps and guidebooks and argued amiably about which routes to follow on their journey to Vienna.

Anthony also had the privilege of seeing them off on the evening of 21st July 1836. His mother, Tom, Tom's friend, Hervieu, and the maid, Cox, made Anthony's rooms in London their rendezvous preparatory to boarding the night mail coach to Dover. He helped them transport their immense amount of luggage to the mail coach terminal at Piccadilly. Among other delights, they were going to sail down the Danube. Would he ever see the Danube? Would he ever visit Vienna? It seemed very unlikely to the young man, once again left behind as his mother jaunted off, accompanied as she so often was by his older brother, Tom. Once again Frances Trollope had '*un voyage à faire*', and a goal even more distant than Paris '*au bout*'.

PART FOUR

A Very Trollope
1836–1863

20

The Danube – Vienna –
Prince and Princess Metternich – Viennese Society

It was Tom's fancy to think of his mother as somewhat timid, frightened by thunderstorms and heights. His mother, who had plunged into the primeval forests of Tennessee, coped with the heat and cold of Cincinnati, slithered down the slippery paths that led to the observation post behind Niagara Falls, and generally dared to do whatever seemed necessary, was pleased to let her son be concerned for her comfort on this journey.

There was the matter of the barge, for instance, on which they planned to travel down the Danube from Ratisbon (now Regensburg) to Vienna. They had followed a devious overland route eastwards from Paris, stopping at Metz, Strasbourg and Stuttgart, then making a detour southwards to visit Salzburg, Mozart's home. The coaches in which they travelled had been slow and elderly, but they had not minded, for the leisurely pace gave them time to enjoy the scenery. Then they came to Ratisbon and the barge that was to add the novelty of river travelling to their expedition.

Fanny's first view of the vessel did dismay her. It was a large flat scow made of rough boards and almost entirely occupied by an arklike shed, which provided shelter for the boxes, casks, and bales being transported down the river. Any passengers who might be making the trip along with the merchandise were expected to sit on the sloping roof of this shed on a bench so close to the edge of the roof that their legs had to dangle over the water. A board with slats nailed on it crosswise led to the deck below and two benches in one corner under the roof where passengers could take shelter in bad weather.

Surveying these arrangements, Fanny felt an inward shudder, but she spoke brightly to Cecilia and the others. Obviously not many people chose to travel to Vienna by barge, but that made it more of

an adventure for them and a pleasantly unusual experience to record
in her book. And she led the way back to the inn where they were
spending the night.

Tom, however, was appalled to think of his mother and sister
travelling for days under such primitive conditions. He had never
envisaged such an unlikely transport when they planned the river
interlude. The next morning he rose at dawn, went to the riverfront,
found the boat master, and by a judicious mixture of persuasion and
bribery obtained the boat master's consent to have a small section
at the bow of the barge made into a nook for the Trollope party.
They would only have to leave it free for the captain for a few
minutes before each landing.[1]

Fanny, Cecilia, and the rest of the party were happily surprised
when they appeared an hour or so later and saw what Tom had
arranged.

'This perch is perfectly delightful in all respects,' Fanny wrote
that afternoon, ensconced in the nook. 'Our fruit, cold meat, wine,
bread, and so forth are stowed near us. Desks and drawing books
can all find place, and, in short, if the sun will but continue to shine
as it do now, all will be well.' She went on to describe further aspects
of her surroundings as the barge moved slowly down the river. 'Our
crew are a very motley set, and as we look at them from our dignified
retirement they seem likely to afford us a variety of picturesque
groups. On the platforms, which project at each end of the ark,
stand the men—and the women too—who work the vessel. This is
performed by means of four immense oars protruding lengthwise,
two in front and two towards the stern, by which the boat is steered.
Besides these, there are two others to row with. . . . It appears that
there are many passengers who work for their passage, as the seats
at the oars are frequently changed, and as soon as their allotted task
is done, they dip down into the unknown region beyond the ark and
are no more seen till their turn for rowing comes around again. I
presume the labour, thus divided, is not very severe, for they appear
to work with much gayety and good-humour.'[2]

The Trollope party, saved by Tom's thoughtfulness from sitting
with their legs dangling over the roof, and surrounded by picnic
paraphernalia, was full of gaiety and good humour also. Fanny was

amused to discover that she and her group were considered eccentric to an extreme, not only by the crew of the barge but by the loungers at every landing place where they stopped to load or unload cargo. Each evening when they disembarked to find an inn for the night, for the barge travelled only by day, they were objects of intense scrutiny by villagers and innkeepers. Nor so many English people were travelling about the Continent in those days. The Trollopes were definitely charting new ground.

On one occasion it seemed likely to be dangerous ground as well. They had dined, spent the night, and had breakfast at a small inn, and Tom had paid the rather exorbitant charges without argument. This lack of haggling had convinced the landlord that these English were not only mad but wealthy beyond imagining and that he had woefully undercharged them. All of the Trollope party except Tom had gone aboard the barge when the landlord came storming down upon Tom, who was still on the landing stage, demanding a sum double that which he had already been paid. Tom shook his head, and the landlord seized him by the throat. Hervieu and Tom's friend leaped from the barge to Tom's rescue. Various bystanders hurried to the landlord's side. Everyone began grabbing, pushing, pulling, in a confused scrimmage. Then the landlord broke away to pick up an axe that was lying nearby.

'Oh, no, stop! Help!' shrieked Fanny on the barge. She had managed to extract a bundle of bills from her handbag and rushed to the captain, imploring him to go and pay the landlord whatever he wanted.

The landlord was advancing on Tom with the axe upraised when the captain jumped from the boat and ran to the scene of the struggle waving the money. The landlord put down his axe to take the bills. Tom was released, and Hervieu and his friend hurried him on to the barge.

Tom found great satisfaction in reporting this incident to the police officials in the next little Bavarian town at which the barge stopped, and he knew even greater satisfaction a few days later after they had crossed the border into Austria and stopped at another small town. There he learned from the local police that the Bavarian officials to whom he had complained had confronted the landlord,

forced him to return the money he had extorted, and given him a
trouncing as well.

Soon after the group arrived in Vienna, Fanny found an apartment inside the city walls. Lodgings within this enclave were hard
to find, and expensive when discovered, but all the advice Fanny had
received in London and Paris had agreed that she would limit her
opportunities for moving in good society if she settled in any of the
suburbs outside the wall. An apartment found and the family settled
in, Fanny sent off her letter of introduction to Sir Frederick Lamb,
the English ambassador to Vienna. Soon a footman arrived with a
dinner invitation from the ambassador and his wife for Mrs Trollope
and her party. The invitation was accepted with pleasure. Fanny
and Cecilia fussed over their toilettes and went out to buy ribbons
and flowers to freshen costumes that had already travelled quite a
distance. On the appointed evening the Trollopes presented themselves at the ambassador's residence to join a gathering of notables,
chief among whom were Prince and Princess Metternich. After proper
introductions and a murmur of small talk, Mrs Trollope found herself being escorted in to dinner on the arm of Prince Metternich.

From the moment of the success of her first book, *Domestic
Manners of the Americans*, there were those who called Frances
Trollope 'clever' but 'vulgar'. These critics were not just Americans,
convinced that no 'lady' could have written at such length about
bugs and spitting, but English compatriots as well. A century and a
half later it is difficult to know what offended them. Perhaps her
sarcasm? A blunt honesty now and then in speaking of matters that
proper ladies veiled in rhetoric? The fact was that she got on very
well with men and women of learning, culture, and polished
manners. She got on beautifully that evening with both Prince
Metternich and his small and lovely wife, Melanie. Before the party
broke up, which in those days in Vienna was immediately after
taking coffee, it had been arranged that Mrs Trollope and her son
and daughter would dine with Prince and Princess Metternich on
the following Monday.[2]

During the next months the Trollopes dined often with the minister and his wife, sometimes at formal affairs for thirty guests or more

and sometimes *en famille*. All of the Trollopes were fascinated by one peculiarity of the Prince. At any dinner he sat at the head of the table, pale, slender, emanating courtesy, but taking nothing from the dishes being served to his guests. He had dined previously and alone at one o'clock. And so 'he had a loaf of brown bread and a plate of butter before him, and while his guests were dining, he occupied himself with spreading and cutting a succession of daintily thin slices of bread-and-butter for his own repast.'[3]

While thus isolating himself from his guests as they dined, he joined them in a web of witty and entertaining conversation, which ranged over the topics of the day, the latest concerts or operas, the books of current interest, the latest art exhibits. The talk skimmed over the grief that all Austrians had felt at the death of the old Emperor Franz, two years before. There were comments on the health of the new Emperor Ferdinand, the forty-three-year-old son of the beloved Vater Franz. His epileptic tendencies had once caused alarm but now, to everyone's relief, they seemed to have abated.

Most fascinating to both Fanny and her son were the anecdotes the Prince would sometimes relate from his years of association with Napoleon Bonaparte. The tales the Prince told were all safely peripheral. They heard no revelations as to why or by what persuasion Emperor Franz had given his daughter to Napoleon in marriage, no clues as to why he had later joined in the European alliance against his son-in-law.

Metternich had amusing stories to tell—of how at a meeting he had had with Napoleon, the Emperor of the French had become enraged and flung his cocked hat across the room and then expected that Metternich would go and retrieve it for him. Smiling a little, the Prince said he believed that this exhibition was simply a piece of play-acting, a show of violence by which he hoped to intimidate his adversary of the moment. The Prince commented that he could not believe Napoleon was a 'gentleman' in any sense of the word. Since everyone knew that Napoleon was technically 'gentle' by reason of his descent from an ancient and noble Tuscan family, the Trollopes realized that Metternich's remark summarized a personal judgment. Was there an echo in Fanny's mind of William of Wykeham's motto, 'Manners makyth man'?

All of this was, of course, fine material for Fanny's travel book, but her relationship with Princess Metternich soon went beyond such collecting of anecdotes. They began to meet as two friends, taking tea together, talking about their children, their hopes, and their sorrows. One day Fanny dared to ask a special favour. She would like to have a portrait of her friend by which to remember her when they parted. Would the Princess consent to sit to Auguste Hervieu for her portrait? Princess Melanie smiled, hesitated, and then said she would be willing to do so if Mrs Trollope kept her company at the sittings and if, in return, Hervieu would also make a portrait of Mrs Trollope as a souvenir for her. After that, Fanny spent several mornings each week chatting with the Princess as Auguste Hervieu sketched, took sightings, rearranged poses, and finally achieved tolerable likenesses of both women.

Sponsored by the English ambassador and Prince and Princess Metternich, Fanny had a full calendar of engagements. She and her family were invited to tea, to dinner, to musicales, by this duke and duchess and the other and were soon familiar with most of the splendid homes within the inner city. Because they were foreigners, she and her family were also entertained by some of the bourgeois families, many of great wealth, who lived outside the wall. Long custom had decreed that the nobility within the walls never mingled with those outside, but some of the noble ladies had great curiosity about the other group. Often when Fanny was visiting in some noble house within the wall she was begged for hints about the lives of the rich families outside. Only foreigners of some note like Fanny, writers, artists, or composers, were able to move freely between the two cities of Vienna.

Just how and by what influence she managed to visit a far more macabre section of Vienna she never divulged. Somehow she achieved permission to visit the catacombs under Saint Stephen's Cathedral. Tom recalled the excursion into those vast, long-unused vaults with a certain horror. Because of special qualities of soil and atmosphere, tens of thousands of corpses that had been deposited there, many during the plague of 1713, had resisted the usual processes of decay and become virtual mummies.

Fanny picked her way through the tunnel with its stacked and piled bodies with a steady step, making mental notes of what she saw for her book, while her son Tom, who went to such lengths to protect her, stumbled along beside her, averting his eyes from the grisly sights.

Later Fanny wrote a detailed description of the catacombs for her book, considering it a necessary *frisson* to enliven the obligatory passages about the scenic and architectural beauties of the city and the reports on schools, hospitals, and insane asylums that every armchair tourist expected.

Not long after that expedition Tom received a letter from Birmingham. The position at King Edward's Grammar School that had been pending so long was confirmed at last. He was to appear in Birmingham as soon as possible. 'Well,' said Tom. 'Well,' said his mother. It really seemed too bad that the summons had to come just now, but Tom was a young man who had to make some place for himself in the world. He packed his trunk, and so did his Oxford friend. Soon Fanny, Cecilia, and Hervieu were bidding the two young men farewell.

But invitations were piled on the mantelpiece of the apartment in the Hohenmarkt—an invitation to Princess Metternich's Christmas party for children, invitations to holiday balls at this great house and that. There would be waltzing and more waltzing.

> Then there's waltzing—that mother has but little skill
> Who can't make the waltz do almost what she will.

Fanny had tossed off the rhyme four years earlier in her *Mother's Manual*, but although Cecilia was twenty now, Fanny had few thoughts about hurrying to find a good match for her. She was pleased to see her young-lady daughter whirling gracefully around a ballroom, swaying, swooping with the music.

The Turkish ambassador, Ahmed Ferih Pasha, invited them to a reception at his residence in the Mariahelf Faubourg, a palace that belonged to Prince Esterhazy, and Cecilia was delighted. She thought the ambassador was 'good fun', for he said such amusing things in his fractured French. But Fanny was touched when the ambassador bowed over her hand that evening and said, 'Providence has accorded you great happiness in letting you see your daughter grow to such perfection.'

Memories of another young daughter, idly blowing soap bubbles, were easier to banish when Fanny had Cecilia near her. In fact, the heroine of her almost completed novel, *The Vicar of Wrexhill,* was very much like Cecilia, beautiful, loving, proper. Perhaps all Cecilia lacked was one of Fanny's own characteristics, one that she hardly thought desirable in a heroine, a sense of mischief.

With the beginning of Lent, Vienna's lavish entertainments ceased, but Fanny and Cecilia still had many things to see and do. Fanny checked on details of buildings, institutions, and roadways for her travel book and worked steadily to complete *The Vicar.*

During Holy Week they attended the traditional religious observances in the Court Chapel, sharing a bench with the Turkish ambassador on Holy Thursday to watch Emperor Ferdinand and his Empress wash the feet of paupers. On Easter Sunday they drove to the Prater, but the weather was cold and rainy. The carriages of the nobility were all closed. No one was promenading.

Fanny's lease on the apartment in the Hohenmarkt expired on the first of May. She and Cecilia spent their last evening with the Metternichs and a few other friends. Princess Metternich's mother, the Countess Zechy-Ferrari, had urged Fanny and Cecilia to visit her at her château in Hungary on their return journey. It was a tempting invitation but would have meant a long detour through somewhat troubled country. So instead, there were sincere regrets, fond handclasps, kisses between Fanny, Cecilia, and the Princess, and promises to write. The next morning, Fanny, Cecilia, Hervieu, and the maid, Cox, started on their journey back to England and the house in Hadley where Fanny would work up her notes into yet another travel book, *Vienna and the Austrians.*

America, Belgium and western Germany, Paris, and now Vienna and Austria—Frances Trollope had visited them all in the last ten years, travelling in almost as many conveyances as the Western world provided—steamboat, barge, Dearborn, stagecoach, wagon, horse, donkey. She had looked at many sights with a bright, enquiring eye and encountered many adventures with no gasps of terror. Her son Tom might consider her timid and try to spare her discomfort, but she had already won such a reputation as a traveller that a few years later a writer describing a difficult journey was sure of being understood when he said that it was something that only 'the most enterprising tourist—a very Trollope' would undertake.[4]

21

A New Reign – 'The Vicar of Wrexhill' –
A New Arrangement

William IV, the rough, bluff sailor prince who had been England's king for the last seven years, was dying. He had fathered ten children by his mistress, Mrs Jordan—ten young Fitzclarences, who roamed about the court seeking money, preferment, titled husbands or wives—but no child by his queen, Adelaide, had lived. The crown would have to pass to the daughter of his late younger brother, the Duke of Kent. William had a long-standing feud with the widow of that brother, the Duchess of Kent, and loathed the thought that his death might elevate her to the status of Regent. He breathed a sigh of relief when his niece, Alexandrina Victoria, celebrated her eighteenth birthday on 24th May 1837. He had stayed alive long enough to thwart any schemes of his sister-in-law. After which he had a new goal, to see June 19th so that he might know one more anniversary of the English victory at Waterloo. He begged his doctor to 'tinker with him' to keep him alive until then. The doctor did his best, and so did William. 'The King dies like an old lion,' wrote the young Benjamin Disraeli to a friend. But having lived through Waterloo day, William breathed his last in the early hours of 20th June 1837. Two hours later the Archbishop of Canterbury, accompanied by the Lord Chamberlain, was ushered in to Kensington Palace to greet the young Princess Victoria as England's queen.

Fanny and Cecilia, home again at Hadley, had a few kind words for the departed William. Not really a bad king, when all was said and done. He had made greater efforts than his self-indulgent brother, George IV, and he had managed to keep an uneasy balance between the Tories and the Whigs as he presided over the passage of a Reform Bill of sorts, a bill that was presumably inevitable. Beyond that, it was more entertaining to speculate about the new queen. She was so young, had led such a sheltered life—what would she make of her awesome new responsibilities? Fanny surmised that she would rely a good deal on her Prime Minister, Lord Melbourne, and hoped that the country would not become too Whiggish as a result.

Anthony came from London at weekends and reported on the preparations for the coronation and then later told of the streets jammed with cheering citizens as the new queen rode from the ceremonies at Westminster Abbey to take up residence in Buckingham Palace.

A new reign—and a young woman wearing the crown, a very proper young woman at that. The situation was provocative and offered possibilities for endless small talk, but it did not impinge very closely on everyday life at Hadley.

The usual pattern was quickly established. Fanny rose at dawn to finish *The Vicar of Wrexhill* so that Anthony could take in the manuscript, along with Hervieu's illustrations, to Richard Bentley. After that, she began at once to work up her book on Vienna and the Austrians.

Early in September of 1837 *The Vicar of Wrexhill* was published and made quite a nice splash. The reviews were generally good, and more to the point, so were the sales. It was the sort of book people talked about, its chief character, the vicar, being very close to a caricature of the sort of Low Churchman that filled non-evangelicals with distaste and dismay. A certain reverend named W. J. Cartwright stirred up a minor storm by declaring he had been the model for the fictional vicar and demanding apologies and retractions. This ill-considered claim did the book no harm. But it was a truer measure of the book's success when the vicar became a generally accepted symbol of a hypocritical clergyman and Sydney Smith, writing to Lord John Russell about a currently debated Church Bill, would say, 'This is a cause worthy of the vicar of Wrexhill himself.'[1]

Rent, food, clothing were assured for a while longer. But Fanny did not slacken her efforts. She had almost finished *Vienna and the Austrians* and was already thinking of a plot for another novel, using Vienna as the background. As she saw it, a novel a year was absolutely necessary if she was to keep herself and her family afloat. If she could manage two, that would be even better. She had the formula down fairly pat by now and knew just how many pages to write to spin out her story so that it would fill three volumes—the accepted format for novels in those days. (If, by chance, some writer could only invent enough plot to fill two volumes, readers were suspicious of being cheated by something flimsy.) She knew how to pace each chapter to a suspenseful break and how to leave one group of characters in a situation fraught with anxiety or danger while she dealt with a subplot, and she knew how to bring each volume to a similar end, presumably having roused her readers to a frantic desire for the next volume, until finally the third volume concluded the story, tying up all the loose ends.

On a trip to London in November she finally had a glimpse of the new Queen. 'The little Queen looked very young, and very pretty yesterday,' she wrote to Tom, but 'the Duke of Wellington got even louder cheers than she did.'

The Christmas holidays of 1837 brought Tom to Hadley from the school at Birmingham, and they turned out to be the happiest holidays the family had known in years. No one was ill. Anthony brought a friend and colleague, John Tilley, home with him. The house was warm and welcoming and full of guests. Fanny flitted about among them, small, energetic, and eager for everyone to have a good time. She arranged all sorts of junkets for the daytime hours and in the evenings urged her visitors to charades or theatricals. During these holidays, even Tom, who observed his fellow beings through a cloud of comfortable classical reference and loved to talk earnestly with pretty women while somehow keeping himself aloof from any real emotion, saw that his sister and John Tilley seemed to have an electric effect on each other. Perhaps, Tom thought, they were falling in love.

His mother was quite sure that this was the case and was generally pleased. Tilley's background was solid if unremarkable. He was a merchant's son, but at twenty-five, after eight years with the Post Office, he had risen to a responsible position with a salary double what Anthony made. He was also a well-mannered, intelligent, and amusing young man. Just what Cecilia needed, Fanny thought. She could begin to contemplate a satisfactory marriage·for her daughter.

Life was serene, sociable, scheduled as it had not been for years. Perhaps its very serenity allowed Fanny the luxury of feeling a little fatigue. She had written and had published nine books in the last eight years, written them while she was nursing first a dying son, then a dying husband, and then a dying daughter. Now and then, in moments of reflection, she remembered she was going to be fifty-eight this March 1838. Before too long Cecilia would be marrying and leaving her. Tom was gainfully employed in Birmingham, Anthony in London—she did not wish anything less for them. But a little shiver of dread shook her as she looked to the years ahead, all alone.

It was at this point that one of Tom's friends, stopping in at the house in Hadley, reported that Tom was so unhappy at the Birmingham school that he was thinking of resigning. Fanny was stunned by these secondhand tidings. Tom had confided at Christmas that he felt not well fitted for the post at King Edward's Grammar School. Most of the boys were sons of tradesmen, and none of them was interested in a classical education. Corporal punishment was the rule, simply to enforce a certain amount of order and silence during school hours, and Tom hated the times, almost daily, when he had to apply the cane. He and a colleague had tried to start a debating society, but few of the 'turbulent Birmingham lads', intent on careers in trade, were interested in such a pursuit. The younger clergy of the city from whom he might have hoped for some support in reaching the 'lads', or even a little social activity for himself, were all Low Church evangelicals, and to Tom, reared in his mother's mockery of evangelicals and full of his own young prejudices, such men and he were an 'oil and vinegar mix'.[2]

Still Fanny was shocked that Tom was contemplating giving up the post with no other plans in mind. She wrote to him expressing her alarm.

'I am fifty-eight years old, my dear Tom. And although, when I am well and in good spirits, I talk of what I may yet do, I cannot conceal from you or from myself, that my doings are nearly over. Believe me, I should be perfectly miserable did I look forward to your remaining where you are; for I see, and feel, that you cannot be happy there. But give me the great comfort of knowing that you have sufficient strength of mind and resolution to stick to it for a little while, till we see our way clear before us.'³

Sensing the hint of panic in his mother's letter, Tom responded promptly. He was not about to resign from King Edward's and did not know who had told his mother that he was. He begged her to stop worrying and also not to listen to any idle rumours she might hear. To this, Fanny replied apologetically. She knew she could trust her son to be steady and responsible, and in due time some solution would present itself.

It is very likely that she already had a glimmering of the plan that might help solve some of Tom's problems and her own, but she kept the scheme to herself for the moment.

One spring day John Tilley came to her, asking in proper fashion for Cecilia's hand in marriage. Fanny was happy to grant his request. She was also pleased that thanks to the funds from her own dowry, which brother Henry had put into trust at the time of Thomas Anthony's bankruptcy, she could offer a decent marriage portion with her daughter. No need for Cecilia to worry about going with inadequate funds to her bridegroom, as Fanny had worried about doing years before.

With kisses and smiles and tears, the engagement was a settled thing. And almost at once Fanny decided that it would be a good idea to move to London for the summer so that they would be near the shops to purchase Cecilia's trousseau. In London she would be closer to her publishers. Anthony would be nearby. London would be a more satisfactory residence in every way, at least for a while.

Tom came home to Hadley from Birmingham when school broke up in mid-June. One afternoon Fanny asked him to walk with her in the garden. They meandered up and down the paths for an hour and more as she slowly and diplomatically worked towards her goal.

She knew Tom was not happy as a teacher. She had heard him speak often of a desire to travel and to write. She could understand such an ambition. She had made something of a career of such activities. So what would he think of combining their careers as writers and travellers?

'Combining them?'

'You need to be free of a regular position if you are really to pursue your ambition. I need something also, especially when I travel. Someone to take care of the details of luggage, reservations, passports, as you did on the trip to Vienna.'

Suddenly, as she mentioned passports, they looked at each other and laughed, remembering one inn in Austria where the Trollope party had been registered as 'Mr. Passport and family'.

Then, serious again, Fanny said she also needed someone to manage her business affairs for her, to help her with proofs and galleys, and to represent her with her publishers. Finally, she disclosed her plan completely. She wondered if Tom would consider resigning his Birmingham post and deferring his academic career altogether for a while to act as her manager, assistant, 'companion and squire', an assignment that would allow him a good deal of freedom for travelling on his own and writing.

Despite his unhappiness at Birmingham, Tom did not agree to the proposition immediately. Already twenty-eight years old, he had to realize that 'deferring' any steps in an academic career might mean its abandonment. He had inherited no money from his bankrupt father. The only money to which he could look forward in the future was his share of his mother's marriage settlement, which had been put in trust. He really had to consider how he would earn his way in the world. As a result, he and his mother took several long, thoughtful walks in the Hadley garden before they came to their 'momentous decision'.

'Audacious rather than prudent,' Tom called it later, but added that he had never once regretted it in the years that followed. Neither he nor his mother ever revealed what sort of financial arrangement they agreed upon that would allow the young man the dignity of independence, but they did settle on something, and Tom sent in his resignation to King Edward's Grammar School.

Cecilia was pleased when she heard of the new arrangement. Now she need not fret about her mother being left alone after her marriage, Tom would be able to do what he liked and would be resuming a role he had played often in the past.

Anthony's reactions were understandably more mixed. He knew it was good that his mother would have someone to look after her, and if he was jealous that once again it was Tom to whom she turned instead of him, the jealousy was a primitive emotion that was difficult to justify. In the last year or two Anthony had done his share of running errands for his mother to various publishers, and he had no desire to make a career of such attentions. At the same time, the sense of rejection he had suffered all his life smouldered within him. 'Yes, it's probably all for the best,' he said to Tom. 'You really do not have the temperament to earn your bread in the routine work of a profession or under the supervision of a superior.'4 Anthony had learned by this time how to get a reaction from his equable older brother.

Years later, Tom was still rebutting Anthony's jibe, insisting that he could indeed have earned his way in a definite profession and under supervision, insisting also that although it might appear to outsiders that his mother had given him a life of leisure, he had never been idle but had worked vigorously and with great productivity through the years when he was his mother's 'squire'. This was true enough. As soon as Tom severed his connections with the Birmingham school, he set aside some time each day for writing. He seemed to write as easily as he talked. Articles, reviews, biographical notices, any sort of squib, flowed even more swiftly from his pen than his mother's novels and travel books did from hers. He submitted these items to whatever magazines or papers seemed likely markets, and before long, various of his productions were finding their way into print. Often they were published anonymously, but that made little difference to Tom just now. He was, he could tell Anthony, 'earning his bread'.

Fanny found a comfortable house for the family at 20 York Street in Portman Square. With Tom on hand to take care of all the tiring details of packing and moving, the shift to London was made easily. In a short time Fanny was established in a new Sacred Den, bringing *A Romance in Vienna* to a conclusion in the early morning hours, and after that going out with Cecilia to visit the London shops. They had all sorts of fabrics and laces and linens to buy, dressmakers to consult, fittings to attend. And, of course, the social life was even more active in London than it had been in Hadley.

A Romance in Vienna was completed in time to be published in the autumn—'another book by Mrs. Trollope' according to most reviewers. Lacking the dark melodrama of *Jonathan Jefferson Whitlaw* or the extravagant satire of *The Vicar of Wrexhill*, it was still an acceptable story, pleasing to a number of readers who enjoyed getting a background of Vienna along with the fiction. As usual, the manuscript was hardly out of her hands before Fanny was beginning a new novel. Again she shifted her scene to America, but this time she was viewing it from a comic angle with a robust and energetic heroine, the widow Barnaby.

Plans for Cecilia's wedding accelerated with the start of the new year, 1839, and suddenly the day itself was upon them. On 11th February 1839, Cecilia Trollope married John Tilley in Saint Mary's Church in Bryanston Square. Two friends from her Harrow childhood, Mary and Kate Grant, were bridesmaids. A Dr Dibdin presided. After the ceremony there was an elegant collation at 20 York Street, attended by a crush of friends, relatives, and acquaintances.

Fanny saw Cecilia and her new husband off with the mixture of emotions usual on such an occasion. She was happy that her daughter had found someone who looked to be a good and loving life's companion. She wept a little because Cecilia and John would not be settling in London after their honeymoon. The Post Office had transferred John to a new post, so the young couple were going to live in Penrith in the Lake District, an area that seemed impossibly remote to Fanny since she had never visited it.

Happily the life she led gave her no opportunity for a letdown. She had a new project in hand for which she had been preparing even as she hurried about making arrangements for Cecilia's wedding. During the last year she had become aware of the terrible abuse of children as workers in the new factories that had changed the face of the Midlands. She was no radical, no reformer. Such sentiments had been burned out in her experiences at Nashoba and in America. She had not cared at all about the Reform Bill, designed to reapportion voting districts so that nobility could not keep boroughs in their pockets and so that the citizens of the new mercantile centres would have a voice in Parliament. But when she heard about children who were forced to work in factories or mines for twelve to fifteen hours a day, she was horrified. Some years before, Frances Wright had excused her defection from Nashoba by saying that if she was not dedicated to principle, still she had a 'good heart'. Years later, her son Anthony wrote that she 'reasoned from the heart'.

The plight of these children, so far from her, living in a different world, touched her heart. In the autumn of 1838, because she was already committed to a novel for Richard Bentley, she went to a new publisher, Henry Colburn, and suggested a novel that would dramatize the pitiful lives of these exploited children. Mr Colburn was interested and gave her a contract. She then got in touch with Lord Ashley (later the Earl of Shaftesbury) who had been sponsoring bill after bill in Parliament designed to limit a child's working day to ten hours. Lord Ashley was eager to help in any way he could. A book by the popular writer, Mrs Trollope, might do a great deal to rouse public sentiment. He wrote a number of letters for her, introducing her to the radicals and agitators in Manchester, Ecclesfield, and other cities where numbers of children were employed, who could give her not only facts and figures but show her the children at their labours and in their homes.

As a result of all this, Fanny's novel *The Widow Barnaby* was progressing very slowly. On 20th February 1839, just nine days after Cecilia's wedding, Fanny put it aside altogether for a while as she and Tom set off for Manchester, where she planned to begin her research.

Tom handled all the details, made arrangements for them to travel on that rather alarming new means of transport, the railway, saw that their luggage was on board, and reassured her as she got into the new conveyance.

She had been quite sure from the beginning that her plan for engaging her eldest son as 'companion and squire' was a good one. She was even more thankful for her inspiration now. His large, placid presence calmed her fears as the engine chuffed out of the station and into the countryside, belching smoke and sparks. Everything was made easy after they arrived at Manchester, thanks to Tom. She knew she could never have made her way to the factories, the homes of the agitators to whom Lord Ashley had given her letters, and the miserable dwellings that sheltered the child workers and their families if Tom had not been beside her.

A new regime had begun for Fanny. She was in command of her own life, and Tom of his too, for that matter—free to pursue his own interests and travels when she did not need him—but when she did need him, he was there, cheerful, accommodating. The young Victoria might have her elder ministers to preside over the details of state. Fifty-nine-year-old Fanny had found a young minister to handle her own administration—her oldest son, Thomas Adolphus.

22

'Michael Armstrong' – Penrith – Paris – Anthony's Illness

Charles Dickens was the new literary sensation in London. He did not exactly 'wake up one morning and find himself famous', but recognition had begun when the *Sketches by Boz* started to appear in 1833. Amusement had become delighted hilarity with the publication of the *Pickwick Papers* in 1836. Then the young writer had astounded his readers by shifting from humour to drama and pathos in the tale of an orphan, *Oliver Twist*, a novel that Richard Bentley began publishing in monthly instalments in 1837. Surprise quickly turned to enchantment as readers followed the adventures of the unfortunate Oliver, and their hearts welled with sympathy and outrage at the manner in which such young creatures could be abused by an uncaring society.

Fanny met Dickens at a party in the spring of 1838. 'He is extremely lively and intelligent,' she wrote to a friend, 'has the appearance of being very young, and although called excessively shy, seemed not at all averse to conversation.'¹

Oliver Twist may have played some part in turning Fanny's attention to suffering children. Its success may have encouraged Colburn to contract a novel with an exploited child as its hero. But Fanny was following her own course as she embarked on her study of the life of a factory child. Unlike Dickens, she had had no experience of working-class life. Her shock was fresh and immediate when, with Tom at her side, she first entered a great, six-storey red-brick factory, where the 'ceaseless whirring of a million hissing wheels seizes on the tortured ear', where reeking scents of 'oil, tainted water, human filth, with that last worst nausea arising from hot refuse of atmospheric air ... render the act of breathing a process of difficulty, disgust and pain.'² She was sickened by the sight of scores of children, thin and pale, with 'a look of hideous premature old age', going numbly about their routine tasks of walking backwards and forwards before the reels, on which the cotton was wound, so as to join the threads when they broke. 'Piecers', they were called. Other children, some of them little girls no older than six or seven, worked as 'scavengers', collecting flying fragments of thread or fluff flung off as the looms crashed back and forth.

After such sights she still had to visit the squalid homes of a few of these children and meet their hopeless parents. Then, gasping for breath in the reeking air, she talked with the men to whom Lord Ashley had directed her, men who told her tales that she could hardly believe of the callous indifference of mill owners. There were, it seemed, factory owners who smugly justified their use of child labour as a sensible way to deal with the excess of population.

Shaken by her immersion into this alien world, Fanny followed her research with a visit to Cecilia and John at Penrith. It was like awakening from a bad dream to come from the mills to the spring-time blue-green of the Lake country and to see Cecilia again, blooming in her role of wife.

Still unwinding, Fanny and Tom walked a few miles one afternoon to visit a colleague of John Tilley's in the postal system, the poet William Wordsworth. Wordsworth held the post of stamp collector for Cumberland and Westmorland, and because of a running dispute about which of the two villages in the district should collect the revenues, he and John Tilley were not on the best of terms. Fanny decided to ignore this small difficulty in her desire to meet the poet. Tom found Wordsworth rather brusque and self-centred, but Fanny enjoyed his long monologue about himself and his writings.

Soon after that, Fanny and Tom returned to London. Fanny set to work to finish *The Widow Barnaby* and to begin her novel about child labour. She invented a rather improbable plot, which had a self-righteous factory owner tricked into adopting a little 'bag of rags out of his own factory'. But the 'bag of rags', Michael Armstrong, was a gallant and likeable little hero. His efforts to bring assistance to his brother, still working in the factory, enabled Fanny to describe the horrors of the mill in detail, and the sympathy he aroused in one of the mill-owner's daughters, who was shocked by her discovery of the source of her family's wealth, would finally allow her to bring everything to a happy conclusion.

Tom, pursuing his chosen career of writing and travelling, managed to achieve a contract for a travel book on Brittany from Colburn that summer and set off with Auguste Hervieu, who was to do the illustrations. Left alone, Fanny finished *The Widow Barnaby* and delivered the manuscript to Richard Bentley. She met Colburn and agreed with him that *The Life and Adventures of Michael Armstrong, Factory Boy* should be published in monthly instalments, following the new fashion, and began sending him chapters as soon as she finished them.

But alone in London, seeing Anthony only rarely, her days seemed long and dreary. When Tom and Hervieu returned from Brittany, they found her ill with tonsillitis. Ill and also restless. Lying in bed, achy and miserable, she had decided that she was tired of this house in York Street, tired of London in general.

Going over the bills that had accumulated in his absence, Tom agreed that living in London was extremely costly. 'Good heavens,' he said, 'look at the charges from the greengrocer alone!' Fanny was roused into defending herself against extravagance.

'Potatoes were very dear this year,'[3] she countered at random. But when Tom stared at her, they both burst into laughter. And whatever potatoes had to do with it, they decided to give up the house in London. Fanny would go for a restorative visit with Cecilia at Penrith, and after that—well, what could be more pleasant than a winter in Paris?

Fanny always enjoyed herself in Paris, but that winter of 1839–1840 turned out to be the most social yet. All the friends she had made in previous years welcomed her. She was again a guest at the salons of Madame Récamier, the Princess Belgiojoso, and Miss Mary Clarke, a clever Englishwoman soon to become the wife of the German Orientalist, Julius von Mohl. She made new friends, among them the British ambassador and his wife, Lord and Lady Granville. She was presented to the 'citizen king', Louis Philippe, who, it turned out, knew her book on America. During his years of exile from France after the revolution, Louis Philippe had spent some months in the United States and had his own memories of Philadelphia and other eastern cities. Smiling, the king asked Mrs Trollope if she would like to revisit the United States. Fanny choked back any mocking answer and responded with an enigmatic smile.

England's young Queen Victoria was married that winter of 1840 to her cousin, Albert of Saxe-Coburg-Gotha. In Paris, Lord Granville and his wife celebrated the event with a grand Valentine's Day ball, and Fanny was a guest. She only regretted that her own young bride, Cecilia, was not present for the gala and that she did not have all three of her sons at her side, for she counted John Tilley as another son now.

A few weeks later, one missing son, Anthony, did appear, to spend his month's vacation from the Post Office with her. Fanny thought she had never seen him in such good spirits. He looked well, was acceptably tailored, and seemed happy to squire her to all the parties to which she had been invited.

As so often before, Fanny was being misled by appearances. Anthony told her nothing about the difficulties from which he was escaping during these weeks in Paris. He said not a word to her, or to anyone, about the moneylender who visited him regularly at the Post Office, insisting on another payment on the loan that Anthony had contracted. Somehow an original loan of sixteen pounds had grown to the immense and improbable total of two hundred pounds. The weekly visits of this moneylender, always taking place under the interested gaze of his fellow workers, were driving Anthony almost to distraction, relegating him again to the humiliation he had known as a 'charity boy' and inflaming all the scars from the impoverished months he had shared with his father at Harrow Weald.

Anthony saw his mother living easily and graciously during that winter of 1840, entertaining at dinners and teas, ordering theatre tickets with abandon, buying trinkets to send to Cecilia, freely spending the money she earned. But Anthony would never do as his brother Tom did—depend on his mother for any portion of his livelihood. He would sooner starve than tell her of his financial difficulties.

Even less could he tell her of another even more alarming problem. Tormenting himself, he tried to remember exactly what he had said to the young country girl he had met one idle afternoon and then seen several times later. He had spoken some flattery, of course. What else did one talk about to simple country girls? But surely he had never said anything about marriage. Then had come the day when her wretched mother, monstrous bonnet askew over straggling hair, market basket over her arm, had come storming into the room where he worked at the Post Office, screeching his name.

'Anthony Trollope! Ah, there you are! Now, young man, when are you going to marry my daughter?'[4]

This was humiliation far beyond any the persistent moneylender could inflict. It was agony for Anthony to know that all his fellow clerks were staring, snickering while the woman was there, and then laughing uproariously after she left. Anthony could hardly remember what he had said to the woman. He lived in terror of her return.

But it was altogether impossible that he should tell his mother about this. So he put on a brave face and fooled her completely. When his holiday came to an end, she kissed him good-bye with a light heart, feeling easier about him than she had for a long time.

The shock was that much greater when Fanny returned to London in June and found Anthony very ill. He was burning with fever, unconscious, sometimes delirious. Frantic, Fanny summoned doctors, who seemed to have no idea what was wrong. He had various symptoms that all led to several possible diagnoses. The doctors prescribed this treatment and that and left, shaking their heads.

Fanny was desperate. Anthony had always been the healthy one, never sick except for the time when the whole family had influenza. She could not bear the thought of losing Anthony as she had lost Henry and Emily.

She called in a Dr Eliotson, a physician whom she had met when Tom was briefly investigating mesmeric phenomena. Dr Eliotson did not attempt any hypnotism of an already comatose patient, but to help Mrs Trollope nurse her son he sent her two young women, the Okey sisters. He neglected to mention that both Okey sisters were given to clairvoyance and often saw a spirit whom they called Jack appear from time to time in company with one person or another. Jack's appearance always presaged death.

Now as Fanny put cool cloths on her son's brow and stared anxiously for signs of consciousness, she was given new causes for terror.

'Look!' one Okey sister whispered to the other, nodding towards the bed.

The other sister stared, rolled her eyes to her sister and whispered. 'Jack.'

'Yes,' whispered the first. 'Yes. You see him too?'

'What? What?' gasped Fanny.

'But look,' said the first sister, 'only at his knees.'

'That's right,' said the other. 'Jack is only at his knees.'

'It's all right,' the first reassured Fanny. 'It's only when we see Jack at someone's shoulder that we know—you know. . . .'[5]

Fanny had come to London with Tom, intending to spend only a few days and then travel on to Penrith. Cecilia was expecting her first child, and Fanny had thought nothing could be more wonderful than to be present when her first grandchild was born. But Cecilia was almost forgotten as Anthony continued so gravely ill.

Word came to her in London that Cecilia's baby was born. She had had a little girl, whom she and John were naming after the grandmother, Frances Trollope Tilley. Fanny nodded and resumed her vigil, eyeing her young helpers with dread as they came in and out of the room. Were they seeing Jack again? Closer to the shoulders now? She did not believe in such things; and yet, to a degree she did—and was frightened. Who knew? Who could be sure?

Fanny was slow to relax as Anthony began to come out of the shadows. 'He's getting better,' Tom tried to reassure her. 'He's going to be all right.' But Fanny had been very frightened. She lingered near her youngest son until he was actually on his feet, walking about, eating three meals a day, and almost ready to go back to his work at the Post Office. Only then was she finally able to leave him and go, along with Tom, to Penrith and Cecilia and the new grandchild.

Leaving Anthony, she still had no idea of the problems that were waiting for him after he recovered—the endlessly spiralling debt, his involvement with the girl who had such a vengeful mother. Anxiety about these problems may have helped to make him ill.

But his mother, so sharp-eyed and observant of the world around her, was not so quick at probing beneath the surface. It seemed never to occur to her to wonder *why* her youngest son was silent and unconfiding, and she could only deplore his sullen and uncommunicative attitude.

The new grandchild was delightful. Life at Penrith with Cecilia and John was wholly agreeable. John was almost as dedicated a walker as Tom, and so when Fanny arose at four or five in the morning, she wakened both the young men, who then set off for long tramps around the lakes while she sat down to her daily writing stint. Tom and John returned, exuding fresh air and virtue, by around eight-thirty or nine, and then it was time for the family breakfast. After that, John took off for his duties as surveyor for the Post Office, Tom went to his writing desk, and Fanny and Cecilia were free to enjoy the baby and plan the social activities for the rest of the day.

Life was so agreeable, in fact, and the area was so picturesque that Fanny began to wonder if she had found the place where she wanted to settle. Autumn came, and Tom began to talk about winter in Paris. Yes indeed, said his mother, Paris was very pleasant in the winter, but this time why did not Tom go by himself and have a real bachelor holiday? Tom was intrigued by the idea and soon departed. Now when Fanny and Cecilia rode out in the gig of an afternoon, Fanny was looking for land to purchase on which to build a house of her own.

The serial publication of *Michael Armstrong* was drawing to a close, and Colburn was planning a hard-cover edition. Fanny, as sympathetic as ever to the plight of exploited children, had become alarmed by various demonstrations in the factory towns and wondered if the book had been a good idea, after all. True, she wanted small children everywhere to have easier lives and not be forced to stand at machines for fifteen hours a day, but she wanted the change to come about quietly, sensibly, with no public disorder. Unlike young Dickens, who gloried in flinging out challenges, never mind what he created, Fanny trembled at shouting crowds; shoving; pushing; the throwing of brickbats, overturning of carriages, and smashing of windows. Manners, manners! And when it seemed that manners were not providing a decent life, mockery was her chosen weapon.

The Widow Barnaby, published in 1839, had become a great favourite of the public. Accordingly, she was now busy writing a sequel to that book, *The Widow Married*. Meantime, she had also begun on still another light novel, *The Blue Belles of Scotland*.

Two novels at once? Yes, of course, for Fanny had at last located three attractive acres in Penrith, not far from Cecilia and John's house, and was eager to buy them and begin building a house there. She had already discussed with Colburn a novel to follow *The Widow Married*, but the Scottish novel was something else entirely, and so, anxious for ready money, she felt justified in offering it to another publisher, Saunders and Otley. When the new publisher announced a forthcoming novel by Mrs Trollope, Colburn was at first astonished, then outraged, crying 'breach of contract' and promising public exposure of Fanny's perfidy.

Fanny begged John Tilley for advice, wrote to her brother, Henry, and to Tom in Paris. Surely Colburn would not dare denounce her publicly as a greedy, grasping, mercenary writer? Surely she had done nothing really wrong? She still planned to deliver to him the novel they had discussed. What should she do? How should she save herself and her reputation?

A flurry of letters, a series of agitated meetings did not really settle anything. However, the fuss gradually died down with none of the scandal Fanny had feared. In due time the new publishers, Saunders and Otley, published *The Blue Belles*. In due time Colburn capitulated and published the novel originally agreed upon.

Long before all that, however, in the winter of 1841, while the charges and countercharges were still being made, Fanny contracted with Richard Bentley for yet another travel book. Threats of revolution in France and general warfare in Italy seemed to have subsided for a while. At last Fanny was going to journey to the country of which she had dreamed since she was a girl translating Dante. There was *un voyage à faire, et Italie au bout!*

She left Penrith on 2nd April 1841 to meet Tom, who had come from Paris to join her in London. Together they journeyed across the Channel to spend some time in Paris and then travel on to Italy.

Milan, Florence, Rome—Fanny and Tom followed the regular pilgrims' route, and Fanny was enchanted by everything.

Letters from home caught up with them erratically. Anthony was not much of a correspondent, and so it was months after the event before Fanny learned that he had done some journeying on his own. Accepting a post nobody else much wanted, he had gone to be a travelling clerk to a surveyor of the postal system in Ireland. The nominal salary was less than he was receiving in London, but travelling expenses as he visited outlying postal offices would more than triple it. Looking forward to four hundred pounds a year, he had gone to the family lawyer to borrow enough money to pay off the persistent moneylender who had persecuted him so long. Anthony had felt great joy in seeing the last of him, and perhaps even greater joy in sailing far beyond the aggrieved young girl who thought he had promised to marry her.

Ireland! From all he had heard, it was a strange, wild, primitive country, and he hoped that what he had heard was true. If ever he was to begin a new life, he thought, such surroundings were what he needed. Half-frightened, half-exhilarated, he arrived in Dublin in September 1841, and before too long he discovered that his hopes were coming true. Ireland, unhappy, neglected, and abused adjunct to the British Isles, became the land where Anthony Trollope found himself.

23

Carlton Hill – Italy Again – And Again – Anthony Married

The situation was beautiful—a rise overlooking the ruins of Brougham Castle and the confluence of the Eden River with the Lowther. The house was built with almost magical swiftness, a gracious foursquare dwelling on the highest part of the site, to take advantage of the view. Fanny and Tom were moving in to the new house in Penrith within months after their return from Italy in the spring of 1842, so that Fanny could be present at the birth of her second grandchild.

Fanny called the house Carlton Hill and laughed when her new neighbour, Sir George Musgrave, warned her that she would not live there long. In the course of arranging for a drive up to the house from the road, a small spring had been diverted. It was a 'holy well', Sir George said, and anyone who tampered with it could never succeed in establishing himself near it. Sir George might well be listened to on such matters. His own manor was Edenhall, and its fortunes (celebrated in a poem by Henry Wadsworth Longfellow) depended on an ancient decorated glass goblet, which bore the legend:

> When this cup shall break or fall
> Farewell the luck of Edenhall.

However, Sir George made no attempt to keep this lucky goblet safe in a locked cupboard but let any visitor handle it. 'You take your chances,' Fanny told him, 'and I take mine'.

Tom embarked on a grand landscaping project for the new residence, planting hundreds of young trees in a long alley to provide a future promenade sheltered from the wind but open to the lovely views. Fanny furnished the interior in her usual easy, comfortable way and was soon entertaining the superstitious Sir George and his wife, Lady Musgrave, and other neighbours at dinners, teas, or evening parties. Her chief joys in Penrith were Cecilia, her two-year-old namesake, Fanny, and the new grandson, Cecil, with whom she spent as much time as possible.

Anthony came on a visit in August. Fanny and Tom were both surprised by the change in him. One year in Ireland and he seemed to move with a new assurance. He liked his work, he said. He rode long hours in the saddle to remote hamlets to check on complaints about mail delivery or to plot more efficient routes for the postmen. The surveyor whose clerk he was allowed him full authority, pleased to have him doing all the hard work. But he did have some free time as well, and Anthony's face had an unusual glow as he told them that he had bought a horse and hunted weekly with the local pack. He did not elaborate, but it was clear that this gave him special pleasure. There was joy in the chase, satisfaction in being accepted as an equal by the hunting gentry of the county where he lived. He liked the Irish people, he told them, the poor, feckless peasants as well as the landowners. He liked the land.

Fanny sighed with relief to see this troubled son happy at last. Who would have dreamed that such a wild, uncivilized place as Ireland could bring him such content? But perhaps its very roughness allowed him to accept his own turbulent nature more easily. For once he was not a misfit.

Old grudges and hostilities between Tom and Anthony seemed to have vanished. Anthony asked his brother if he would like to go with him when he returned to Ireland, to see the country and to join him in a good, strenuous walking tour of the Killeries. Tom accepted the invitation, and soon Fanny was saying good-bye to both her sons, now united in a new fellowship.

The two young men had a splendid time. Tom was impressed with the reliance placed on Anthony by his supervisor, and he was startled by Irish poverty. Then they had their 'grand walk' over the mountains above the Killeries. Tom never forgot 'the truly grand spectacular changes from dark, thick, enveloping cloud to brilliant sunshine, suddenly revealing all the mountains and the wonderful colouring of the intertwining sea beneath them, and then back to cloud and mist and drifting sleet again'. They returned from a walk, wet to the skin, to dine at a local inn. Wrapped in blankets like Roman senators, they feasted on roast goose and whiskey punch.

Fanny wrote steadily every morning. She had completed *A Visit to Italy* soon after returning to England in the early spring, and Bentley had duly published it. She had been in awe of Italy for so long and read and heard so much about it that her observations were rather routine and secondhand. But it was another book by Mrs Trollope, so people bought it and read it. Now, because the widow Barnaby had been popular through two appearances, Fanny was inventing more adventures for her and the confidence man she had married, once again sending her heroine to the United States. *The Barnabys in America* occupied her early morning hours. But after that, the day stretched out before her. She was discovering a dearth of company in Penrith. The weather was cold, grey, and mean, discouraging for rambles or any sort of outdoor activity.

By the time Tom returned from his visit to Ireland, his mother was beginning to talk wistfully about the Italian sunshine they had enjoyed at the same time the year before. The winter seemed endless. When spring finally came, Fanny's mind was made up. She had had enough of living at Penrith. Never mind that she had built Carlton Hill at some expense not a year before. Never mind all the trees and shrubs Tom had planted. Let Sir George say that the curse of the 'holy well' had been fulfilled. Let anybody who wanted call Carlton Hill another Trollope's Folly. She did not care. She was through with it.

Soon after her sixty-third birthday she kissed Cecilia, John, and the babies good-bye, left Tom to dispose of Carlton Hill and its furnishings, and departed to visit Cousin Fanny Bent at Exeter. Two months later, his mission completed, Tom joined her at Exeter. Always ready with some classical allusion, Tom had his own valediction for Carlton Hill. He and his mother had simply decided 'the sun yoked his horses too far from Penrith town'.

The Barnabys in America was finished and in Colburn's hands, and Fanny was already busy with another novel. But she could write anywhere. Tom also could write his essays, sketches, and squibs at a desk in any location. Fanny and Tom walked up and down a quiet lane in Exeter, discussing this city and that as possible residences for the next year. They talked of Dresden; they spoke of Rome; they both loved Paris and thought of spending a year there. But Fanny was eager for winter sun, and she wondered about Florence. They had liked it so much when they visited it on their Italian tour and had made friends among the sizeable English community there. Furthermore those friends had indicated that living was cheap in Florence. If they could settle where basic costs were minimal, they would have that much more money for extensive travels in the summertime. They decided to try Florence for a while.

They left England in early September 1843, prolonged their journey by a tour of Savoy, and finally arrived in Florence where they found an apartment in Via dei Malcontenti, so named because the road led eventually to the local prison. But the rooms of the apartment were large and cool and gracious, and Fanny refused to find the address ominous. She and Tom settled in and Fanny resumed her regular schedule of rising at dawn to write on the current novel-in-progress. Afternoons and evenings were soon as social as even Fanny could wish.

Lord Holland was the British minister to Florence at the time, and he and his extremely pretty wife were lavish in their hospitality. Their '*omnium-gatherum* dinners and receptions' were of the most generous and catholic sort. From time to time they also entertained more select groups, which led some wit to declare that Lady Holland received in two fashions—*en ménage* and *en ménagerie*. Since Fanny and her son were invited to entertainments in both styles, they could find the much repeated joke amusing.

One surprise was again meeting a friend from the months in Cincinnati—the talented Hiram Powers, now perfecting his skills as a sculptor in Florence. Astonished at renewing their acquaintance in such a different situation, Fanny and Hiram reminisced about Dorfeuille's 'Hell', the young Hiram's ingenious waxwork and electric contrivances, and Fanny's translation of Dante for the visitors to the Infernal Regions. For the first time in years Fanny allowed herself to remember the ill-fated bazaar she had built in that far-off city. To Hiram, who had been there also, she could speak with some bitterness about the comments Harriet Martineau had made in the book she had written after her return from a tour of the United States. 'A deformity' Miss Martineau had termed the bazaar, and she hardly wondered that the natives called it Trollope's Folly.¹ But Hiram had shared in some of the imagination and hope that had gone into its erection. He had been nearby throughout the dreadful days when it failed before it was fairly started. With Hiram, Fanny could even speak a little about Henry, dead ten years now, for Hiram remembered him as a cheerful youth, clever at theatricals.

The great event of the winter, the event by which Florentine residents dated what had happened before and after, was the flooding of the Arno. A series of heavy rains caused the catastrophe, the river rising swollen until it was pouring out over a third of the city. Gazing out of the windows of the apartment in Via dei Malcontenti, Fanny had watched the water advancing, then lapping at the foundations of the house in which she sat, then rising and still rising until five feet of water washed through the ground floor. Tom, of course, was soon out in a boat, making his way to Giotto's tower to survey the scene from that vantage point. He came back to his mother with a great many stories to tell, but the most remarkable tale was of a cradle with a crying baby in it, floating down the river on the flood. Someone on a lower storey of the tower had acted promptly, thrown out a rope, lassoed the cradle, and brought it and its occupant to safety. Gradually, the waters subsided, and the slime left behind was cleaned away, the damage repaired.

Charles Dickens and his wife, Kate, came to Florence after the flood and called upon Mrs Trollope. It was Tom's first meeting with the novelist, and he was surprised by what seemed like 'a dandified, pretty-boy-looking sort of figure . . . with a slight flavour of the whipper-snapper. . . .' Further acquaintance, and ultimately friend-ship, led Tom to change those first impressions. As Dickens grew older, he lost his delicate, almost fragile look and became bronzed and reddened by wind and weather. But Tom would always remem-ber Dickens's eyes, 'not blue, but of a very distinct and brilliant hazel—the colour traditionally assigned to Shakespeare's eyes'. And from the first meeting in Florence, on through the years, he was dazzled by the charm of Dickens's manner. 'There was a peculiar

humorous protest in it when recounting or hearing anything specially
absurd, as who should say, "Pon my soul this is *too* ridiculous! This
passes all bounds!" and bursting out afresh as though the sense of
the ridiculous overwhelmed him like a tide. . . . His enthusiasm was
boundless.'[2]

Perhaps Fanny talked a little with Charles Dickens about the
repercussions that resulted when one wrote about some social issue.
All through the previous year Colburn had been issuing her latest
novel, *Jessie Phillips, A Tale of Today*, as a monthly serial. Despite
her reluctance to make propaganda in this book, Fanny had attacked
the new Poor Law through the story of her pathetic heroine. This
year Colburn was publishing it in book form, but Fanny almost
wished the whole thing forgotten. Once again she seemed to have
stirred up agitation. Hard to believe, but there were actually people
who felt the poor did not have any '*right* to a sufficiency of necessary
food to sustain the life that God has given them'.[3] Dickens might
enjoy stirring up controversies, but Fanny did not. As a result, she
was determined not to let her sympathies dictate themes for her
books any longer. She would write purely romantic fiction, with the
satirical overtones she could not resist. Currently she was working on
such a novel, *The Laurringtons: or Superior People*.

Letters came frequently enough from England to keep her informed of the welfare of Cecilia, John, and the Tilley children. She
heard less often from Ireland, and not until the spring of 1844 did
she learn that Anthony was planning to be married.

In the new world he had found for himself, Anthony had met
Rose Heseltine before he had been there a year. She was not an
Irish girl but the daughter of a bank manager in Rotherham, in
Yorkshire, holidaying with her family at the seaside resort of
Kingstown, near Dublin. Secretive Anthony had not said a word
about her when he visited Penrith in September 1842. He and Rose
had already pledged themselves to an engagement, but Anthony
seemed to have some need for a life wholly apart from his family.
He had taken Tom with him for a walking tour of the Killeries but
confided nothing about Rose. Almost with reluctance, he wrote two
years later to inform his mother that he would be getting married in

June at the home of Rose's parents. He did not urge his mother or brother to be present.

Rose Heseltine. Anthony's mother puzzled over the name, which was all Anthony gave her to go by. Was she tall, short, beautiful, homely, bright, dull? How like Anthony to tell her nothing, she who loved detail, anecdote, gossip.

Actually, Rose Heseltine was a moderately pretty young woman, five years younger than Anthony, with a steadiness of character that seemed to be just what he needed. She dressed nicely, was competent at all wifely duties, and totally loyal. A young woman wholly different from the mocking, here-today-gone-tomorrow woman that Anthony knew as his mother.

Anthony was still withholding something in the letter announcing his forthcoming marriage. He did not mention the fact that he had begun a novel. His work for the Post Office was arduous and time-consuming. He loved those days of the month when he could ride himself half-blind at the hunt. But stories and fantasies had been simmering in his imagination for years. He had made a few stabs at writing during the London days. Then, in September 1843, an old Harrow friend, John Merivale, had visited him in Ireland. On one of their walks through the countryside they had come upon a deserted house of some former elegance. The grounds were overgrown with weeds, the drive only an echo of a road. Something in the sight had stirred Anthony's heart. Was he remembering one house after another in which he and his family had lived when he was a child and then deserted? Whatever the unconscious motivations, he was seized with the desire to re-create the story of this house, the people who had lived in it, and the reasons why they had left it.

He was well into his first novel, *The Macdermots of Ballycloran*, when he wrote to his mother in Florence, in the spring of 1844. But of this he told her, the author of dozens of books by now, not one word.

24

Anthony – Theodosia Garrow – Cecilia

'I acknowledge the weakness of a great desire to be loved,—of a strong wish to be popular with my associates. No child, no boy, no lad, no young man, had ever been less so.'[1]

Anthony confessed the truth in the autobiography he wrote when he was sixty-one. At that age the 'years of suffering, disgrace, and inward remorse' that he had known as a child and young man were still sharp in his memory. 'There had clung to me a feeling that I had been looked upon always as an evil, an encumbrance, a useless thing,—as a creature of whom those connected with him had to be ashamed.' Perhaps it was as well that his mother never had to read those words. Careless and thoughtless she might have been during his childhood, and sometimes mocking of his awkwardness, but could she ever have regarded him as 'an evil'?

'Even my few friends who had found with me a certain capacity for enjoyment were half afraid of me,' Anthony recalled. 'But from the day on which I set my foot in Ireland all those evils went away from me. Since that time who has had a happier life than mine?'[2]

Rose Heseltine helped make it so, of course, though Anthony wrote nothing about her. Some students of his novels, charmed by such heroines as Lily Dale and Lucy Robarts in the Barchester series, or Lady Glencora, of the political, or Palliser series—all of whom brightened their propriety with glints of mischief—like to surmise that Rose was the inspiration of their special liveliness. It may be. No one knows enough about Rose Heseltine to argue. But one does know enough about Frances Trollope to hear a faint echo of her voice when Lady Glencora lightly and lovingly rebukes an over-solemn friend with a periodic 'Oh, don't be so stupid'.

'My marriage was like the marriage of other people,' Anthony wrote, 'and of no special interest to any one except my wife and me.'

But it was of some interest to his mother. She met the bride when she and Tom visited England and Penrith in the summer of 1844, shortly after Anthony's marriage. Anthony and Rose travelled to Penrith from Rotherham where the marriage had taken place, so Rose could meet Anthony's family. Fanny seems not to have been dazzled by Rose, but she liked her and called her 'an excellent little wife'. In her turn, Rose was charmed by her mother-in-law. She was amazed by Fanny's industry, loved to hear her talk, and was impressed by the energy with which she organized picnics and excursions.

During that visit in 1844, Anthony said nothing about the novel on which he was working and which was only half-completed. It was not until almost a year later—after he and Rose had spent the first months of their marriage at Anthony's new post in Clonmel, in southern Ireland, and after Fanny and Tom had spent another winter in the apartment in Via dei Malcontenti in Florence, that they all met again in Penrith. Cecilia, John, and the children had now moved into the house Fanny had built, Carlton Hill.

By this time Anthony had finished his novel and brought it with him to entrust to his mother 'to do with it the best she could among the publishers in London'. No one had read it, he said, but his wife. Handing it over to his surprised mother, Anthony suggested that 'it would be as well that she should not look at it before she gave it to a publisher'.

Still defensive more than twenty years later, Anthony wrote, 'I knew that she did not give me credit for the sort of cleverness necessary for such work. I could see in the faces and hear in the voices of those of my friends who were around me at the house in Cumberland—my mother, my sister, my brother-in-law, and I think, my brother—that they had not expected me to come out as one of the family authors. There were three or four in the field before me, and it seemed to be almost absurd that another should wish to add himself to the number. My father had written much— those long ecclesiastical descriptions—quite unsuccessfully. My mother had become one of the popular authors of the day. My brother had commenced, and been fairly well paid for his work. My sister, Mrs. Tilley, had also written a novel, which was at the time in manuscript—which was published afterwards without her name, and was called *Chollerton*. I could perceive that this attempt of mine was felt to be an unfortunate aggravation of the disease.'[3]

Ireland had changed Anthony, but not altogether. In the company of his mother, brother, and sister, he still felt himself the odd child out—it seemed to him 'absurd' that he should want to be one of the family authors. Never mind that Cecilia, who had recently become very, very High Church, had written a book that was basically a religious tract. Never mind that Tom's writing to date, although he was paid for it, was both wordy and fugitive. Anthony felt them all staring at him in amazement and disapproval.

His mother took him at his word and did not read the thick manuscript he gave her. However, when she went in to London on her way back to Florence, she placed it with a man named Newby, who had also published Anne and Emily Brontë's novels, and reported to her son that he was printing it at his own expense and that Anthony would receive half the profits.

As it turned out, there were no profits,[4] but Anthony accepted that stoically and had already begun on another novel, *The Kellys and the O'Kellys*, again a story with Irish characters and background. In a curious parallel to his mother's experience, the shock of moving to a new and totally foreign country and observing unfamiliar ways and manners was what started Anthony to writing in earnest. For his mother, America, which she disliked, had been the catalyst. Anthony liked Ireland. To be sure, he was distressed by the general poverty, but he was even more amazed by the cheerful bravado with which most people bore it. He was amazed by the open show of emotion around him. Tears were as close to the surface as laughter. Rage exploded and was dissipated. Tenderness was freely expressed. All of this seemed to raise some shutter in Anthony's mind. He began to observe his fellow humans more objectively than he had ever done before. Their behaviour was no longer filtered through the screen of how it reflected on him. He stood aside and apart—not a misfit, for he had been accepted by gentry and ordinary folk alike—but a tolerant and fascinated onlooker. America had unleashed his mother's mockery and sarcasm. Ireland released Anthony's humanity.

Tom, in Florence, was not standing aside for once. At thirty-five he was at last falling in love. To his own surprise, his love was not beautiful by any of his previous standards. She was, instead, an exotic.

Mr and Mrs Joseph Garrow had come with letters of introduction to call on Fanny at the apartment in Via dei Malcontenti, not long after the flood in the spring of 1844. They were an unusual couple. Joseph Garrow was the son (illegitimate according to some reports) of an English civil servant stationed in India and a high-caste Brahmin woman. He had been sent to England as a youth to be educated for the law but was more interested in playing the violin and drawing. Both his parents had died while he was at school, after which he was supported by his father's English kin. Then, still a relatively young man, he had married a wealthy widow, Theodosia Fisher, who had been born Theodosia Abrams. She was twenty-three years older than he and already had a grown son and daughter. The son had severed all family ties by becoming a Roman Catholic priest, but the daughter, Harriet Fisher, was a plain, sweet-tempered young woman who lived with her mother and continued to do so after the marriage.

The birth of a daughter to Mr and Mrs Joseph Garrow in 1825, when Mrs Garrow was fifty-nine years old, startled everyone who knew them. In Torquay, where the Garrows had an estate called The Braddons, people looked at each other in amazement and surmise and then frequently glanced towards the self-effacing Harriet Fisher. Fortunately, Mrs Garrow had enough money to frighten speculation to a muted whisper.

The child was named Theodosia, after Mrs Garrow. She was tenderly cared for by her half-sister, Harriet, and it was this Theodosia, grown to be a slender, tawny, nineteen-year-old with great grey eyes, who gradually wakened Thomas Adolphus Trollope to love.

Thomas Adolphus, whose nature it was to ignore anything unpleasant, seems not to have been aware of any speculation about Theodosia's parentage. He wrote in a forthright way about the close 'union and affection' that existed between the half-sisters, Harriet Fisher and Theodosia Garrow. Harriet, who was seventeen or eighteen years older than Theodosia, was, according to Tom, 'the most absolutely unselfish human being I ever knew, and one of the most loving hearts. . . . She was simply nobody in the family save the ministering angel in the house to all of them. . . . *Her* life was not made brilliant by the notice and friendship of distinguished men. Everything was for the younger sister. And through long years of this eclipse, and to the last, she fairly worshipped the sister who eclipsed her.'⁵

He wrote in quite a different vein about Mrs Garrow. For once he abandoned altogether his equable tone for a harshness so unique that one would wonder about the Garrow family even without other hints. Mrs Garrow was 'not an amiable woman'. In her late seventies when Tom met her, she was still vigorous, with a pair of 'still brilliant and fierce black eyes'. But she was 'in no wise a clever woman', while her husband and young Theodosia were both markedly clever, and 'thus produced a closeness of companionship and alliance between the father and daughter which painfully excited the jealousy of the wife and mother'. Plain, good-hearted Harriet tried to mediate between the angry old woman and the other members of the family, particularly defending Theodosia, but it was not easy. 'I am afraid', Tom wrote, 'that Mrs. Garrow did not love her second daughter at all.'⁶ Taking after his mother to a degree, Tom seemed never to ask why such an extraordinary emotional situation should exist in the Garrow family.

But there was more to Theodosia Garrow than the emotional tangle of her family background. She was indeed clever, as Tom wrote, with a talent for poetry, for sketching, for playing the piano, and for singing.

Theodosia had been a child at Torquay when the poet, Elizabeth Barrett, spent a summer there. Miss Barrett was an invalid, but Theodosia, who had read Miss Barrett's poetry, insisted that her big sister, Harriet, take her to visit the ailing celebrity, though she hardly ever received visitors. They were not admitted. Determined to be noticed, the child gathered white violets and returned home to spin out a rhyming tribute to accompany the flowers, which she delivered later to the Barrett house. Mortality and impending death were common poetic subjects in the 1830s, but even so, Theodosia's invocations to an 'innocent life, ebbing so swiftly away. . . .' and 'innocent beings like thee fade with gentle decay,' must have been less than consoling to Elizabeth Barrett.[7]

Miss Barrett acknowledged the flowers and the poem with a polite note. Years later, after she had become acquainted with an older Theodosia Garrow in Florence, she would assess her as 'very clever —very accomplished—with talents and tastes of various kinds—a musician and linguist, in most modern languages, I believe—and a writer of fluent graceful melodious verses,—you cannot say more.'

Thomas Adolphus Trollope was not aware of love at first sight when he met her in the spring of 1844. Attuned to all sorts of social nuances, he noticed that she and her half-sister, Harriet Fisher, were dressed very dowdily by Florentine standards. But there was a charm in Theodosia's soft voice, a response to Tom's conventional remarks that made him feel that he 'had got hold of something of a quite other calibre of intelligence from anything I had been recently accustomed to meet with in those around me.'[8]

As the weeks passed, Theodosia, a quick study of her surroundings, improved her wardrobe. Soon Tom saw her looking very much the reverse of dowdy when he spied her in Florentine drawing rooms. Watching her increasing popularity, he thought she was becoming like a new 'Corinne' in the little English community. He began to seek her out and to spend as much time as possible at her side.

But he was still not ready to admit anything like love. In the summer of 1844 Fanny and Tom had travelled to England to meet Anthony and his new bride, Rose, at Penrith. In the summer of 1845 they were again in England (this was the year that Anthony gave his mother his first novel, asking her to find a publisher for it). Though Tom saw Theodosia frequently during the winter months, there is no record that he was unduly disturbed by the summer partings or suffered any of a lover's anguish.

In the spring of 1846 Anthony and Rose's first child was born, a boy whom they named Henry Merivale, after one of Anthony's few friends in his childhood years at Harrow. This summer Fanny and

Tom did not return to England but spent the warm months touring the mountains of Tyrol and Bohemia with a group of friends.

Through this time, as always, Fanny was at her desk each morning. The novels followed each other, three full fat volumes each, year after year. Colburn published *The Attractive Man* in 1846 and also a brightly satirical account of British bad manners abroad, *The Robertses on Their Travels*. Fanny had also completed a series of sketches called *Travels and Travellers*, which Colburn had published. No wonder a critic would write of 'a very Trollope' and know that his readers understood exactly what sort of indefatigable traveller he meant.

Fanny and Tom finally made their way to England again in the spring of 1847, after visits to the Riviera and a stay in Paris. They had a host of friends to see in London and parties to attend almost every night. Fanny saw her brother, Henry, again and was distressed that he did not look well. Then they travelled on to Penrith to visit Cecilia, John, and the children and to greet Anthony, Rose, and their small son, who were also visiting Carlton Hill.

Anthony had some of the first copies of *The Macdermots of Ballycloran* with him and gave one to his mother. But there was too much going on every day for her to read the book just then. Perhaps the constant activity prevented her also from noticing that Cecilia was alternately excited and fatigued in a way she had not been before.

Fanny and Tom were stopping at Baden-Baden, slowly making their way back to Florence, when Fanny had a letter from John. Cecilia was ill. The doctor had advised her to winter in a warm climate, and so John was sending her to her mother in Florence. He did not say so, but with a terrible premonition, Fanny knew that Cecilia had the same disease that had killed Henry and Emily. She rushed Tom back to England to meet Cecilia and escort her to Florence while she hurried on to Italy to make everything ready. The result of Tom's impetuous journey was that he missed Cecilia at Southampton and never caught up with her on the way to Florence.

But Fanny was in Florence to greet her daughter and hurry her to bed and then to call in a local doctor. By the time Tom arrived,

Fanny had the doctor's opinion. Rome would be a better place than Florence for Cecilia to spend the winter. Fanny had already arranged for an apartment in Via delle Quattro Fontane. Tom had only to help her and Cecilia make the move.

Tom made one diffident request. He wondered if his mother would invite Theodosia Garrow to spend the winter with them in Rome. Sure that his mother had no idea of his interest in the young woman, he was surprised that she accepted his request so quickly and urged Theodosia to join them.

Mr Garrow, a doting father, was reluctant to have his daughter away from him all winter, and Mrs Garrow, an unloving mother, was unwilling to grant Theodosia any special pleasure. But Harriet Fisher was an ally. She had seen the growing attachment between Thomas Trollope and her young half-sister, and as Tom saw it, she was 'the good fairy. Without the strenuous exertion of her influence on her mother and Mr. Garrow the object would hardly have been accomplished. Of course the plea put forward was the great desirability of taking advantage of such an opportunity of seeing Rome.'⁹

And so they departed for Rome—Fanny, her ailing daughter, Tom, and Theodosia Garrow.

For Tom, the wonder of that winter was the friendship that was formed between Theodosia and Cecilia. He could hardly imagine two young women more different. Cecilia, pale, blonde, and very English, was a strict observer of High Church rituals. Theodosia, dark-haired, olive-skinned, with a mixture of Indian, English and Jewish heritages, had no interest in organized religion. Her 'faith' was poetry, music, art—and Italian independence, a new passion she had acquired since coming to Italy. Somehow Cecilia and Theodosia found a bond in their shared emotionalism, softly and sympathetically expressed.

Tom was not so surprised that his mother also appeared to like the young guest. His mother got on well with most people. Still, it was now his conclusion that 'it would have been very difficult for any one to live in the same house without loving her'.¹⁰ His own opportunities for enjoying Theodosia's company extended through the day as he escorted her to the various galleries and antiquities that it was obligatory for a visitor to see.

Fanny worked each morning on the latest novel-in-progress, a story set in the Regency years, the period of her own youth. The rest of the day she devoted to Cecilia, doing what she could to amuse her daughter while she rested in the sun. They talked idly of all sorts of things, even speculating now and then about the revolutions that were simmering all over Italy that winter, and they commented on Tom's new revolutionary zeal, acquired under Theodosia's spell. But Cecilia's talk drifted most often to her babies back in England. She wondered how they were growing, what they were doing. She talked of John and how kind and considerate he was, reporting how he wrote in his letters that he was considering giving up the house in Penrith and finding a house in London where Cecilia would be nearer to good medical care when she returned. Fanny nodded and agreed, and was willing to talk endlessly about John and the grandchildren. But all the while she watched anxiously for signs that Cecilia was growing stronger and healthier. She must be. Impossible that Cecilia should be doomed as Henry and Emily had been.

Towards the end of the winter, Mr Garrow arrived in Rome to escort his daughter back to Florence. His arrival brought Tom to a decision at last. He loved Theodosia Garrow. He wanted to marry her and was ready to make a formal request of her hand.

There was a scene in Rome; and then, after Tom followed Mr Garrow to Florence, another one there. Mr and Mrs Garrow finally based their objections on financial grounds. Theodosia had only one thousand pounds in her own right. Thomas Adolphus possessed nothing except what he might inherit at the death of his mother and in the meantime what he could earn from 'the farm which he carried under his hat'. Mr and Mrs Garrow did not think this made Tom much of a match. But Theodosia talked privately with Harriet Fisher, and whatever Theodosia wanted, Harriet wanted for her. With that strange influence she was able to exert now and then, the usually self-effacing half-sister won parental consent.

After that, Tom acted quickly. He saw no need for an elaborate ceremony, no need to summon his mother and sister from Rome. On 3rd April 1848, he and Theodosia Garrow were married in the British minister's chapel in Florence. The small group that was present went to breakfast afterwards at the Garrow house. Then Tom swept his young bride off for a walking tour of Tuscany.

Fanny and Cecilia were apprised of the marriage by letter. They smiled, happy for Tom. Surely it was time that he, almost thirty-six, should be getting married. If Fanny had any small worry, it concerned how her convenient arrangement with Tom might be upset by marriage. She hoped she had made it clear, without saying so directly, that she would be delighted to share a home with Tom and his wife just as she had with Tom alone.

Tom and Theodosia reappeared in Rome rather sooner than expected, as Theodosia was not quite ready for the full course of one of Tom's strenuous walks. Fanny and Cecilia greeted them with hugs, kisses, and congratulations, and Fanny was soon reassured to learn that the newly married couple would be living with her.

But her greater anxiety persisted. Cecilia had not noticeably benefited by the months she had spent in Rome and was almost as frail and easily exhausted as she had been upon arrival. However, by now her longing for her husband, her children, and her own home was so great that Fanny could not argue long against her determination to return to England. The arrangements were made. Fanny, Tom, and Theodosia saw her aboard the ship that would carry her home, and Fanny's heart was heavy as she kissed her good-bye.

25

Deaths – New Arrangements – Birth

It was a shock to all who knew her when Harriet Fisher, Theodosia's doting half-sister, contracted smallpox and died in the autumn of 1848. Theodosia was stunned, but now she had the support and sympathy of both her husband, Thomas Adolphus, and her mother-in-law. A further surprise about Harriet's death did not come until some time later when her will was read. Then her family learned that she had left all her money—of which she seemed to have a great deal more than anyone suspected—to Theodosia. This last gesture of affection would, in due time, make life much easier for both Thomas Adolphus and Theodosia.

Before that came about, however, Mr and Mrs Garrow had departed from Florence to take up residence again in their house near Torquay. For a while Fanny thought of making the journey with them. The turmoil across Europe that had made travelling difficult for the past year seemed to have subsided. The fighting in the streets of Paris, the disturbances in Rome and Naples, and the revolution in Venice, led by Fanny's old friend, General Pepe, had all died down. Still, Fanny lingered in Florence. Not until late February of 1849 did she, Tom, and Theodosia finally agree on plans. Fanny had one chief goal—to go to England and see Cecilia. Tom planned a sightseeing tour in France for Theodosia and himself. They decided to travel together as far as Aix-en-Provence. From there Fanny continued on her own to Ostend, the Channel crossing and the trip to London.

She had received no letters from Cecilia or John for several weeks and was haunted by fear of what she might find when she arrived at the house in Kensington that John Tilley had taken after Cecilia became so ill. It was late in the evening on her sixty-ninth birthday, 10th March 1849, when she arrived at the Tilley house, and it seemed a birthday present in itself that Cecilia was alive to greet her and whisper how very glad she was to see her mother again. But Fanny's relief was soon submerged in the awareness that she had arrived just in time.

On 4th April 1849, Cecilia died.

Anthony wrote from Mallow, the Irish seaside town that was his newest post:

> My dear John,
>   I cannot say that I have been sorry to get your last letter—I have felt so certain that since Cecilia's last relapse, that she could never recover, that I have almost wished that her sufferings should end. I know, that although you have expected her death, it will still come to you as a great blow—but you are not the man to give way to sorrow—You will be absent from your office, I suppose, for a month or six weeks—bring mama over here—it will be infinitely better for you—for you both—than remaining alone in the house which must for a time be so sad a place for you. . . . God bless you my dear John—I sometimes feel that I led you into more sorrow than happiness in taking you to Hadley.[1]

More letters were exchanged between Anthony and John. Anthony and Rose even offered to adopt one of the now motherless Tilley children. John appreciated the thought but could not agree to adoption. However, he would take it kindly if Anthony and Rose would keep the youngest child, Edith, for a while. Anthony was reluctant to commit himself to such an arrangement, fearing he would grow too attached to a child he must ultimately lose. Finally, in spite of Anthony's fears of emotional investment, he and John agreed that young Edith should stay with him for a time and that her grandmother would accompany John and the child to Ireland.[2]

The country that had inspired Anthony to novel writing interested Fanny but did not touch her deeply. She saw what was picturesque but hardly seemed aware of the poverty that was destroying the people. As always after a loss, she made no great show of grief but Cecilia's death had been a deep wound. Of the seven children she had borne only two were left to her, her eldest and youngest sons. And the curious distance that had always existed between her and the youngest still prevailed. Anthony was far more confident now than he once had been. A settled man with a good, pretty wife, two healthy little sons, he was making a name for himself as an efficient Post Office official, a man to rely on in spite of his often bluff manners. He was satisfying some enormous hunger for gentlemanly violence with his weekly hunting. He was also gratifying some other need by releasing his visions of the human scene into the novels on which he worked in the early hours of the morning.

One might have thought that the mother, who had written thirty-three books in the last seventeen years, and the son, who had now published two novels and was working on a third, would have had that interest in common. But writing is basically a lonely business, with nothing much to be said about it until the work is done, and then, for all the elaborate comments critics may make, the judgment still lies with the public. Fanny may have suggested to her son that English readers were not enticed by stories about Irish characters, Irish problems, Irish tragedies. Romance, a little comedy, and happy endings—those were what readers wanted. She herself was working on a new novel to be called *Petticoat Government*. After they had discussed their various writing projects, what more could they say? There was never the easy, idle chatter between Anthony and his mother that there was between her and Tom.

Tom was the one she fretted about during the weeks in Ireland. He and Theodosia had finished their ramble in France and were visiting the Garrows at Torquay. Letters from there reported that Mrs Garrow was so ill that they dared not leave her to join Fanny in Ireland. Fanny felt a jealous sense of rejection. Impossible that the disagreeable Mrs Garrow was going to die—she would live for ever. Fanny was the one who needed Tom and Theodosia, and if they were not going to make the journey to Ireland, she would certainly expect to see them when she returned to London.

When she arrived there, she received news of the death she had not expected.

Wrote Anthony to his brother from Mallow,

Dear Tom,
    I cannot pretend to condole with you on Mrs. Garrow's death, for it is impossible that it should be a subject of sorrow for you. But of course Theodosia must feel it. . . . Where do you mean to go?[3]

Where indeed? That was the question that was soon agitating Fanny to the exclusion of any other. Tom wrote that Mr Garrow was urging him and Theodosia to make their home in Torquay and that they were considering the proposition.

Fanny saw the little world she had built for herself dissolving. Tom leaving, Tom who had been her mainstay for the last eleven years? Theodosia leaving, the soft, pretty daughter-in-law, with whom she got along perfectly? She herself all alone? She reached frantically for some other solution, and an idea came to her. Instead of Tom and Theo joining Mr Garrow at The Braddons, Mr Garrow should join Tom, his wife, and Fanny in Florence. By this time they had all had news of Harriet Fisher's bequest to Theodosia. If Tom and Theodosia, Mr Garrow and Fanny, pooled their resources, they could live in splendid style. She wrote asking Tom and Theodosia to meet her in London for a conference.

They came to London, heard Fanny's plan, and were persuaded. Tom was, after all, a confirmed Florentine by now, charmed by the society there, endlessly fascinated by the small revolutions continually exploding in one Italian kingdom after another. Theodosia also loved the city and the place she had won in society there. Her one-time idol, Elizabeth Barrett, now married to Robert Browning, was a new resident. Dozens of other members of the English colony, including the ageing Walter Savage Landor, admired her greatly. Would she find the same ambience of culture, literature, and admiration in Torquay?

All that remained to do was convince Mr Garrow, and this proved not too difficult. By the spring of 1850 Tom, Theo, Mr Garrow, and Fanny were all in Florence. Before too long they had acquired the villa later to be known as Villino Trollope, and Tom and Theo had begun to furnish it according to their luxurious tastes, which Harriet Fisher had made it possible for them to gratify.

Fanny had what she wanted—Tom nearby and a nucleus of a

family, a book on which to work in the morning, and later a variety of social entertainments to keep her amused.

'We were great at picnics in those Florence days,' Thomas Adolphus wrote. 'Perhaps the most favourite place of all for such parties was Pratolino, a park belonging to the grand duke, about seven miles from Florence, on the Bologna road. . . . About three miles farther, still always ascending the slope of the Apennine, is a Servite monastery which is the cradle and mother establishment of the order. Sometimes we used to extend our rambles thither. . . . A much more favourite amusement of mine was a picnic arranged to last for two or three days, and intended to embrace objects farther afield. Vallombrosa was a favourite and admirably well-selected locality for this purpose. And many a day and moonlight night never to be forgotten have I spent there.'⁴

But picnics, even those extending for two or three days, were not the whole of Florentine amusements. 'Among the other things that contributed to make those Florence days very pleasant ones, we did a good deal in the way of private theatricals.' *The Rivals* was a popular choice, often repeated. Tom appeared once as Bob Acres but was not much of a success. Later, in another production, he took the part of Sir Anthony Absolute, in which he did better, and his mother was an enormous success as Mrs Malaprop.

There was talk of attending the Great Exhibition in London in the summer of 1851. Anthony wrote, urging them to come. But so much money had been spent in furnishing the Villino Trollope that Tom, Theodosia, and Fanny decided they could not afford the journey.

'I grieve to find that you and Theodosia do not intend coming to London next summer,' Anthony wrote to Tom in March. 'Your stay in Italy will, I presume, occasion my mother's. And there is our pleasant party broken up!' Rose was going to exhibit a threefold embroidered screen, and Anthony wrote self-mockingly that he meant to exhibit 'four 3 vol. novels—all failures!—which I look on as a great proof of industry at any rate'. He wondered if there was no such thing 'as a cheap trip from Florence by which a man could come to London and go back within a fortnight or so.' Eventually Tom, as much 'a very Trollope' as his mother, discovered such a trip and visited the Great Exhibition briefly.

The two novels regularly expected of Fanny appeared that year, *Mrs. Mathews, or Family Mysteries* and *Second Love, or Beauty and Intellect*. Tom was beginning to appear in print with large and serious volumes, mostly concerned with Italian or Florentine history. In the meantime, Anthony, who had been sent to the west of England on a special mission for the Post Office, was letting his writing lapse for a while. The new mission was demanding. It was all he could do to get in a few days of hunting now and then. But then, in the spring of 1852, he was inspired by a newspaper story about a good man caught in a situation where he took public money for a job that entailed no effort at all. Suddenly Anthony was envisaging an imaginary English county where such a situation was taking place. He saw the cathedral, the close, and not far away, the hostel for indigent old men where the innocent hero was employed. It was the birth of Barsetshire, a locale that inspired him to a series of novels about its inhabitants.

In the autumn he had a surprising bit of news from John Tilley. John had been walking in Kensington Gardens and met a friend who had told him that Theodosia Trollope was expecting a child. Anthony thought it was a curious way to receive the information and wondered it if was true. 'If so, why has not Tom told us what we should have been so glad to learn from him?' he wrote to his mother in Florence.

His mother wrote back, and so did Tom, confirming the news. After five years of marriage, Tom was to become a father. Anthony responded with a letter of congratulations in what he considered a joking vein. 'I am glad you are to have a child. One wants some one to exercise unlimited authority over, as one gets old and cross. If one blows up one's servants too much, they turn round, give warning, and repay one with interest. One's wife may be too much for one, and is not always a safe recipient for one's wrath. But one's children can be blown up to any amount without damage,—at any rate for a considerable number of years. The pleasures of paternity have been considerably abridged, since the good old Roman privilege of slaying their offspring at pleasure, has been taken from fathers. But the delights of flagellation, though less keen, are more enduring.'[5]

It was simply one of the baffling contradictions about Anthony that even as he was beginning to write a novel with the special sort of evenhanded grace that would characterize his fiction, he could be so misguided in an attempt at humour in a personal relationship.

Receiving such a letter, what could Tom do but shake his head, smile, and say, 'Well, that's Anthony.' And his mother, reading the letter, could only shake her head in agreement. She never had understood Anthony and never would.

'A daughter, I fear,' Anthony continued, 'does not offer so much innocent enjoyment. But some fathers do manage to torment their daughters with a great deal of evident and enviable satisfaction. I have none, and therefore have not turned my attention to that branch of the subject. . . . You don't at all say when you expect to see your child, but from Mama's letter to Rose I presume it will be early in the spring. I shall be very anxious to hear that Theo and her baby are well and out of danger. Alas, alas, the Duke of Wellington is dead, or of course you would have had him for a godfather.'

The baby did arrive in the early spring, in March, very near the time of Fanny's seventy-third birthday. And it was a girl, who was named Beatrice Harriet Catherine—an imposing name which was soon shortened to Bice by her adoring parents.

Hardly a month after young Beatrice's birth Anthony and Rose arrived for their first visit to Florence and the Villino Trollope.

26

Villino Trollope

A handsome marble staircase led to a large reception room. A long, dim library was filled with hundreds of books. Tiled hallways were studded with painted chests, suits of armour, statues of marble or terra cotta, or dark paintings of virgins or martyrs. The galleries and terrace looked out on the surrounding garden, formal with fountains, statues, cypress trees, and yew, and colourful with flowers. Beyond the garden, sheltered from the winds, was a small orange and lemon grove. Theodosia's inheritance, enhanced by the income from Fanny's writings and Tom's, contributions from Mr Garrow, and some returns from the sale of fruit from the little grove, had resulted in a richly beautiful residence on the Piazza dell' Independenza in Florence.[1]

Anthony and Rose were astonished by the magnificence of the Villino Trollope. None of the letters from Fanny or Tom had prepared them for such opulence. Their own lodgings, which had improved a great deal since the first days of their marriage, were humble compared to this. But Anthony's taste, and Rose's also, ran to English-country-house comfort rather than splendour, so they both admired the Villino Trollope without envy.

Theodosia was still somewhat an invalid after the birth of the baby. There was a pallor under the olive of her skin, but her dark hair blazed and crinkled, and her grey eyes were an astonishment in her oval face. She looked very foreign to Anthony and Rose. But she was so gently welcoming, so eager for them to enjoy their first visit, that they were charmed.

It is unlikely that either Anthony or Rose heard any echo of some gossip that had drifted through the English community during the last winter when a few of its members were amusing themselves by wondering about Theodosia Trollope's pregnancy. After all, she and Tom Trollope had been married for five years, hadn't they? with no sign of such an event before. Tom was fifteen years older than Theo, and had he not been away on one of his frequent junkets during most of the summer? There had been speculation as to who might have been a favoured visitor at the Villino Trollope during that period. The gossip was not really ill-natured, just an amusing way to pass the time, reminiscent of the sort of chat that had entertained the court circles in England forty years before, during the Regency. After the child was born and visitors decided that the baby favoured its mother but had no signs of Trollope heritage, the whisperers smiled and made a few more quiet remarks to each other. None of these insinuations seemed to reach any of the Trollopes, either those in residence or the visitors from England. Only a few cryptic remarks in letters that never met their eyes linger to tantalize later generations.[2]

Nothing spoiled Anthony's and Rose's visit to Florence. They said goodbye to Fanny, to Theo, to Tom and Mr Garrow and returned to England, pleased with their first view of foreign scenes and equally pleased to be going home. Soon after their return Anthony's special mission in England was completed. He and his little family went back to Ireland, where he was transferred from headquarters in Belfast to Dublin. He and Rose found a comfortable house in the suburb of Donnybrook, after which Anthony spent some time learning the geography of his new district. Then he resumed the habit of writing each morning. By late autumn he had finished *The Warden*.

At Villino Trollope, Fanny also continued to write. Her old publisher in London, Colburn, had been taken over by a new firm, Hurst and Blackett. Her novel, *The Young Heiress*, was published by them in that year of 1853.

Fanny was seventy-three. She suffered somewhat from arthritis and was having trouble with her teeth, which were being extracted one by one. But she was still faithful to her early morning stint at her desk, and then eager as always for each day's adventures. And she did not forget to be good company to Mr Garrow, whose consent to join the group had enabled her to keep a family around her.

Such an easy family to live with too. Tom made everything agreeable. Incipient crises vanished under his calm, beneficent approach. Maids might quit, cisterns spring leaks, gardeners run amok—it did not matter. Tom could cope.

Theo, delicate as a hothouse flower, was also easy. She never had tantrums or fell into rages or sulks. When she was well enough, she was busy with her own writing or translating. And could anyone call it a fault, least of all a grandmother, that Theo doted almost too fondly on her daughter? Young Beatrice, whom Anthony liked to call Bimba, but who was still Bice to her mother and father, was growing from an infant into a toddler and then into a small girl. Whether Theodosia was well or only mildly ill, her greatest joy was to be with the child and watch her play. Again, as in the days when she adored Elizabeth Barrett, Theo was inspired to poesy and wrote sixteen stanzas of verse about her daughter.

> In the noonday's golden pleasance,
>   Little Bice, baby fair,
> With a fresh and flowery presence,
>   Dances round her nurse's chair,
> In the old grey loggia dances, haloed by her shining hair. . . .

The tone was rather different from the rollicking one Fanny had conjured up years before at 16 Keppel Street when Tom and Henry had been children and she had sung and clapped:

> A captain bold in Halifax
> Who dwelt in country quarters . . .

But Fanny found no fault in the greater delicacy and refinement exhibited by her daughter-in-law. She had no fault to find with any of the arrangements in her life. Tom's taste and Theodosia's might be responsible for the richness of the Villino Trollope. It was certainly a far different setting from the vicarage at Heckfield where she had spent her girlhood, different from the spare but elegant comfort she had tried to achieve in London, different from the country-house luxury at Julians, which she had tried to recapture at Julians Hill, and again at Hadley, and again at Carlton Hill. Well, she had created, flung together, or improvised many different homes by now—in America and Belgium as well as in England. She was content to let others make the effort. She had dreamed of Italy as a young girl when she was translating Dante and Tasso. By some alchemy of life she had been transported into that landscape of her dreams and was an inhabitant of a villa that was almost a redundancy of the ancient Italian beauty she loved.

But she was still a traveller—'a very Trollope'. There were always journeys in the summer to escape the heat of Florence. Sometimes all the Trollopes, and Mr Garrow as well, travelled to the baths at Lucca, a favourite resort of the English residents in Italy. In the summer of 1855 Anthony and Rose made another European tour, this time in the company of John Tilley, and Fanny and Tom met them in Venice. Fanny was pleased that she could still walk along the Lido and climb all the stairs as briskly as always. After that, Fanny and Tom accompanied Anthony, Rose, and John back to England. It was Fanny's first visit there since Cecilia's death in 1849. She found some pleasure in seeing a few old friends, but too many were gone, among them her brother, Henry, who had died a year after Cecilia. She felt no urge to make England her home again.

One highlight was an afternoon with the new wonder of the world of spiritualism, Daniel Home. Tom arranged for the invitation to meet the young Scottish prodigy, fresh from American triumphs, at the home of his host in England, a Mr Rymer who lived in Ealing. A proper high tea began the proceedings, but then the lanky, red-headed, rather consumptive youth was summoned to preside over the real business of the gathering. Everyone was seated around a large mahogany table, awaiting some manifestation from the spirit world.

Tom, who could glide over almost any sort of emotional disturbance in everyday life, was a dedicated investigator of the material manifestations of so-called psychic phenomena. He and another guest were soon on their knees underneath the big table, trying to ascertain whether or not some physical tricks were being used to levitate it. The table did rise and fall, and both men were baffled at their inability to discover how or why. Fanny was merely wondering if it really was possible to have some word with those who had 'crossed over'. There were so many with whom she would like to speak. And once or twice it did seem someone was trying to reach her, but she could not be sure.

Spiritualism was the vogue. Back in Florence, Fanny found Elizabeth Barrett Browning very curious to hear all about Daniel Home and his powers. Fanny was not sure exactly what she thought, any more than she had been when the Okey sisters had stood beside Anthony's bed years before, when he had been so ill, and seen Jack at his knee but never so far as his shoulder. But she had no objections when, a year or so later, Tom, having heard that Daniel Home was going to visit Italy, invited him to spend a month at the Villino Trollope.

Interest among the English Florentines was so great that Tom and Theo had to set a limit of eight guests each evening. Each evening, with the pale, strained Mr Home at the table around which everyone sat, there were curious manifestations, crackings, and oscillations of the table and then distinct raps. Messages appeared to be coming through from somewhere, often from people long forgotten by those to whom their words were directed.

Theodosia, full of sensibility as she was, was repelled by these evening seances and tried, in vain, to find some way to discredit Mr Home. Tom continued fascinated and finally decided that the movements of the table could not be produced by any 'fraud, machinery or trickery'. But he was unable to decide what he believed about the messages from the spirit world.

Fanny sat at the table, listened, and hoped again for some word from one of the many who were gone. And this time it seemed she did hear the voices of Cecilia and of Emily and Henry. Fanny's eagerness to believe made Theodosia wonder if age was at last beginning to tell on her mother-in-law. She was almost seventy-six after all.

She sent off her last book, *Fashionable Life, or Paris and London*, to her publishers in London in 1856. Yes, not just her latest but her last book. She made no more special drama out of laying down her pen after finishing that forty-first book than she had made out of picking up a pen twenty-five years before to rescue herself and her family from penury. There was no longer any real financial need for her to write. She was still receiving royalties from books she had written. Tom was doing very well with his articles and books. Theo's translations and articles brought in further sums. Life at the Villino Trollope could continue along its rich, civilized course without her aid. Besides, she no longer felt any necessity to unburden herself of her opinions on unmannered people or the various injustices of society.

Unmannered people were everywhere, heaven knew; in fact, they proliferated, and so did social injustices. But Frances Trollope had said all that she cared to say publicly. She would still react privately to boors and bores, mocking or teasing them or simply ignoring them, but she was through with writing about them.

In 1856, the year in which Fanny's last novel was published, her son, Anthony, in Ireland, was completing the novel, *Barchester Towers*, which would bring him his first recognition and fame.

It is impossible to romanticize the idea of some sort of literary torch being handed down from mother to son. The mother had paid little heed to the son's writing activities and probably did not even know that his novel, *The Warden*, had won him his first favourable reviews. The son, for a long time, had not read his mother's yearly novels. During his first, unhappy years as a Post Office clerk he had devoted a surprising amount of time to studying the satirical poem his mother had written back in the Harrow days, about the hypocrisy surrounding the burial arrangements for Byron's young daughter, Allegra. Filling the tedious evenings when he was alone in his rooms, he had annotated the poem, criticized the metre of various lines, and approved or disapproved of various characterizations. But it is impossible to believe that Anthony learned anything about writing from that Byronic imitation.

What he might have learned from his mother, though he was years in finding his way to it, was the ability to see his fellow humans objectively. His mother's offside stance often led her to mockery and to the portrayal of characters that was close to caricature. Anthony at last was beginning to write about ordinary human beings, some with better manners than others, all with characteristics that made them unique, but few with personalities so distorted as to make them bizarre.

An easy conversational style of writing also linked Anthony with his mother. Fanny seemed to have fallen into that style by instinct with her first book, *Domestic Manners*. Her eldest son, Thomas, copied it but carried it to an extreme, becoming so digressive, discursive, and allusive that his writing developed a wearying loquacity. Anthony, whether by study or luck, hit the balance between his mother and Thomas. He was conversational without being either sarcastic or long-winded.

'Dearest mother,' Anthony addressed his letters to Fanny these days. Finding the way to a success of his own in the world, he had no more need for jealousy and resentment.

He and Rose visited the Villino Trollope for the second time in 1857, soon after *Barchester Towers* was published. This book had not only received excellent reviews but a host of readers was discovering it with enthusiasm. Anthony may not have wakened one day to find himself famous, but he had at last found success. He brought copies of the book for her and Tom and Theo, but Tom also had a new book out, *The Girlhood of Catherine de Medici*, which had also received good notices. It was a standoff between Anthony and his older brother once again.

But Fanny had never been sensitive to the rivalry between her two sons, never aware of the terrible favouritism she had shown. And now, at last, she was growing old. She was quite bent with arthritis. Her teeth were all gone, and the replacements had left her lips pulled in and her cheeks sunken. She looked ancient. For a good part of each day she was alert and amused, eager for talks and walks and drives. Still, it was a sign of the change in her that she had given up whist, the game with which she had beguiled hundreds of Friday evenings. For entertainment, she was content to watch her granddaughter, Bice, at play and to enjoy the times when Elizabeth and Robert Browning's small son, nicknamed Penini (Pen), spent the afternoon at the villa and she could smile as the little boy and girl bickered and laughed and chased each other around the garden.

The years began to slide together. Anthony in his turn was becoming a 'very Trollope' for travelling. He was sent as an emissary of the Post Office to Egypt to see about expediting the transit of mails across that country on their way to India and Australia. He had a splendid journey, returning by way of Malta and Gibraltar. After that, the Post Office sent him on another mission to study the postal service in Spanish Cuba and Panama. During all his travelling Anthony devoted most of the time not given to official business to working on more novels.

His mother was not always sure of where he was nor of what he was writing. Books by one or another of her sons or by her daughter-in-law were always appearing. How could she keep up with them? She was pleased when she was told that one or another of the books had been well reviewed, but she kept no strict count any more than she had done with her own.

In the autumn of 1860 Anthony and Rose again visited the Villino Trollope. Much had happened since their last visit. A flurry of wars had finally achieved the goal for which so many, including Fanny's old friend, General Pepe, had struggled so long—a united Italy. Tom and Theodosia had both written reams of material for magazines and newspapers, reporting on the exciting events they were able to witness. Theo was publishing a book of essays on the subject. Tom had published two more historical works.

The Villino Trollope was now one of the established houses in Florence. Every English and American notable visiting the city hoped for an invitation. Harriet Beecher Stowe, who had gone to Cincinnati a few years after Fanny's departure and spent long years there, had her own memories of that city on the Ohio and the remarkable building known as Trollope's Folly. She had to share these recollections with Tom Trollope, who had known Cincinnati only briefly, because Fanny was not really paying attention. George Eliot and her husband, George Lewes, were visitors from England who became close friends of Tom and his wife, Theo.

And Fanny? Somewhere along the way she had slipped out of it. Mr Garrow died suddenly one day when Tom was away. Fanny did not die. She grew very deaf.

'Dead?' said old Walter Landor to Tom one day when he had asked after Tom's mother. 'Well, I wish I were too.'

'No, no,' shouted Tom, 'not dead. Deaf'.

Her memory seemed to go with her hearing. So much to remember, and no more recollection.

Tom and Theo were kind and loving. Young Bice, growing to be seven, then eight, was a joy to witness each day, even if Fanny could not remember one word the child had said the day before.

She was not really aware of Anthony's journey to the United States in 1861 and his plan to write a book on his impressions of that country that would counteract the bad feelings his mother's book had created thirty years before.

What a 'quiz' Fanny might have thought it once—her awkward, hobbledehoy son smoothing over feathers she had ruffled years before. Once she would have mocked at the idea of smoothing them. Who cared if the Americans had been offended by what she wrote? She had been offended by *them* and their bad manners.

What a 'quiz' all around that someone so observant, so mocking and laughing and teasing as Fanny Trollope should still live but observe and laugh and tease no more. And then, early in October of 1863, she was briefly ill. On 6th October 1863, she died. A few days later she was buried in the little English cemetery in Florence overlooked by the Apennine Mountains.

Anthony, stern and objective twenty years later, noted in his *Autobiography* that she had 'continued writing up to 1856, when she was seventy-six years old,—and had at that time produced 114 volumes, of which the first was not written till she was fifty. Her career offers great encouragement to those who have not begun early in life, but are still ambitious to do something before they depart hence.'

He gave her what he thought was her due. 'She was an unselfish, affectionate, and most industrious woman, with great capacity for enjoyment and high physical gifts. She was endowed, too, with much creative power, with considerable humour, and a genuine feeling for romance. But she was neither clear-sighted nor accurate; and in her attempts to describe morals, manners, and even facts, was unable to avoid the pitfalls of exaggeration.'

Tom, remembering 'many, many journeyings, and more tête-à-tête walks, and yet more of tête-à-tête at home hours,' felt that she had died 'in a ripe old age after a singularly happy, though not untroubled, life'.[3]

27

Afterword

For those who have stayed with the story this far . . . Anthony, of course, went on to become one of the most popular novelists of the latter half of the nineteenth century. Not all of his books were successful, but he wrote seventy in all, and at least two dozen of them have become minor classics. He tried his hand at playwriting, but the plays he wrote were failures. Fascinated by politics, he stood for Parliament in 1865, in the district of Beverley, in the East Riding, but was defeated. He sublimated this interest into a series of political novels, which featured such characters as a charming MP from Ireland, Phineas Finn, and the aristocratic Plantagenet Palliser, nephew of the Duke of Omnium, and his wife, Lady Glencora.

Like his mother, he did much of his writing in the hours before dawn and had his manservant waken him each day at 4 a.m. He trained himself to write a certain number of pages each day, and when he began to travel for the Post Office, he wrote on board ship and on trains, keeping to his schedule. Feeling secure of his income from writing, he resigned from the Post Office in 1867 so as to become editor of a magazine. This was not an altogether successful venture, but he went on writing novels. He began to worry about glutting the market with Trollope novels, and in fact, by the time of his death in 1882, when he was two books ahead of his publisher, his popularity had begun to decline.

Anthony's eldest son, Henry, studied for the bar (following in the footsteps of his grandfather, Thomas Anthony Trollope), but he did not care for the law. He worked for a few years in a publishing house and then turned to writing. He wrote an unsuccessful novel and a competent biography of Molière. After his father's death he edited and had published his father's *Autobiography*, a cranky, aggressively defensive work that almost ruined Anthony Trollope's reputation for the next fifty years.

Anthony's second son, Frederick, did not like school and migrated early to Australia, where he became a sheep farmer and the father of a large family. One of his sons ultimately inherited the family baronetcy and became Sir Frederick Ferrand Trollope.

Rose Trollope lived to be a very old lady, outliving Anthony by thirty-five years and dying in 1917.

Theodosia Garrow Trollope, whose very strength seemed to lie in her fragility, shocked everyone by dying in 1865. Anthony and Rose worried about Tom, desolate and alone in Florence with his small daughter, after the deaths of Mr Garrow, Fanny, and Theo. Finally they persuaded Frances Eleanor Ternan, a sister of Ellen Ternan, who was the great love of Charles Dickens's later years, to go to Florence as the governess for young Bice. Before too long their secret hopes were realized. Frances Ternan became the second Mrs Thomas Trollope.

Frances Ternan Trollope was a talented but steady young woman, very good for Tom. She was a writer. Dickens published a number of her stories in the various magazines he edited. She also wrote novels and finally wrote the only semi-contemporary biography of Frances Milton Trollope, the mother-in-law she had never known. She drew on Tom's recollections, letters, and memorabilia for her story of Fanny's life.

Bice grew up, beautiful, talented, and delicate as her mother had been, to marry the Right Honourable Charles H. Stuart Wortley (Lord Stuart of Wortley). She died giving birth to a daughter, also named Beatrice, who grew up to marry into the famous Cecil family.

Auguste Hervieu, who had been such a support to Fanny Trollope in America and who had illustrated so many of her books, gradually drifted away from close intimacy with the family. He married a young Swiss woman in 1848.

Frances Wright, the 'angel' who led the way to America, did take the blacks she had gathered at Nashoba to Haiti and placed them under the protection of the governor. She was accompanied by the Frenchman Guillaume Phiquepal D'Arusmont, her assistant at New Harmony. In the summer of 1830, while Fanny Trollope was touring the eastern seaboard, Frances Wright and her sister Camilla left the United States and settled in Paris. Camilla died there the next winter, 1831. D'Arusmont had already joined Frances in Paris. When Frances discovered she was pregnant, she married D'Arusmont and legalized their relationship. Her first child died at birth, but a second daughter, named Frances Sylva, was born in April 1832. In 1835 Frances Wright returned to the United States to continue her lecturing and missionary activities. In 1850, partly as a legal manoeuvre to recoup some of her American investments, she divorced D'Arusmont. She died in 1852.

La Fayette read Fanny Trollope's *Domestic Manners* in 1832, soon after the book was published, and urged Frances Wright to respond to the harsh comments on the Nashoba settlement, but Miss Wright was too busy with other concerns to do so. La Fayette had emerged from retirement in 1830 to head the National Guard in the revolution against Charles X. He died in 1834.

Thomas Adolphus Trollope wrote his memoirs, *What I Remember*, in two volumes, the first covering his life from childhood through the deaths of his mother and Theodosia, in 1863, the second chronicling his life after his second marriage to Frances Eleanor Ternan. He was accorded many honours in Italy for his sympathetic writings about the country's history and struggles for independence, but his books, although almost as numerous as his mother's and younger brother's, are no longer read. He died in 1892 at the age of eighty-two.

With his death the great gush of literary works by Trollopes, which had begun with Frances Trollope's *Domestic Manners of the Americans*, came to an end.

Trollope's Folly in Cincinnati, Ohio, was demolished in 1898. Fanny Trollope's most famous book and many of her son Anthony's are less destructible.

Notes

1. *Heckfield Vicarage—'Manners Makyth Man'—'Au-mieux-ing'*

1. The Reverend William Milton and his inventions are described in Thomas Adolphus Trollope, *What I Remember* (London: Richard Bentley and Son, 1887) vol. 1, pp. 19–21.
2. Mrs George Mitford to her daughter Mary, 14th November 1802, A. G. K. L'Estrange, *The Friendships of Mary Russell Mitford* (London: Hurst & Blackett, 1882), p. 10.
3. Ibid., p. 8.

2. *London—Thomas Anthony Trollope—Letters*

1. Frances Eleanor Trollope, *A Memoir of Frances Trollope, Her Life and Literary Work (From George III to Victoria)* (London: Richard Bentley & Sons, 1895), p. 12.
2. The courtship letters of Frances Milton and Thomas Anthony Trollope are recorded in F. E. Trollope, *A Memoir*, pp. 15–22; and in Michael Sadleir, *Trollope, A Commentary* (London: Constable & Co Ltd, 1927), pp. 30–41.

3. *Marriage—Children—Social Life*

1. Sadleir, *Trollope*, p. 48.
2. F. E. Trollope, *A Memoir*, p. 36.
3. Mr Trollope's penurious ways in small matters are described in T. A. Trollope, *What I Remember*, vol. 1, p. 4.
4. Ibid., p. 12.
5. The letters between Fanny and her husband when she was at Heckfield in 1810 are recorded in F. E. Trollope, *A Memoir*, pp. 39–41.

4. *Harrow—Loss of Inheritance—Evangelicals—Grief*

1. The decision to move to Harrow is the first in a series of decisions about which Trollope biographers disagree. Michael Sadleir credits Mr Trollope with the decisions to move and to build the expensive house on rented land. The Stebbinses feel that he may have decided on the move but that his wife insisted on the large house. C. P. Snow believes that both as to the move and the house there is 'a reasonable suspicion that much of the blame rested on Mrs Trollope'.
2. The excerpts from Fanny's poem are quoted by permission of N. John Hall, who published it in its entirety in *Salmagundi, Byron, Allegra, and the Trollope Family* (Princeton, N.J.: Beta Phi Mu, 1975).
3. The rituals at Winchester are fully described in T. A. Trollope, *What I Remember*, vol. 1, p. 96 onwards.
4. Ibid., p. 299.

5. *Paris—Frances Wright—La Fayette*

1. F. E. Trollope, *A Memoir*, pp. 66–67.
2. Anthony's experiences at Sunbury are related in Anthony Trollope, *An Autobiography* (London: Oxford University Press, 1947), pp. 3–6.

6. *An Unhappy Man—Poverty—Decisions*

1. Anthony Trollope, *The Last Chronicle of Barset* (London: Smith, Elder, 1867).
2. T. A. Trollope, *What I Remember*, vol. 1, p. 58.
3. Frances Milton Trollope, *The Refugee in America* (London: Whittaker, Treacher, 1832).
4. F. E. Trollope, *A Memoir*, p. 78.
5. Sadleir, *Trollope*, p. 65.
6. Anthony Trollope, *An Autobiography*, pp. 7–8.
7. The decision to leave Julians for Julians Hill is another of the moves for which biographers have conflicting theories.
8. 'Why not?' This and the scene that follows are surmise. There is no direct evidence as to whether it was Fanny or her husband who first thought of a venture in America. Some chroniclers credit Mr Trollope with the entire inspiration. C. P. Snow accuses Mrs Trollope of 'the scattiest idea yet'. On the evidence of Fanny's letter to Julia Garnett (Helen Heinemann, 'Mrs Trollope: The Triumphant Feminine in the 19th Century', *Radcliffe Quarterly* 60, no. 4 [1974]: 4–9) rhapsodizing

about Frances Wright's compelling personality, as well as Fanny's lifelong tendency to move somewhere else when things became difficult, it is this biographer's belief that hers was the initial impulse to follow Frances Wright to America. It seems likely that Mr Trollope was convinced that a Wykehamist and barrister like himself could handle lesser activities such as farming and merchandising almost offhand, and that he had the idea of a commercial venture in the United States.

9. Frances Wright's letters to Julia Garnett reflect her doubts about Mrs Trollope's qualifications for life at Nashoba. (Cecelia Payne-Gasposch-kin, 'The Nashoba Experiment', *Harvard Library Bulletin* 23, nos. 3 & 4 [1975]: 221–251, 429–461).

7. *New Orleans—Mississippi Steamboats Memphis*

1. Frances Wright, *Views of Society and Manners in America* (Cambridge, Mass.: Harvard University Press, 1963), pp. 8–10.
2. Frances Milton Trollope, *Domestic Manners of the Americans* (London: Whittaker, Treacher & Co, 1832), vol. 1, p. 2.
3. Frances Wright letter to Julia Garnett (Payne-Gasposchkin, 'The Nashoba Experiment').
4. Fanny's impressions of New Orleans are all from *Domestic Manners*. The further quotations throughout the chapter (except for Henry's likely comment about the skill of their driver) are also from this source.

8. *Nashoba*

1. F. M. Trollope, *Domestic Manners*, vol. 1, p. 38.
2. Ibid.
3. This is likely dialogue for a scene implied in F. M. Trollope, *Domestic Manners*.
4. F. M. Trollope, *Domestic Manners*, vol. 1, p. 38.
5. Ibid.
6. Ibid., p. 30.

9. *Cincinnati—American 'Help'*

1. All the quotations in this chapter are from F. M. Trollope, *Domestic Manners*, except for Henry's ad.
2. *Cincinnati Gazette*, March 1828.

10. *Dorfeuille's 'Hell'—Lectures—'Dropping In'—Revivals*

1. *Cincinnati Gazette*, April 1828.
2. On the evidence, it seems likely that Fanny was the one who envisaged the particular kind of commercial venture that the Trollopes should establish.
3. F. M. Trollope, *Domestic Manners*, vol. 1, p. 63.
4. Ibid., p. 96.
5. Ibid., p. 99.
6. Ibid.
7. Ibid., pp. 142–144.
8. Ibid., p. 104.
9. Ibid., p. 106.
10. Ibid., p. 113.

11. *Anthony—The Bazaar—Andrew Jackson*

1. Anthony's misadventures and unhappiness are described in A. Trollope, *An Autobiography*, pp. 8–9.
2. T. A. Trollope, *What I Remember*, vol. 1, pp. 156–163.
3. F. M. Trollope, *Domestic Manners*, vol. 1, p. 202.
4. Basil Hall, *Travels in the United States*, vol. 2 (Austria: Akademische Druch- und Verlagsanstalt, 1965), p. 25.

12. *Disaster*

1. Various English travellers in the United States who visited Cincinnati commented on Mrs Trollope's bazaar. Capt. Frederick Marryat (1795–1848), who was in Cincinnati in the mid-1830s, wrote in his *Diary in America* (1st Series, II [London, 1839] pp. 152–153): 'Mrs Trollope's bazaar raises its head in a very imposing manner; it is composed of many varieties of architecture; but I think the order under which it must be classed is *preposterous*. They call it "Trollope's Folly".'
2. F. M. Trollope, *Domestic Manners*, vol. 1, p. 252.

13. *Harrow Weald—Travels in America—Slavery*

1. Anthony describes Harrow Weald in *An Autobiography*, p. 11: 'The farmhouse . . . was one of those farmhouses which seem always to be in danger of falling into the neighbouring horse-pond.'

2. F. M. Trollope, *Domestic Manners*, vol. 1, p. 219.
3. Ibid., p. 261.
4. Ibid., p. 262.
5. Ibid.
6. Ibid., p. 283.
7. F. M. Trollope, *Domestic Manners*, vol. II, p. 3.
8. Ibid., p. 24.
9. Ibid., p. 12.
10. Ibid., p. 11.

14. *Return to England—'Domestic Manners of the Americans'*

1. T. A. Trollope, *What I Remember*, p. 240.
2. Lady Milman (widow of Sir Francis, who had been a physician to George III) was a longtime friend of Frances Trollope's. The Reverend Henry Hart Milman (1791–1868), her youngest son, was Professor of Poetry at Oxford for some years and in 1830 had published *The History of the Jews*, the first of many works that included drama, epic poetry, and hymns.
3. F. M. Trollope, *Domestic Manners*, vol. II, p. 294.
4. Ibid., p. 301.
5. Ibid., p. 303.
6. F. E. Trollope, *A Memoir*, p. 150.
7. Ibid.,
8. Ibid., p. 151.
9. Ibid., p. 150.

15. *Fame—Criticism—Julians Hill—'The Refugee in America'*

1. Sadleir, *Trollope*, pp. 85–86.
2. *Quarterly Review* 47, (March 1832): 39–80.
3. Charles Dickens visited America in 1842. His *American Notes* were published later the same year. *Martin Chuzzlewit* was published in monthly instalments, beginning in 1843.
4. F. M. Trollope, *Domestic Manners* (London: Whittaker, Treacher, 1832; New York: Reprinted for the Booksellers, 1832).
5. Mrs Trollope's name, originally hissed at in America, gradually took on additional meanings, both as a noun and as a verb. People called, 'A Trollope! A Trollope!' to anyone behaving in an unseemly manner in a theatre. To 'trollope' became synonymous with spitting or otherwise acting boorishly. Such usage may have had some effect in improving American manners.

6. F. E. Trollope, *A Memoir*, p. 164.
7. This verse and the ones following can be found in Frances Milton Trollope, *The Mother's Manual: or Illustrations of Matrimonial Economy, an Essay in Verse* (London: Treuttel and Würtz and Richter, 1833).

16. *Travels in Belgium—'The Mother's Manual'—'The Abbess'—Eviction*

1. Frances Milton Trollope, *Belgium and Western Germany in 1833* (London: John Murray, 1834).

17. *Exile—Illness—Henry's Death*

1. Anthony describes the episode in *An Autobiography*, pp. 23–25.
2. Ibid., pp. 33–34.

18. *Paris—Madame Récamier—Chateaubriand—Thomas Anthony's Death*

1. Frances Milton Trollope, *Paris and the Parisians in 1835* (London: Richard Bentley, 1836).
2. Ibid.
3. Jeanne Françoise Julie Adélaide Récamier (née Barnard) (1777–1849) was in exile during most of Napoleon's ascendancy but returned to Paris after the restoration of the monarchy. In the 1830s she was living in apartments in the convent Abbaye-aux-Bois. The Princess Cristina Belgiojoso (1808–1871), the daughter of an ancient Lombard family, was an ardent supporter of Italian independence. She was involved in Carbonari activities in the revolution of 1830, and when this was put down, she fled to Paris. She was a writer, historian, pianist, and feminist of sorts, much admired by Heine, Balzac, Musset, and Liszt, among others.
4. A. Trollope, *An Autobiography*, p. 47.
5. T. A. Trollope, *What I Remember*, vol. I, p. 270.
6. F. M. Trollope, *Paris*.
7. T. A. Trollope, *What I Remember*, vol. I, p. 296.

19. *England—'Jonathan Jefferson Whitlaw'—Emily's Death—Vienna*

1. Frances Milton Trollope, *The Life and Adventures of Jonathan Jefferson Whitlaw: or Scenes on the Mississippi* (London: Richard Bentley, 1836).

2. Ibid.
3. Ibid.
4. 'Fifteen years later, Harriet Beecher Stowe was to write in *Uncle Tom's Cabin* a simpler story with many points of resemblance. Hers was the better tract, but Mrs Trollope's was the greater novel.' (Lucy Poate Stebbins and Richard Poate Stebbins, *The Trollopes: The Chronicle of a Writing Family* [New York: Columbia University Press, 1945], p. 79.

20. *The Danube—Vienna—Prince and Princess Metternich—Viennese Society*

1. The journey down the Danube is described in Frances Milton Trollope, *Vienna and the Austrians* (London, Richard Bentley, 1838) and in T. A. Trollope, *What I Remember*.
2. The Stebbinses quote from Princess Melanie Metternich's diary: 'She has made a conquest of my husband, and he appears to have made one of her. She is a good-natured woman, very simple and natural, an attentive listener, and grateful for every mark of interest. She is 45 or 50 years old [actually she was almost 59] and though she looks a trifle common, her conversation bears the marks of the best education.' (L. P. and R. P. Stebbins, *The Trollopes*, p. 87).
3. T. A. Trollope, *What I Remember*, vol. I, p. 334.
4. 'Of these abominable political turnpike gates no less than ten are to be met along the distance of scarcely as many miles between Sargano and Pontremoli . . . and if we recollect that no less than three of these irksome houses bear the cognisance of Este we may easily conceive that the most enterprising tourist—a very Trollope—would give up the excursion in despair.' (*The New Monthly Magazine*, July 1847, quoted by Sadleir, *Trollope*, p. 89.)

21. *A New Reign—'The Vicar of Wrexhill'—A New Arrangement*

1. Quoted in F. E. Trollope, *A Memoir*, p. 158.
2. T. A. Trollope, *What I Remember*, vol. I, p. 353.
3. F. E. Trollope, *A Memoir*, p. 285.
4. This scene is paraphrased from T. A. Trollope, *What I Remember*, vol. I, p. 356.

22. *'Michael Armstrong'—Penrith—Paris—Anthony's Illness*

1. F. E. Trollope, *A Memoir*, p. 295.

2. Frances Milton Trollope, *The Life and Adventures of Michael Arm-strong, the Factory Boy* (London: Colburn, 1840).
3. T. A. Trollope, *What I Remember*, vol. II, p. 69.
4. Anthony's indebtedness and romantic involvements are related in A. Trollope, *An Autobiography*, pp. 43–44.
5. T. A. Trollope, *What I Remember*, vol. I, p. 370.

23. *Carlton Hill—Italy Again—And Again—Anthony Married*

1. Harriet Martineau (1802–1876), a writer in a moralistic and philosophic vein, spent two years (1834–1836) in the United States. After her return to England she wrote *Society in America*, published in 1837, and *Retrospect of Western Travels*, published in 1838. In the latter book she wrote of Mrs Trollope's bazaar in Cincinnati: 'This bazaar is the great deformity of the city. . . . From my window at the boarding-house it is only too distinctly visible. It is built of brick, and has Gothic windows, Grecian pillars, and a Turkish dome, and it was originally ornamented with Egyptian devices, which have, however, all disappeared under the brush of the whitewasher.' (Harriet Martineau, *Retrospect of Western Travels*, vol. 2 [London: Saunders and Otley, 1838] p. 54).
2. T. A. Trollope, *What I Remember*, vol. II, pp. 111, 114.
3. Frances Milton Trollope, *Jessie Phillips: A Tale of the Present Day* (London: Colburn, 1843).

24. *Anthony—Theodosia Garrow—Cecilia*

1. A. Trollope, *Autobiography*, p. 54.
2. Ibid.
3. Ibid., p. 67.
4. *The Macdermots of Ballycloran* was not a bad novel, nor was Newby at fault, as he seems to have been in some of his dealings with the Brontë sisters. English readers simply were not interested in reading about Irish problems.
5. T. A. Trollope, *What I Remember*, vol. II, p. 152.
6. Ibid., p. 156.
7. Poems by Theodosia Garrow, written when she was thirteen and fourteen, were published in such annuals as *Heath's Book of Beauty* (1839) and *The Keepsake* (1841), popular sentimental staples of the time.
8. T. A. Trollope, *What I Remember*, vol. II, p. 157.
9. Ibid., p. 166.
10. Ibid.

25. *Deaths—New Arrangements—Birth*

1. A. Trollope, *Letters of Anthony Trollope*, edited by Bradford Allen Booth (London; Oxford University Press, 1951), p. 14.
2. John and Cecilia's youngest daughter stayed with Anthony and Rose in Ireland for some months but returned to England when her father married again. His second wife was Mary Anne Partington. Her relationship to the Miss Partington who became Frances Trollope's stepmother is unknown but she was the daughter of Thomas Anthony Trollope's sister, Penelope, hence a cousin of Cecilia's and of all of Fanny's children.
3. A. Trollope, *Letters*, p. 16.
4. T. A. Trollope, *What I Remember*, pp. 215–216.
5. A. Trollope, *Letters*, p. 21.

26. *Villino Trollope*

1. The Villino Trollope was described by a young American writer who became a special favourite of Anthony, Kate Field, in 'English Authors in Florence', *Atlantic Monthly* 14 (December 1864).
2. A letter from Robert Browning to Isabella Blagden, a talented member of the English community in Florence and a friend both of the Brownings and the Trollopes, written in 1867, after the death of Tom's first wife and his remarriage, recalls the gossip in Florence in 1853, fourteen years earlier, when Beatrice Trollope was born. This 1867 letter tells of Browning's meeting Thomas Trollope in London, 'looking out of sorts and worn'. Later, at his club, Browning heard that there 'had been a great quarrel [between Thomas and his second wife], revelation of the past misfortunes of which T. had been ignorant altogether, and a separation.' The story was further confirmed by someone who had heard it from 'Anthony T.—I think in Paris'. Browning went on: 'If things have gone so—if the wife did enlighten poor T. for the first time on the paternity of the child, and so on—I hardly ever knew so deplorable a case. I take it that people's tongues, never very tight, were absolutely loosened by Theo's death—as if it didn't matter holding them any more.' Of course, this proves nothing about the paternity of Beatrice Trollope, only that there had been a good deal of speculation about it in 1853 (Robert Browning, *Letters of Robert Browning*. Collected by Thomas Wise [New Haven, Conn.: Yale University Press, 1933]).
3. T. A. Trollope, *What I Remember*, vol. I, p. 295.

Bibliography

Primary Sources

Trollope, Anthony. *An Autobiography*, with an Introduction by Michael
  Sadleir. London: Oxford University Press, 1947.
——*Barchester Towers*. London: Longman, 1857.
——*Doctor Thorne: A Novel*. London: Chapman & Hall, 1858.
——*The Last Chronicle of Barset*. London: Smith, Elder, 1867.
——*Letters of Anthony Trollope*. Edited by Bradford Allen Booth.
  London: Oxford University Press, 1951.
——*Orley Farm*, London: Chapman & Hall, 1862.
——*The Small House at Allington*. London: Smith, Elder, 1864.
——*The Warden*. London: Longman, 1855.
Trollope, Frances Eleanor, *A Memoir of Frances Trollope, Her Life and
  Literary Work (From George III to Victoria)*. London: Richard
  Bentley & Sons, 1895.
Trollope, Frances Milton. *Domestic Manners of the Americans*. London:
  Whittaker, Treacher, 1832.
Trollope, Thomas Adolphus. *What I Remember*. London: Richard
  Bentley & Sons, 1887.

Other Contemporary or Near-Contemporary Sources

Browning, Robert. *Letters of Robert Browning*. Collected by Thomas J.
  Wise. New Haven, Conn.: Yale University Press, 1933.
Hall, Basil. *Travels in the United States*. Philadelphia: Carey, Lee &
  Carey, 1829.
L'Estrange, A. G. K. *The Friendships of Mary Russell Mitford*. London:
  Hurst & Blackett, 1882.
——*The Life of Mary Russell Mitford Told by Herself in Letters to Her
  Friends*. New York: Harper & Bros., 1870.
Wright, Frances. *Views of Society and Manners in America*. Cambridge,
  Mass.: Harvard University Press, 1963.

Secondary, Non-Contemporary Sources

Bigland, Eileen. *The Indomitable Mrs. Trollope*. London: Barrie, 1953.
Escott, T. H. S. *Anthony Trollope; His Work, Associates and Literary Originals*. London: 1913.
Hall, N. John. *Salmagundi, Byron, Allegra, and the Trollope Family*. Princeton, N.J.: Beta Phi Mu, 1975.
Heineman, Helen. 'Mrs. Trollope: The Triumphant Feminine in the 19th Century'. *Radcliffe Querterly*, September-December 1974.
Hennessy, James Pope-. *Anthony Trollope*. London: Cape, 1971.
Payne-Gasposchkin, Cecelia. 'The Nashoba Experiment', *Harvard Library Bulletin* 23 (1975).
Perkins, A. J. G. and Wolfson, Theresa. *Frances Wright, Free Enquirer*. Philadelphia: Porcupine Press, 1972.
Sadleir, Michael. *Trollope, A Commentary*. London: Constable, 1927.
Snow, C. P. *Trollope, His Life and Art*. London: Macmillan, 1975.
Stebbins, Lucy Poate, and Stebbins, Richard Poate. *The Trollopes: The Chronicle of a Writing Family*. New York: Columbia University Press, 1945; London: Secker and Warburg, 1946.

Chronological Bibliography of Frances Milton Trollope's Works

Domestic Manners of the Americans. With illustrations by A. Hervieu. 2 vols. London: Whittaker, Treacher, 1832.
The Refugee in America: A Novel. 3 vols. London: Whittaker, Treacher, 1832.
The Mother's Manual: or Illustrations of Matrimonial Economy. An Essay in Verse. With illustrations by A. Hervieu. London: Treuttel and Würtz and Richter, 1833.
The Abbess: A Romance. 3 vols. London: Whittaker, Treacher, 1833.
Belgium and Western Germany in 1833. 2 vols. London: John Murray, 1834.
Tremordyn Cliff. 3 vols. London: Bentley, 1835.
Paris and the Parisians in 1835. With illustrations by A. Hervieu. 2 vols. London: Bentley, 1836.
The Life and Adventures of Jonathan Jefferson Whitlaw: or Scenes on the Mississippi. With illustrations by A. Hervieu. 3 vols. London: Bentley, 1836. (Reissued in 1857 under the title *Lynch Law*.)
The Vicar of Wrexhill. With illustrations by A. Hervieu. 3 vols. London: Bentley, 1837.
Vienna and the Austrians. With illustrations by A. Hervieu. 2 vols. London: Bentley, 1838.
A Romance of Vienna. 3 vols. London: Bentley, 1838.

The Widow Barnaby. 3 vols. London: Bentley, 1839.

The Widow Married: a Sequel to The Widow Barnaby. With illustrations by R. W. Buss. 3 vols. London: Colburn, 1840.

The Life and Adventures of Michael Armstrong, the Factory Boy. With illustrations by A. Hervieu, R. W. Buss, and T. Onwhyn. London: Colburn, 1840.

One Fault: A Novel. 3 vols. London: Bentley, 1840.

Charles Chesterfield: or the Adventures of a Youth of Genius. With illustrations by 'Phiz'. 3 vols. London: Colburn, 1841.

The Ward of Thorpe Combe. 3 vols. London: Bentley, 1841. (Reissued in Ward, Lock's Parlour Library and later as a Routledge Railway Novel under the title *The Ward*.)

The Blue Belles of England. 3 vols. London: Saunders and Otley, 1842.

A Visit to Italy. 2 vols. London: Bentley, 1842.

The Barnabys in America: or Adventures of the Widow Wedded. With illustrations by John Leech. 3 vols. London: Colburn, 1843.

Hargrave: or the Adventures of a Man of Fashion. 3 vols. London: Colburn, 1843.

Jessie Phillips: A Tale of the Present Day. With illustrations by John Leech. 3 vols. London: Colburn, 1843. 1 vol. 1844.

The Laurringtons: or Superior People. 3 vols. London: Longman, Brown, Green and Longmans, 1844.

Young Love: A Novel. 3 vols. London: Colburn, 1844.

The Attractive Man. 3 vols. London: Colburn, 1846.

The Robertses on their Travels. 3 vols. London: Colburn, 1846.

Travels and Travellers: A Series of Sketches. 2 vols. London: Colburn, 1846.

Father Eustace: A Tale of the Jesuits. 3 vols. London: Colburn, 1847.

The Three Cousins. 3 vols. London: Colburn, 1847.

Town and Country: A Novel. 3 vols. London: Colburn, 1848. (Reissued in 1857 under the title *Days of the Regency*.)

The Young Countess: or Love and Jealousy. 3 vols. London: Colburn, 1848. (Reissued under the title *Love and Jealousy* in Ward, Lock's Railway Library, and later by C. H. Clark.)

The Lottery of Marriage: A Novel. 3 vols. London: Colburn, 1849.

The Old World and the New: A Novel. 3 vols. London: Colburn, 1849.

Petticoat Government: A Novel. 3 vols. London: Colburn, 1850.

Mrs. Mathews, or Family Mysteries. 3 vols. London: Colburn, 1851.

Second Love, or Beauty and Intellect: A Novel. 3 vols. London: Colburn, 1851.

Uncle Walter: A Novel. 3 vols. London: Colburn, 1852.

The Young Heiress: A Novel. 3 vols. London: Hurst and Blackett, 1853.

The Life and Adventures of a Clever Woman. Illustrated with Occasional Extracts from her Diary. 3 vols. London: Hurst and Blackett, 1854.

Gertrude: or Family Pride. 3 vols. London: Hurst and Blackett, 1855.

Fashionable Life: or Paris and London. 3 vols. London: Hurst and Blackett, 1856.

Index